River of Love in an Age of Pollution

River of Love in an Age of Pollution

The Yamuna River of Northern India

David L. Haberman

UNIVERSITY OF CALIFORNIA PRESS
Berkeley · Los Angeles · London

Frontispiece: Two women making offerings in the
Yamuna near Vrindaban. Photo by David Haberman.

University of California Press, one of the most distinguished university presses in the United States, enriches
lives around the world by advancing scholarship in the
humanities, social sciences, and natural sciences. Its
activities are supported by the UC Press Foundation and
by philanthropic contributions from individuals and
institutions. For more information, visit
www.ucpress.edu.

University of California Press
Berkeley and Los Angeles, California

University of California Press, Ltd.
London, England

Library of Congress Cataloging-in-Publication Data

Haberman, David L., 1952–.
   River of love in an age of pollution : the Yamuna
River of northern India / David L. Haberman.
      p.   cm.
   In English, Hindi and Braj; includes translations from
Hindi and from Braj.
   Includes bibliographical references and index.
   ISBN 978-0-520-24790-1 (pbk. : alk. paper)
   1. Yamuna River (India)—Religious life and customs.
   2. Yamuna River (India)—Environmental conditions.
   I. Title.

BL1215.R5H33   2006
294.5'3509542—dc22   2005029654

Manufactured in the United States of America

15   14   13   12   11   10   09
10   9   8   7   6   5   4   3   2

This book is printed on New Leaf EcoBook 60,
containing 60% post-consumer waste, processed chlorine
free; 30% de-inked recycled fiber, elemental chlorine free;
and 10% FSC-certified virgin fiber, totally chlorine free.
EcoBook 60 is acid-free and meets the minimum
requirements of ANSI/ASTM D5634–01
(*Permanence of Paper*). ∞

For Nathan, my young son,
delightfully aware of the magic of the river
and compassionately aware of
the sickness of the river

And in memory of the one whose ashes
floated away on the river

She shimmers as her abundant foamy water
  cascades down the peak of Mount Kalinda.
Playfully she descends the high rocky slopes,
  moving eagerly for love.
She flows as if riding in a swinging palanquin,
  dashing over uneven ground while singing
  songs of love.
All glory to Yamuna, Daughter of the Sun,
  who increases love for Krishna.

      Vallabhacharya, *"Yamunashtakam"*

The life of every river sings its own song, but in
most the song is long since marred by the discords
of misuse.

    Aldo Leopold, *A Sand County Almanac*

Contents

Illustrations

Acknowledgments

To write this book, I conducted ethnographic and textual research primarily during the years between 1999 and 2003, with a period of writing extending over the next couple of years. Although I am responsible for the representations that flow in the major current of this volume, I have a flood of gratitude for all those who contributed to the many tributaries that made extensive reflection on the Yamuna River possible. I began preliminary research on this river with a bicycle expedition from its Himalayan source to the religious center of Vrindaban in October 1996. I thank the Friends of Vrindaban for organizing this expedition, Michael Duffy for leading the ride, and my colleagues Robert Orsi, Jan Nattier, Rebecca Manring, and Rob Campany for covering my courses at Indiana University for the three weeks I was away for this journey. I was able to devote an entire year to research in India in 1999–2000 with the aid of an ACLS/SSRC National Endowment for the Humanities International Postdoctoral Fellowship. This kind of federal support is essential to current scholarship and greatly appreciated. Indiana University provided funding for a research stay in India during my sabbatical in the fall semester of 2001 and for two monthlong trips to India over the winter breaks of 2002 and 2003.

I owe huge thanks to Shyam Das for introducing me to much of the literature on Yamuna and for reading many of the poems in the Braj Bhasha language with me. Although I conducted my own interviews in Hindi, I thank Jagannath Poddar for his assistance in interviewing

Bengali-speaking worshippers of Yamuna in Vrindaban and Deepu Pandit for his help with interviewing Gujarati Yamuna worshippers in Gokul. I am grateful to Shrivatsa Goswami for hosting me at his Shri Caitanya Prema Samsthana on the bank of the Yamuna in Vrindaban and for allowing my family to live in his family's house in the priestly compound of the Radharaman temple.

I am grateful to the late Dr. Vedaprakash Khanna for opening up to my family his Himalayan home located on the edge of a deer park above Almora, enabling me to write the initial draft of this book in a peaceful and natural setting where I could be inspired by the feel and sound of cool summer breezes moving through pine trees. And I thank Andy Mahler and Linda Lee, owners of the Lazy Black Bear, for offering me refuge in their forest tower office in southern Indiana to work on the final drafts of this book while staying in touch with the wonderful and powerful forces of nature I ponder in it.

Early drafts of this text were read by Jack Hawley, Sarah Pike, Sandra Ducey, and two readers for the University of California Press. UC Press editors Reed Malcolm and Jacqueline Volin were a pleasure to work with, and Bonita Hurd made my prose more crisp and clear with her insightful copyediting. I am deeply grateful to all for their valuable suggestions. My wife, Sandra, daughter, Meagan, and son, Nathan, accompanied me during my full year of research in India and put up with my absences during my return visits to India and during my long periods of writing. I appreciate their adventurous spirits and continual support.

Finally, I am immensely grateful to the priests of the Yamuna temples in Yamunotri and in the area of Braj, as well as to the many worshippers of Yamuna who took the time to share generously with me their thoughts and feelings about Yamuna as a remarkable river and loving goddess. I hope that some of the wonder they conveyed about this sacred river has seeped into this book.

Note on Translation and Transliteration

The translations in this volume are mine unless otherwise attributed. I have included the original Hindi or Braj Bhasha in the notes or text in the case of rare texts, posted signs, and technical words or phrases. In an effort to make this book more accessible to a wider readership, I have eliminated the diacritical marks; UC Press editors requested that I also eliminate them in the notes. Combining transliterations of Sanskrit, Hindi, and Braj Bhasha leads to a certain amount of inconsistency. I have transliterated words from these languages in a manner that attempts to represent actual pronunciation, following the standard system as closely as possible without making use of diacritics (thus *puja* instead of *pooja*, although in this case the long *u* will not be differentiated from the short *u* of *Purana*). Consonants have been selected and medial and final vowels have been dropped when such practice more closely reflects local pronunciation (thus, *Braj* instead of *Vraja*). The final vowel, however, has been retained in a few words that have become familiar to English-speaking readers in such spellings (e.g., *moksha, Purana, Yama*). Medial and final vowels have also been retained in Sanskrit technical terms (e.g., *adhibhuta, adhidaivika, svarupa*). A glossary of frequently used names and terms appears at the end of this book.

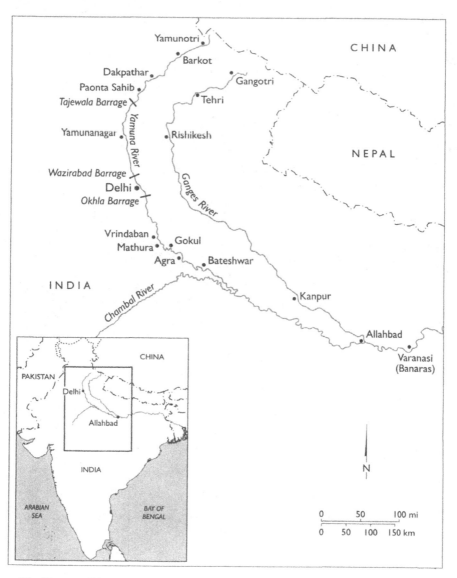

The Yamuna River

Introduction

This is a book about the Yamuna, a river that has been celebrated in India as an aquatic form of divinity for thousands of years. Although rivers have been worshipped as sacred entities for millennia worldwide, river worship is a more prominent feature of Indian culture than of any other culture in the world today. Signs of river worship can still easily be found throughout the South Asian subcontinent; this is certainly true of the Yamuna River, which is conceptualized religiously as a divine goddess flowing with liquid love. Today, however, we live in a complicated world, a world in which sacred rivers have become severely polluted. This too is true of the Yamuna.[1] The current degradation of the Yamuna, however, is not just an ecological problem; it also involves a religious crisis, bringing into question the very nature of divinity. Furthermore, the religious culture of sacred rivers in India offers a unique avenue for approaching environmental restoration today. For these reasons, I situate my examination of this river in the context of the growing interest in the overlap between religion and ecology, which I introduce in chapter 1.

Beginning with chapter 2, I explore the complex religious world of the Yamuna, investigating the stories, theology, and religious practices connected with the worship of the Yamuna river goddess, which I encountered not only while reading texts associated with her that were written over several millennia but also while talking with pilgrims, priests, and worshippers during many visits to various pilgrimage sites and temples on the river's banks. This is necessary, for as Lance Nelson has argued, "anyone wishing to understand the relation between religion and ecology in India, or to think or act ecologically in an authentically Hindu context, must come to grips with the mythic and sacred dimensions within which Hindus function—and the ecological implications thereof."[2] Although this study includes the older pan-Indian sites referred to in early scripture and literature, I focus particular attention on the region and religious views of Braj, a cultural region south of Delhi where the theology of the Goddess Yamuna was most fully developed during the cultural renaissance that began there in the sixteenth century and continues to be expressed today in sophisticated philosophical literature, delightful poems and songs, everyday conversations, and daily rituals.

After looking at the current environmental condition of the river in some detail, I examine how the religious perspectives, practices, and sentiments associated with the Yamuna are affected by its massive pollution. I also explore the responses emerging in reaction to this situation in the religious communities that worship the Yamuna as a goddess. This will take us into the world of Indian river environmentalism, a world that in many ways is quite different from its Western counterpart. I conclude with a consideration of what a study of the Yamuna has to offer those with a general interest in Indian religious culture, as well as those concerned with what is happening to rivers and other aspects of our environment worldwide.

I began this study with great concern about the environmental deterioration taking place in the region of Braj—a major site of my research for more than twenty years—and, for that matter, throughout the entire world. All who have eyes open to seeing it are well aware that we are already moving rapidly into a serious environmental crisis that threatens the very future of most life-forms on the planet. One of my reasons for researching and writing this book is that I saw it as a way to deal with a growing state of despair about what humans are doing to their environment everywhere, but specifically in northern India, which has become a second home for me. I have now observed how the lives of my friends in the region of Braj have been adversely affected by environmental degradation, and I have listened to them express serious worries about the land they love and fears for their children's future. In part, my inquiries were motivated by an interest in finding ways to appreciate the wonder of the world in a manner that neither denies nor is defeated by the serious problems we face today. As I ventured deeper into this study, my attention increasingly turned to tracking an elusive balance point between the differing perspectives I encountered in my research. I found myself repeatedly moving back and forth between contrasting views: between the crystal clear waters of the Yamuna flowing freely high in the Himalayan mountains and the dreadfully reduced and polluted stream that emerges downstream from the metropolis of Delhi; between the most beautiful poetic and theological literature ever written about a river goddess and alarming scientific reports about the current water conditions of the Yamuna; and between discussions with devoted worshippers of the river and talks with environmental scientists. How is it possible to hold these differing perspectives together and live in an authentic and responsible manner that remains open to the wonder of the natural world around us? Or perhaps more simply: how are we to live in an age of pollution?

Since no other study of this sacred river exists in English, I introduce the reader to the Yamuna's major geographical features, from its source high in the Himalayan mountains to its confluence with the Ganges on the plains far below. The Yamuna has a long history on the South Asian subcontinent. About fifty million years ago, the large land mass we now call South Asia slammed into the Eurasian plate. Several hundred miles of the Indian subcontinental plate have subsequently been subducted beneath the Eurasian plate, resulting in the uplifting of the latter plate and the creation of the Himalayan mountain range. Since that time, great rivers have formed to direct the water off the southern slopes of what is now the largest mountain range in the world. The rich alluvial soil carried off the Himalayas by these rivers made the plains of northern India some of the most fertile land on the planet. The origin of the Yamuna River, in the central Himalayan region, is thought to date from the mid-Miocene epoch, during which time it was part of the Indus River system, which drained into the Arabian Sea. Because of subsequent plate tectonic activity, however, the Yamuna shifted course, and today it forms the largest tributary of the Ganges system that flows into the Bay of Bengal.[3]

With a catchment area of 142,827 square miles, or 366,223 square kilometers, the total length of the Yamuna from its source at Yamunotri to its confluence with the Ganges at Allahabad is about 853 miles, or 1,376 kilometers.[4] I have traveled the full length of the river several times. I made my first visit to Yamunotri while participating in a bicycle expedition that consisted of a group of international riders who were concerned about the deteriorating quality of the river.[5] We traveled by mountain bike along the course of the river for about half its length, starting just below Yamunotri and ending in the Braj pilgrimage town of Vrindaban. I later returned to Yamunotri and the upper Yamuna valley for several more visits, once with my entire family. I have traveled the remaining half of the river on several occasions by car (and small sections by boat), sometimes with family or friends, and sometimes alone. I lived on the bank of the Yamuna in Braj for more than four years and have visited it yearly for more than two decades, spending much time observing, studying, discussing, swimming in, worrying about, and simply enjoying this magnificent river. My time with the Yamuna has yielded much familiarity and affection.

The Yamuna River is considered one of the holiest rivers of India. Much Hindu scripture identifies it and its sister, the Ganges, as the most eminent of all the sacred rivers. Many temples in India feature these two goddesses standing on both sides of the doorway to the inner sanctum.[6] The Yamuna has played a major role in the political history, religious culture, and economy of the heart of India. One out of every twelve people alive today lives in the Gangetic basin, of which the Yamuna is a part, and about sixty million people are dependent on water solely from the Yamuna.

The Yamuna originates from the Yamunotri glacier 20,000 feet above sea level. This glacier is nestled into a steep slope just below the crest of Mount Kalinda, located about six miles west of the Bandarpunch peak (20,735 feet), the dominant mountain in the central Himalayan region of Garhwal, which divides the watershed of the Yamuna from that of the Ganges. The Yamuna gushes out of the morainic snout of the glacier to fill a pond named Saptarishi Kund and from there cascades down the southern face of Mount Kalinda in an impressive series of waterfalls to join boiling water bubbling from a hot spring that flows out of the stone wall of a canyon at the base of the chute. Here, at an elevation of about 10,500 feet, is located the Yamunotri pilgrimage complex. Pilgrims have been coming to this site for centuries to worship Yamuna at her source and to seek her blessings. The pilgrimage complex of Yamunotri is described in chapter 2.

The Yamuna descends rapidly from the Yamunotri pilgrimage complex as a freely flowing and crystal clear mountain stream, carving a valley through the scenic Garhwali hills. It cuts through solid rock in its uppermost region, often exposing bright red layers of ancient sediment. The steep slopes of the valley are covered with brown oaks and the evergreen Himalayan yew trees. A few small settlements, such as Hanuman Chatti, have sprung up in the upper valley to serve the large number of pilgrims who make their way to the blessed source of the river. The river widens as it leaves the higher elevations, and small villages can be found in the valley, where residents have devised ways to make a living in terraced fields dug into the steep slopes. Turquoise waters wrap around yellowish green rice fields with white sand beaches on the opposite shore. White-cheeked and red-vented bulbuls contribute birdsongs to the beauty of the valley. The Yamuna is joined in the mountains by several tributaries that add volume to its current. The most important among them is the Tons, which merges with the Yamuna from the northwest at Kalsi, an old historic town in which stands a rock edict of the great emperor Ashoka. The upper Yamuna valley stretches about 100 miles through the Himalayas before the river forces its way through the foothills known as the Shivaliks and emerges onto the Indo-Gangetic plains at the town of Dakpathar.

Here a great change takes place, for at Dakpathar the Yamuna leaves the wild mountains and enters the "civilized" plains. Here it is transformed from a free river to a stream managed by and for humans. Dakpathar marks a boundary: located on the border of the mountains and plains, it signals a transition from the natural to the industrial, from river worship to river management, from the aesthetic to the utilitarian, from Yamuna as a majestic, unharnessed river to Yamuna as a greatly reduced stream. At Dakpathar, a huge barrage has been built across the entire river, and a great majority of the water is removed from the riverbed to be channeled off into utility canals.[7] Only 10 percent of the water will reach Delhi, the capital city about 150 miles downstream, which was built on the bank of the Yamuna centuries ago because of the river's beauty and bounty.

Believing that India's future depended on rapid industrialization, Prime Minister Pundit Jawaharlal Nehru laid the foundation stone for a hydroelectric dam at Dakpathar in 1948. Although the project was not completed until 1965 because of financial problems and disputes between the states of Punjab and Uttar Pradesh, this was one of the first of Nehru's big dam projects after independence in 1947. Nehru was well known for saying that "dams are the temples of a modern India."[8] Today the Dakpathar Barrage spans almost a third of a mile (516.5 meters), with twenty-five huge bays to control the river, and almost all the water is diverted by means of this barrage into a power channel to generate electricity, before some of it is returned further downstream.

From Dakpathar, the diminished Yamuna flows over a rocky riverbed through a series of low hills to Paonta Sahib, a town on the west bank of the river in the state of Himachal Pradesh that is of great significance for the religious community of Sikhs.[9] In the seventeenth century, the local king of this region invited the tenth guru, Guru Gobind Singh, to live here in his kingdom. Guru Gobind Singh visited this site in 1685 and was so impressed with the magnificence of the river that he decided to stay. The name *Paonta* means "a place to keep the feet." Later that year the guru laid the foundation stone for a fortified town. Sikh poets and saints began to visit this place, drawn by its natural beauty and the attractive personality of Guru Gobind Singh, and soon Paonta Sahib became a great center of literature and learning. The guru himself stayed here for more than four years, composing much of his famous poetry on the bank of the Yamuna.

Paonta Sahib became famous for poetry contests; Guru Gobind Singh gathered fifty-two court poets around him and erected a platform called the Kavi Darbar Asthan on the bank of the Yamuna; poetry contests are still held here at every full moon. The most impressive building at Paonta Sahib, however, is the Gurdwara Harmandir Sahib, a large temple first established by Guru Gobind Singh and enhanced during the reign of Ranjit Singh, the famous Sikh emperor who ruled over an independent Sikh kingdom in northwest India in the early nineteenth century. This temple, which features a large white dome and houses weapons used by Guru Gobind Singh, is a major pilgrimage site for Sikhs today. The Guru Granth, the holy book of the Sikhs that contains the words of the gurus, rests on an elaborately decorated dais in the center of the temple.

About ten miles downstream from Paonta Sahib, the Yamuna reaches Tajewala, site of another huge barrage that dams the river and channels its water into two irrigation canals: the Western and Eastern. The Western Yamuna Canal was originally built in the fourteenth century by Firuz Shah Tughluq, the sultan of Delhi, to support irrigation schemes designed to bring barren lands into productive use and supply water to his new fort west of Delhi at the town of Hissar.[10] By the sixteenth century, Firuz Shah's canal had become so silted that it was no longer functional. The Mughal emperor Akbar ordered the restoration of the canal during his reign, in the latter half of the sixteenth century, so that it could once again carry water for irrigation to the dry regions west of Delhi.[11] Modification of the canal was begun in 1638, during Shah Jahan's time as Mughal emperor. The result of this alteration was that the canal's terminal point was shifted from Hissar to the royal city of Delhi itself, for the purpose of supplying freshwater to the new fort constructed there by Shah Jahan.[12] Over time, however, this new course, too, fell into disrepair. Work began in 1817 under the British governor Lord Warren Hastings to reopen the canal for the purpose of irrigating the regions west of Delhi; this project was completed in 1825. Today, the Western Yamuna Canal flows through the industrial towns of Yamunanagar, Karnal, Panipat, and Sonepat and is maintained by the state government of Haryana to support the extensive agricultural projects of the so-called green revolution in this region.

The Eastern Yamuna Canal, which began operation in the 1830s, also starts at the Tajewala Barrage, and it follows the route of an earlier canal built during the reign of Shah Jahan. This canal supplies water for irrigating the western Uttar Pradesh districts of Sahranpur, Muzaffarnagar, and Meerut and is currently maintained by the state government of Uttar Pradesh. Previously this canal was called the Doab Canal, since it irrigated the fertile region between the Yamuna and Ganges Rivers known as the Doab, or "Two Rivers." These two canals have been used to supply water for the green revolution in the regions surrounding the banks of the Yamuna just north of Delhi.

By means of modern agricultural techniques and the abundant use of water from the Yamuna for irrigation, India has been able to feed a larger number of people than ever before. The introduction of modern technological farming techniques in the region has not been without problems, however, as we shall see in chapter 3. So much water is extracted from the main riverbed for the Western and Eastern Yamuna Canals that, during the dry season, no water flows downstream from the Tajewala Barrage. The river recharges itself somewhat from groundwater, and a few tributaries enable it to regain some water from the mountains. Nonetheless, only 10 percent of the volume of water leaving the mountains ever reaches Delhi, and during the dry months of the year no water at all flowing from Yamunotri reaches the capital city. Clearly, dams have an enormous effect on the life of this river.

Downstream from the Tajewala waterworks, the Yamuna flows through flat, rich agricultural land—planted with abundant wheat, tall sugar cane, and yellow mustard flowers—for some 140 miles and arrives in Delhi, the huge megalopolitan capital of India originally built on the bank of the Yamuna because of its attractiveness and seemingly endless supply of freshwater. Here, two more barrages break the flow of the river, at the city's water-supply intake point of Wazirabad and at the lower end of the river's passage through Delhi at Okhla, where the stream is channeled into the Agra Canal for additional irrigation. Almost all the water remaining in the river is extracted at this point; the darkened water that dribbles out of the Okhla Barrage consists primarily of human waste and industrial effluents. The quality of the water in the Yamuna once it leaves Delhi is said to be the worst of any river in India.[13] The tale of what happens to the Yamuna in Delhi is told in chapter 3.

Delhi's long and fascinating history is intimately linked with the Yamuna. Indian mythology records that this was once the site of Indraprastha, the capital built by King Yudhishthira, the eldest of the five Pandava brothers who are the heroes of the great Hindu epic the *Mahabharata*.[14] By the time a Muslim ruler from Afghanistan conquered this region in the late twelfth century, Delhi was already inhabited by Tomar Rajputs, a military clan from Rajasthan that had settled here because of the protection provided by the barren Aravalli Hills and the cool life-giving water afforded by the Yamuna River. The first of the so-called seven cities of Delhi was built on the west bank of the Yamuna at the end of the twelfth century by Qutbuddin Aibak, the Turkish slave-general of Muhammad Ghuri who defeated the Rajputs and took possession of the kingdom of Delhi.[15] Muhammad Ghuri was assassinated soon after, and Qutbuddin constructed a fort near the Yamuna, proclaiming himself sultan of Delhi. Thus began the Delhi Sultanate, three centuries of rule in India from the bank of the Yamuna by Turks with ties to central Asia. Five more cities were built near the river at Delhi by succeeding sultans. Then, in the early sixteenth century, the Turkish sultan of Delhi, Ibrahim Lodi, was defeated by the invading Afghan forces of Babar, who established what was to become the Mughal Empire, which would last another three centuries. Shah Jahan, Babar's great-great-grandson and the grandson of the famous Akbar, built the magnificent seventh of the old cities of Delhi in the mid-seventeenth century. This city represented the very zenith of Mughal architecture: it featured wide streets, luxurious residential quarters, artistic mosques, and busy bazaars. The city hugged the western side of the forbidding sandstone Red Fort, which was built directly on the bank of the Yamuna and cooled with water pumped from its bed. The British assumed military control over much of northeast India in the late eighteenth century and, in the middle of the nineteenth century, took charge of Delhi after exiling Bahadur Shah II, the last of the Mughal rulers.[16] Deciding to shift India's capital from the older colonial city of Calcutta, the British began in 1911 to build New Delhi to take its place. Throughout the period of British colonial rule, which ended with Indian independence in 1947, the Yamuna was navigable, allowing passengers to travel from Calcutta to Delhi by boat. The rapid decline in water flow and quality has long since eliminated this possibility. After independence, Delhi quickly sprawled out on both sides of the Yamuna. The city received a large number of refugees from the partition of Pakistan and India and a major portion of the economic and technological development and population explosion that characterized the latter half of the twentieth century. This megalopolis is now the chief source of pollution in the river that runs through it.

From Delhi, the Yamuna flows about one hundred miles downstream to meander past the ornate temples and red sandstone ghats of the pilgrimage centers of Vrindaban, Mathura, and Gokul in Braj, the important cultural region associated with the popular Hindu deity Krishna. The concentration of Yamuna temples and devotees in this region is greater than in any other. Although this section of the river is now the most polluted, ironically it is here that Yamuna is most celebrated as a goddess and her theology and worship have been most fully refined. In Braj she is regarded as an exquisite goddess of supreme love, and an encounter with her in this region is believed by many to be the most transformative. The well-developed theology and religious practices present in Braj are the subject of chapter 4.

Traveling the twelve miles from Vrindaban to Mathura by boat provides a wonderful opportunity to observe the abundant variety of wildlife in and along the Yamuna. I undertook such an excursion with my family during the first month of the new millennium, and I include a description of our journey to give a sense of the fauna that can still be found along the river. We departed midafternoon from Keshi Ghat in Vrindaban in a wooden boat with these Hindi words painted on its inside walls: "O Yamuna-ji, please grant me life after life of living near you. All glory to Shri Yamuna, Chief Lover of Krishna!" January can be quite pleasant in Braj. The day was sunny and warm, and many people sat on the ghats enjoying the mild winter weather; several noted our plans with envy. Bar-headed geese were basking in the sun on a wide expanse of white sand on the opposite shore while we settled into our boat. I had observed a large group of painted storks resting there the previous day. As we pulled away from the ghat, I saw a flash of silver in the river and recognized it as one of the flat-bodied fish that inhabit these waters. We soon ducked under a pontoon bridge that allowed traffic to cross the river during the months with little rain. Several turtles, the animal companions of Yamuna, had climbed out of the water to sun themselves on low sandy cliffs just past the bridge. A short distance downstream we encountered a small flock of spoonbills feeding in the shallow water at the edge of the river. A pied kingfisher was performing impressive aerial dives into the water ahead of the boat, and cormorants bobbed in the current all around us. Plump orange-colored Brahminy ducks with green-marked wings called out from the shore, and the grand silhouette of a gray heron captured our attention a short distance beyond. As the Yamuna snakes slowly through the countryside, graced this time of year with brilliant yellow mustard fields in full bloom, it is frequently lined with a great variety of waterbirds. The "Yamunashtakam," a devotional hymn written by the sixteenth-century saint Vallabhacharya, identifies these birds as Yamuna's companions who accompany her as she travels to meet her beloved.

A little more than twenty miles from the Yamuna, and well within its watershed, is the Bharatpur Bird Sanctuary, located within the Keoladeo National Park. This World Heritage site is one of the finest bird sanctuaries in India and is home to more than four hundred species of birds during the winter months. Most famous among these are the Siberian cranes, tall white cranes known for their magnificent dance, which migrate across almost half the globe from their breeding grounds in Siberia to winter at the wetlands of Bharatpur. A great many of the birds that frequent the Bharatpur sanctuary can be seen on the shores of the Yamuna. About halfway through our journey, we approached small dirt cliffs formed where the river had cut into the surrounding fields. Colonies of cliff swallows, fast-moving, gregarious birds that skim along the surface of the river in search of insects, make their home in these banks. A colony of weaver birds had woven grass nests with long entrance tubes that hung from the nests' bottoms in a tree at the top of the bank. Once we cleared the bend formed by these low cliffs, we were in for a real treat. A flock of large white pelicans occupied this quiet stretch of the river; some were floating in the water, others were basking in the sun on shore. These huge birds, which have pinkish white plumage and large pink feet, have a wingspan of about six feet. Further downstream, two nilgai—large elklike animals—surprised us by plunging into the water and swimming across the river directly in front of our boat. We arrived at Vishram Ghat in Mathura at dusk, welcomed by the lights of a long string of sandstone temples and the sound of the gongs from evening services. Although pollution in this part of the river has reached life-threatening levels, the wildlife on the shores of the Yamuna in this region is still splendid.

The Yamuna leaves the pilgrimage towns of Braj and winds its way through badlands marked by dry arroyos. This area is famous for bandits who take advantage of the harsh environment to evade the law.

After flowing in a southerly direction for half of its length, here the Yamuna begins to turn eastward. Forty miles downstream from Braj, the Yamuna passes near the celebrated Taj Mahal, built in the seventeenth century by Shah Jahan as a loving memorial for his beloved queen, Mumtaz Mahal, the "Jewel of the Palace." This white-marble-domed mausoleum has drawn a steady stream of visitors to the bank of the Yamuna from all over the world. Shah Jahan had planned to build his own tomb in black marble on the opposite bank of the Yamuna and link the two with a bridge over the river as a symbol of transcendent love, but his plans were never realized. His son Aurangzeb seized the throne and imprisoned his father in the Agra Fort, a structure with magnificent views of the Yamuna built by the great Mughal emperor Akbar.

Forty miles downstream from Agra, the Yamuna makes an abrupt turn back to the north before resuming its southeasterly journey, creating a crescent moon shape just as the Ganges does at Banaras or Kashi. For this reason, this place has become known as the "Kashi of Braj," but it is better known as Bateshwar, named after the main Shiva temple located here. Deep ravines covered with thick foliage dominate the surrounding terrain. Austere yogis have carved caves into the hard dirt of the hillsides, and this area too is a favorite haunt of bandits. On the day I visited, children were floating on inflated inner tubes and splashing about in the water. A string of 108 beautifully whitewashed Shiva temples lines the crescent curve of the river.[17] The people of this area consider Bateshwar to be part of the cultural region of Braj, and they say that this is where the wicked King Kansa's body was found after Krishna killed him and threw him in the river at Mathura.[18] Also located here is Shauripur, an important pilgrimage site for Jains. Ancient scriptures declare that a visit to the Yamuna at Bateshwar destroys all sins.[19]

Fifty miles downstream from Bateshwar, the Yamuna is joined by the Chambal River, which drains the eastern slopes of the Aravalli mountain range in southeastern Rajasthan. The Chambal, 430 miles long, is the biggest of the Yamuna's tributaries. The large quantity of water flowing in the Chambal replenishes the Yamuna after the latter's massive depletion upstream for agricultural irrigation and Delhi's water demands. The Central Pollution Control Board reports that "the Chambal contributes 5 to 10 times more water to the Yamuna river than its own flow in dry weather."[20] The Chambal revives the Yamuna, as the Yamuna revives the Ganges further downstream. Three more major tributaries enter the Yamuna before it merges with the Ganges; the Sind, Betwa, and Ken all drain the northern slopes of the Vindhya mountain range in the state of

Madhya Pradesh into the Yamuna. After joining with these tributaries, the Yamuna runs with a more forceful flow of fresher water. By the time she reaches her point of confluence with the Ganges at Allahabad—another 290 miles downstream from her junction with the Chambal—the Yamuna is considerably larger than her sister river.

The confluence of the Yamuna and the Ganges is a remarkable sight. Water from the Yamuna is deep blue in color, whereas water from the Ganges is a chalky white; the two meet to form a wide expanse of water at Allahabad that is divided by a clearly distinguishable line. Many consider this to be one of the most sacred sites in all of India. The *Narada Purana* states: "Great sages say that the confluence of the Ganga and Yamuna is the most excellent of all sacred spots, and the most sacred of all holy places."[21] Accordingly, this is a favorite bathing spot for the many pilgrims who come to this site for what they call a "holy dip."

The older, pre-Muslim name for Allahabad is Prayag.[22] The word *prayag* literally means a "place of sacrifice," but its common usage refers to a pilgrimage place at the confluence of two or more rivers. Prayag's importance extends beyond the fact that it is the confluence of the two most sacred rivers of northern India: local lore and Sanskrit scripture have it that a third sacred river, the Sarasvati, joins the Yamuna and Ganges at this location. Although satellite photography has confirmed the existence of the ancient Sarasvati River in the desert of northwest India, she is said to join the other two rivers here from a subterranean source.[23] Popular posters available in Allahabad depict the three river goddesses coming together at this site: Yamuna comes from the northwest seated on a turtle, Ganges comes from the northeast seated on a crocodile, and Sarasvati appears in the middle seated on a white swan.[24] In a poster I purchased at the confluence, the goddesses are four-armed and dressed in red. However, a local Hindi booklet titled the *Greatness of Prayag* states, "Ganges comes here wearing white garments; Yamuna flows here wearing a blue sari; Sarasvati meets them here in a hidden form. The three sisters reveal themselves here beneath the Banyan Tree."[25] The booklet identifies this famous tree as the only thing that will remain once the world is reabsorbed at the time of the great destruction. A remnant of this immortal tree stands on the bank of the Yamuna just inside the fort of Allahabad. This used to be a popular destination for pilgrims, but access to it is now blocked; believing this tree to be a direct link to heaven, some people in the past would jump from it, plunging into the Yamuna and drowning themselves.

Because this is the most important sacred confluence in India, it is a major pilgrimage site, particularly in the lunar month of Magh (around February). The *Padma Purana* proclaims that a person who bathes here is even more fortunate than some of the minor gods: "That holy place called Prayag, where Ganga, Yamuna, and Sarasvati are flowing, is the best and is inaccessible even to gods. . . . A man who bathes at Prayag during the month of Magha has no limit to the number of fruits he obtains."[26] Every twelve years this site is home to the Kumbha Mela, the largest gathering of human beings on the planet. Holy men and women from all over India, along with their followers, numbering in the millions, camp for a month on the sands of the rivers and bathe in their confluence. By this act the bathers are said to be cleansed of all sins and to become recipients of powerful life blessings. The *Padma Purana* explains that all the other holy places on Earth come to the confluence of these three rivers in Prayag to be cleansed of the sins they accumulate by their contact with sinners.[27] No temple has been constructed in Allahabad to celebrate the river goddesses, for the water itself is usually viewed as the primary divinity. The *Greatness of Prayag*, for example, declares, "The original deity of the confluence of Ganges and Yamuna is in the form of water [*jal rup me*]."[28]

Although in name the Yamuna ends at Allahabad, devotees of this river insist that the combined rivers are "Ganges in name, but Yamuna in form."[29] There is much truth to this claim, for about two-thirds of the water flowing into the confluence comes from the Yamuna riverbed. This means the river that flows past the famous sacred city of Varanasi, more commonly known as Banaras, and empties into the Bay of Bengal at Gangasagar (some five hundred miles downstream) is to a large degree the Yamuna, although it is called the Ganges downstream from Allahabad.

Such is the course of the mighty Yamuna, which flows through stunning mountain territory from her source at Yamunotri and passes the megalopolis of Delhi, the sacred land of Braj, and the Taj Mahal on her way to her confluence with the Ganges in Prayag, or Allahabad. From here she is joined with her sister the Ganges to run alongside the holy city of Banaras, and eventually she unites with the ocean at the Bay of Bengal. There is a mighty tale that accompanies her as she winds through several thousand years of history. This tale promises to yield many lessons for those concerned with the fate of rivers in our world today.

CHAPTER I

A River of Delights,
a River of Troubles

We are slow to realize water, the beauty and magic of it. It is
interestingly strange to us forever.

                                        Henry David Thoreau

I hold the hand of my five-year-old son, Nathan, as I walk down a
twisted alley that winds through a maze of ancient red stone temples
and leads to the bank of the Yamuna River in the northern Indian town
of Vrindaban. The sun is low on the western horizon, casting a pinkish
golden hue on the rippling surface of the water. Bright green rose-ringed
parrots squawk noisily as they flutter about the buildings behind us, a
koel bird sings its fluty cuckoo call from the tall grasses on the other
shore, and a gray heron wades in the shallow water nearby, hunting for
fish. We settle down on a sandstone platform near three Shiva lingams
to appreciate the sights and sounds of the evening. We are both drawn
to the peace of this place and remain quiet. A turtle pokes its head out
of the water and stares at us for a few moments before disappearing
into the depths. The river is calm in April, and its mirrorlike surface
reflects the ever-changing play of light. We both comment on how beautiful the river looks this evening. Nathan calls it "magical." Reflecting
on all the devotional literature I have been reading, I find it easy in this
moment to understand why for centuries this river has been worshipped
as a goddess. Beauty abounds; this is indeed a world blessed with a river
of delights.

 After some time, however, my gaze shifts from distant to near. I look
down directly into the water and see that it is dark in color—too dark
for natural water, even for a river known to be dark. A large drain carrying untreated sewage empties into the river a hundred yards upstream

from where we sit. Suddenly everything I have been reading about the
environmental condition of this river comes crashing into my consciousness. The flow of the river is diminishing rapidly, because of the
increasing demand for water for domestic use by a growing population
and for irrigation by modern farming techniques. Pesticides seep into
the river from the surrounding farmland, and frightening amounts of
untreated sewage and toxic industrial effluents pour into it continually
from Delhi, a city of more than fifteen million people located one hundred miles upstream.

I struggle to hold onto the magical beauty I experienced with Nathan
a few minutes earlier. It is wonderful to see this river through the eyes
of a child, especially a child open to its stories; but he too is aware of
this other perspective. He points to some trash floating past us in a plastic bag. "Yamuna-ji has a sickness," he says. "People are mean to her."
When he first arrived in Vrindaban, he wanted to swim in the river,
delighted by its sight and my own accounts of swimming in the river
twenty years ago. But my awareness of the pollution loads the river now
carries prohibited me from allowing him this simple pleasure. Joyful
delight gives way to sadness and anger. I follow these feelings and my
knowledge of the river's pollution into a sober consideration of a flood
of troubles.

Rivers are now under threat worldwide; freshwater is becoming
scarcer and more polluted. Although we humans recognize that life on
Earth would be nonexistent without freshwater, we disregard this fact
by abusing our rivers and other sources of freshwater. *The World Watch
Reader* reports, "The Nile, the Ganges, the Amu Dar'ya and Syr Dar'ya,
the Huang He (or Yellow River), and the Colorado are each now so
dammed, diverted, or overtapped that[,] for parts of the year, little or
none of their freshwater reaches the sea. Their collective diminution
portends not only worsening water shortages and potential conflicts
over scarce supplies, but mounting ecological damage."[1] Moreover, the
remaining freshwater that the rivers of the world carry is often so
severely polluted by domestic sewage and industrial poisons that rivers
now threaten the very life they once nurtured. "Eighty percent of all disease in developing countries is spread by unsafe water. . . . In Russia, the
very rivers that people depend on for life—the Volga, the Dvina, the
Ob—are now hazardous to public health."[2]

And it is not just the water; we are now in the process of changing the
Earth's atmosphere. Human activity in the latter half of the twentieth
century increased the concentration of carbon dioxide in the atmosphere

by nearly 30 percent. The result is a global warming that threatens to challenge all life-forms with severe weather and radical climate change.[3] The protective ozone layer is rapidly being depleted because of our fossil-fuel burning and our use of chlorofluorocarbons and other ozone-depleting substances. We are contaminating our air, soil, water, and bodies with toxic chemicals. Safe food is disappearing, the cancer rate is skyrocketing, forests are being clear-cut, the amphibian population is crashing, and biodiversity is plummeting. Many scientists contend that we are now in the throes of one of the fastest mass extinctions in the planet's history.[4] Granted, death and destruction are a natural feature of the biological process; nonetheless, the rate of extinction and radical environmental change today are clearly driven by human activity. Scientists now concur that biodiversity is necessary for the overall health of all species, and the increasingly rapid loss of biodiversity now taking place is one of the greatest threats to life on Earth. All those who are courageous enough to pierce through socially sanctioned denial and acknowledge the vast sea of troubles we face today know that the very future of a healthy humanity is in question.[5] There is no more important challenge today than to find a way out of this life-threatening nightmare and into a nurturing world of sanity in which all life can flourish.[6]

Today we live in a complicated world: a world of delight—perhaps more delight than we ever imagined—and a world of trouble, perhaps more trouble than we ever bargained for. What follows relates to my own struggles to understand and negotiate this contemporary dichotomy in human experience, using the sacred Yamuna River of northern India as a focusing lens. From the outset, I want to make clear that I do not mean to be overly critical of India: the problems of river pollution are found everywhere in the world today. Nonetheless, although the Yamuna is a river of delights—many in India see it as a liquid form of love—today it is also a river with a great many troubles. An examination of the Yamuna River, then, affords a look at both rivers and river pollution from the distinctive perspective of the Hindu religious cultures of northern India.

Why do we humans produce a river of troubles when offered a river of delights? Any answer to this question necessarily is complex, but certainly one contributing factor is that we largely lack an awareness of and appreciation for the interdependence and preciousness of all life-forms. Contrary to the information biologists now provide, human beings often assume their superiority over and independence from other life-forms.[7] Indu Tikekar, a religious scholar and Gandhian environmentalist living in the Himalayas, told a group of bicyclists riding for the purpose of raising awareness about the plight of the Yamuna, "All the expressions of nature are all expressions of one reality. Therefore, humans are members of one family. Why are we then creating havoc within our family? Because we have lost the sense that we are part of one family. Our problem is that we think that we are the center of life. The solution is to realize that we are all part of one single reality."[8] Reflecting on the troubles of the Ganges River, Lina Gupta writes, "From an ecofeminist perspective, pollution is the result not only of inappropriate technologies and mismanagement of resources, but also a failure to be connected with, to, and for one another and the rest of the planet. External pollution begins with internal pollution, the pollution of thinking we are utterly separate from the rest of existence."[9] These insights invite consideration of the role of religion in the current environmental crisis.

What does religion have to do with the health of a river? The contemporary science of ecology is producing many new ways of thinking. A new field of inquiry now in the process of emerging in religious studies, and which is generally known as Religion and Ecology, recognizes that religious worldviews play a major role in shaping human attitudes toward the natural environment. This field analyzes religious texts, both written and ethnographic, to explore how an expressed worldview determines particular beliefs, practices, and interactions regarding the nonhuman world. Different religious traditions establish and promote very different human perspectives on the natural environment. Some religious worldviews regard the health of a river, for example, as religiously unimportant, whereas others consider the well-being of a river to be essential. Religion and Ecology examines such differences and investigates their implications and consequences in the arena of human behavior, for the human effect on a river today is considerable. Those who consider a river sacred treat it differently than do those who regard a river in strictly utilitarian terms. This book explores how the religious culture associated with the Yamuna increasingly serves as a valuable resource in efforts to protect and restore the river.

The emerging field of Religion and Ecology has its origin in the work of the medievalist Lynn White and other scholars concerned with the environmental crisis in the late 1960s. White published a seminal article in 1967 titled "The Historical Roots of Our Ecologic Crisis" and a subsequent article in 1973 titled "Continuing the Conversation."[10] In the first of these articles, White remarks, "What people do about their ecology depends on what they think about themselves in relation to things around them. Human ecology is deeply conditioned by the beliefs about our nature and destiny—that is, by religion."[11] Here White articulates a foundational idea: that religious beliefs influence human treatment of the natural world.[12] White's primary focus is European (and thus American) Christianity. According to him, Western Christianity's dominant theology, which has tended to profess a God who transcends all nature, as well as its strong anthropocentrism, which insists that the physical creation has no value except to serve human purposes, has contributed significantly to the destructive environmental practices we observe today. White, however, does not view religion only as a problem: it may also be part of a solution. "More science and more technology are not going to get us out of the present ecologic crisis until we find a new religion, or rethink our old one. . . . Since the roots of our trouble are so largely religious, the remedy must also be essentially religious, whether we call it that or not."[13] Acknowledging the historically diverse character of Christianity, White promotes a side of this tradition that he identifies as its "recessive genes," exemplified by Saint Francis of Assisi.[14] Importantly, White represents the current ecological crisis as a "religious problem," since for him "every culture, whether it is overtly religious or not, is shaped primarily by its religion."[15] Accordingly, White looks to "religion, including crypto-religion, as a source for historical explanations."[16] With these assertions, he established an approach to environmental considerations in which religion is taken seriously. The conversation White and others began in the late 1960s has certainly continued; although the new field of Religion and Ecology is still in its infancy, it has established a firm foothold in the American academy.[17]

Parallel with the development of the academic study of religion and ecology has been a change in the religious traditions themselves. Although White became the most well known, he was only one of many in the 1960s who criticized the dominant trends of Western Christianity for contributing to the ecological crisis. The assertion that Christianity was largely responsible for attitudes that led to environmental destruction caused some within Western societies to abandon Christianity in search of more eco-friendly ideas in Asian and Native American religious traditions. But many who accepted the critique of Christianity chose to remain within the circles of Christian theology. This latter group of reformers engaged in efforts to rethink the current Christian tradition and articulate a new understanding of it in light of the ecological crisis. This development has been labeled by some as the "greening of religion."[18] While acknowledging that Christianity has been a causal problem in the ecological crisis, those involved in this project agree with White that it may also serve as a creative solution. This leads them to engage in both deconstructive and constructive work.

A general consensus emerged in the late 1960s that identified several negative aspects of Western Christianity contributing to the environmental crisis. First is that Christianity has been highly anthropocentric (the belief that humans are separate from and superior to all other life-forms), a tenet that has led to a disregard for the value of other life-forms.[19] Second, Christianity stripped nature of any sacrality, making way for the exploitation of nature in a mood of indifference.[20] Third, Christianity identified technological progress with religious virtue, thereby legitimizing technological developments that have proved to be harmful to the environment. Fourth, Christianity rejected the notion of metempsychosis, a belief that allowed recognition of a nonhuman being as a relative. For Christianity, the good soul was destined only for heaven, not the body of an animal or plant, thus removing another restraint to harming nonhuman life-forms. Fifth, Christianity often tended to view wilderness as a cursed land. Paradise was conceived of as either a garden (Eden) or a city (New Jerusalem). This fostered a move toward the domestication of all wild land and its inhabitants. Sixth, otherworldliness is pervasive in Christianity; because we are temporary sojourners in this world, our ultimate destination is assumed to be elsewhere. Such a belief is often linked to a radically transcendent view of God or the sacred, and it fosters an attitude whereby this world is greatly devalued in favor of a home far removed from this one.[21] In addition, the charge was made that Christianity eradicated many different cultures that had more this-worldly, or eco-friendly, attitudes. Although the initial critique of religion from an environmental perspective was first applied to Christianity, it was extended over time to include aspects of any religious tradition that might be viewed with suspicion by someone concerned about the environmental crisis. For those receptive to this new avenue of religious criticism, an opportunity presented itself for fresh and creative theological reflection.

Because Christianity was the initial target of criticism by White and others, much creative theology has emerged in Christian circles in response. A common goal of this endeavor is to identify sources within Christianity that can be used to foster a more ecologically positive view of the world. Despite conservative resistance, eco-theology is thriving in American Christianity today.[22] This collective work calls for a move beyond anthropocentrism and for a reenchantment of the world that honors the intrinsic value of the nonhuman and celebrates all life by asserting that the whole of nature is sacred. The theologian Rosemary Ruether, for example, uses lessons from modern science to help accomplish this. "One of the most basic 'lessons' of ecology and spirituality is the interrelation of all things. Both earth science and astrophysics give us extraordinary and powerfully compelling messages about our kinship, not only with all living things on earth, but even with distant stars' and galaxies. A profound spirituality would arise if we would attempt to experience this kinship and make it present in our consciousness. . . . Recognition of this profound kinship must bridge the arrogant barrier that humans have erected to wall themselves off, not only from other sentient animals, but also from simpler animals, plants, and the abiotic matrix of life in rocks, soils, air, and water. Like the great nature mystic, Francis of Assisi, we may learn to greet as our brothers and sisters the wolf and lamb, trees and grasses, fire and water."[23] In the works of many contemporary Christian theologians, we observe a religious perspective that takes seriously the sacrality of the entire world, and an ethical call for a loving care that extends beyond humans.

Trends observed in Western religions are also discernible in philosophy, most specifically in the area of ethics.[24] Throughout much of the history of Western philosophy, ethicists have tended to focus on the behavior of people toward other people. Traditional moral philosophy showed little regard for the nonhuman world. Driven by serious concerns about the environmental crisis, however, environmental philosophy and ethics came into being in the early 1970s.[25] In general, this development in ethics involved widening the circle of moral concern to include all life. More radical environmental philosophers proposed extending the moral horizon to include rocks, soil, rivers, forests, and even entire ecosystems. Representative of this movement are those who identify themselves as "deep ecologists."

The recognized founder of the philosophical movement of deep ecology is Arne Naess, an eminent Norwegian philosopher and mountaineer. Naess coined the term *deep ecology* in a seminal article published in 1973 in which he distinguished the deep ecological movement from the "shallow" ecology movement. The latter, according to Naess, is concerned primarily with resource depletion and pollution control via technological innovations that still favor continuous economic growth and avoid seriously questioning the fundamental values that brought us to the current crisis. The deep ecological movement, on the other hand, through a process of deep questioning seeks to transform problematic sociopolitical systems and achieve an environmentally sustainable, socially equitable, and spiritually rich way of life.[26]

Naess was influenced heavily by Gandhi, who defined the spiritual and ethical life as a process of "self-realization," a Vedantic concept whereby one moves progressively from an identification with the limited ego sense of self to identify ultimately with the unlimited wholistic Self, known in the Hindu tradition as the *atman*.[27] Self-realization, for Gandhi, is rooted in a unified, or nondual (*advaita*), understanding of reality: "I believe in *advaita*. I believe in the essential unity of man and for that matter of all that lives."[28] For Naess, self-realization is a process in which one identifies with a larger and larger sense of self until finally one identifies with all living beings; he calls this larger self the "ecological self." "We under-estimate ourselves," he claims. "Human nature is such that with sufficient all-sided maturity we cannot avoid 'identifying' our self with all living beings, beautiful or ugly, big or small, sentient or not."[29] For Naess, all love and compassion depends on some kind of identification. This leads Naess to articulate not only the spiritual dimension of self-realization, whereby one overcomes painful disconnection by identifying with the All, but also the ethical dimension of environmental activism. For Naess, care of the environment does not require some dutiful sacrifice, but rather comes naturally from joyful identification. The deep ecologist Bill Devall elaborates: "As we discover our ecological self we will joyfully defend and interact with that with which we identify."[30]

Deep ecologists aim to replace what they perceive to be the arrogance of anthropocentrism with the all-embracing eco-centric virtues of humility, wider vision, reverence, and loving care. This has serious implications for rivers. The first of Naess's eight deep ecological principles reads: "The well-being and flourishing of human and nonhuman Life on Earth have value in themselves (synonyms: intrinsic value, inherent value). These values are independent of the usefulness of the nonhuman world for human purposes."[31] To check current anthropocentric tendencies and stress the all-inclusive nature of this eco-centric statement, he adds, "the term 'life' is used here in a more comprehensive nontechnical way to refer also to what biologists classify as 'nonliving': rivers, landscapes, ecosystems. For supporters of deep ecology, slogans such as '*Let the river live*' illustrate this broader usage so common in most cultures."[32] Deep ecology, however, does not stop with thought; the eighth and final principle demands action. "Those who subscribe to the foregoing points have an obligation directly or indirectly to try to

implement the necessary changes."[33] Deep ecology, which is now a
global movement, is not a disembodied philosophy, but rather strives
for implementation through direct environmental action.[34] Later in this
book I discuss environmental movements in India that align themselves
with such deep ecological principles.

What all three of these movements—the emerging academic field
of Religion and Ecology, the greening of religions, and environmental
philosophy—have in common is that they are driven by a deep concern
for what is happening to the life-support systems on Earth, and they all
acknowledge that worldviews significantly shape attitudes and behavior
toward the environment.[35] Although such thinking has been developed
primarily within Christian circles, it has by no means been limited to
this religion. Every religion on the planet is now challenged to rethink
itself in light of the environmental crisis. What about Hinduism? How
does it look from an ecological perspective? In the spirit of Lynn White,
we might ask: Is Hinduism eco-friendly?

One would be justified in rejecting this question altogether, for it is a
misleading question that both reduces a complex tradition to a singularity and expects an answer never intended by any tradition. Like all
world religious traditions, Hinduism is a multifaceted cultural phenomenon made up of many varied and sometimes contradictory voices.
There is plenty of evidence for what we today might identify as ecologically destructive views and practices within Hinduism,[36] and there is
abundant evidence for what we might identify as ecologically friendly
views and practices within Hinduism. In an effort to "dethrone" what
they call the "oriental ecologist," Ole Bruun and Arne Kalland argue
that "Asian philosophies and cosmologies seem to have had little effect
in preventing over-exploitation of soils, over-grazing, erosion, deforestation, pollution of waters and other environmental disasters—by
which a number of Asian societies are acutely threatened."[37] The Hindu
ecofeminist Lina Gupta acknowledges ecologically destructive elements
in Hinduism, which she labels "patriarchal," but she also writes, "Still,
I believe that Hinduism, though containing its own patriarchal aspects,
offers as well some resources for assisting us to move beyond patri-
archy. Hinduism can help us awaken to the deep connections that
already exist, if we have eyes to see."[38] In a similar vein, after noting
that many aspects of Hinduism are detrimental to the environment, Rita
Dasgupta Sherma insists, "In the case of Hinduism, resources exist for
the development of a vision that could promote ecological action." She
especially emphasizes the goddess-worshipping traditions of Hinduism

for their ability to "offer a rich and nuanced resource for the construction of an eco-conscious spirituality."[39]

We must also keep in mind that the present scope of the environmental crisis is a radically new human experience that demands new responses; thus no religious tradition in its present form is prepared to address the current problems. As Poul Pedersen reminds us, "No Buddhist, Hindu, or Islamic scriptures contain concepts like 'environmental crisis,' 'ecosystems,' or 'sustainable development,' or concepts corresponding to them. To insist that they do is to deny the immense cultural distance that separates traditional religious conceptions of the environment from modern ecological knowledge."[40] Religious traditions are always changing as they move into new historical circumstances, and one of the greatest challenges they face today is the environmental crisis, which is already reshaping traditions worldwide. Nevertheless, with these cautionary points in mind we can proceed to examine certain dimensions of the Hindu tradition that might serve as resources for those who employ a Hindu cultural perspective in their struggle with the environmental crisis.

Before beginning this task, it might be worthwhile to acknowledge that, in much of the literature which examines religions from an ecological perspective, the answer to the question "Is Hinduism eco-friendly?" has frequently been: "No."[41] Whereas Buddhism, Taoism, and Native American religions are almost always depicted as being eco-friendly, Hinduism is not. On the contrary, in many Western representations Hinduism is typically assumed to be an ascetic, world-renouncing tradition that views the natural world of multiple forms as a valueless illusion. If this were indeed the case, one might wonder why Hindus would even want to save a river. This is, however, not at all true of many types of Hinduism.[42] It is therefore necessary to clear up widespread confusion on this issue before examining the religious culture associated with the Yamuna River.

Although any scholar of Hinduism must certainly acknowledge the existence of strong and important world-renouncing dimensions in this tradition, by no means can Hinduism be reduced to a single position. Hinduism is a pluralistic tradition with many world-affirming schools of thought and action. In fact, numerically speaking, world-denying asceticism is a minority position overshadowed by a plentitude of world-affirming temple cults. Unfortunately, this latter fact has been missed by many of those considering religious traditions from an ecological perspective. In *The Lost Gospel of the Earth,* for example,

Tom Hayden writes that any reverent attitude toward nature in Hinduism has "to be retrieved from a long Hindu tradition of viewing the earth as illusion to be transcended."[43] The operative assumption here is that schools within Hinduism which view the world as an illusory trap to be escaped, such as the religious system of Advaita Vedanta articulated by the well-known ascetic philosopher Shankaracharya (also known simply as Shankara), represent the sole Hindu position on the value of the world. This assumption, a product of Oriental scholarship driven by particular philosophical commitments and the political agenda of British colonialism, informs many understandings of Hinduism. The truth is that there are many schools of thought within Hinduism. There are even many schools of Vedanta, a variety of religious systems based on early scriptures that establish the unity of all reality. Shankara's specific school of Advaita Vedanta, which rationalizes renunciation of an illusory world, represents only one of the many schools of Vedanta. The Vaishnava schools of Vedanta all tend to assert that the world is real, and thus promote a more this-worldly form of Vedanta.

In his insightful study of deep ecology, Warwick Fox considers the nature of Hinduism while examining Gandhi's influence on Arne Naess. Following other scholars, Fox argues that Gandhi had rendered radical changes in Hindu thought, thus making it more appealing to the ecologically minded Naess. Specifically, Hinduism had to be transformed into a this-worldly religious tradition. Fox writes, "While Indian thought emphasizes repelling and overcoming the forces of life, Gandhi accepts the reality of this world and, proceeding on this basis, insists on remaining in this world and seeking salvation through serving the world."[44] Gandhi's perspective is represented here as a radical deviation from "real" Hinduism. Fox contends that "Gandhi's Hinduism is heavily influenced by Buddhism."[45] He even identifies Buddhism, a tradition assumed by many to be eco-friendly, as the positive transformative force, claiming that "the path of seeking self-realization through serving the world—the upshot of Gandhi's version of Indian thought—is most readily associated with the Bodhisattva ideal, which is the ideal of Mahayana Buddhism, rather than with the more Hindu-inspired ideal, which is strongly associated with Hinayana Buddhism, of seeking one's own salvation first and foremost, and even withdrawing from the world to do so."[46] Regarding Gandhi's specific brand of Hinduism, Fox presumes that "Gandhi was committed to Advaita Vedanta," the "dominant traditional Indian metaphysics" established by Shankara that "impugns the reality status of the empirical world."[47]

Fox makes a big mistake here. In his personal writings, Gandhi clarifies that his own thinking about Vedantic issues was influenced by his Vaishnava background, which holds the world to be real and is therefore deeply invested in life. Nonetheless, because Fox makes the mistake of reducing Vedantic systems of thought to Shankara's alone, he assumes that it was necessary for Gandhi to affect radical changes in Hinduism. Fox remarks that Gandhi "went against the grain of that tradition in the extent to which he endorsed the reality of the phenomenal or empirical world."[48]

In sum, Fox assumed that Naess and anyone else who has a positive ecological view of the world would be attracted only to the eco-friendly version of Hinduism worked out by Gandhi, and not to the traditional otherworldly form of Hinduism that constitutes the real tradition. In condensed form, Fox articulates something commonplace and highly problematic in many representations of Hinduism, particularly in textbook representations that fail to examine critically the scholarship of previous generations on which much of this is based. To be sure, Hinduism does include important ascetic and world-denying schools such as Shankara's Advaita Vedanta, but it also includes much more that frequently gets left out of secondary representations of Hinduism: specifically the lived traditions of theistic or temple Hinduism that typically view the world as a manifestation of the highest divinity. How did the reductionistic views of Hinduism so prevalent in ecological considerations of Hinduism come into being? In many ways this is a story of how a relatively minor part of the tradition came to represent the entire tradition in scholarly literature during the nineteenth and early twentieth centuries.

Scholarship during the colonial period of the late nineteenth and early twentieth centuries was influenced by eighteenth-century European historians who had a nostalgic commitment to recapturing a glorious past. In the normative studies of religion at the time, this meant that authenticity was equated with antiquity, and the "original" aspects of a religion were assumed to be the truest. Early Orientalist scholars working within India, such as William Jones and Henry Colebrooke, constructed a golden age of Hinduism located deep in the past and fashioned a portrayal of the Vedic age that is still widely accepted in the West today.[49] Colebrooke published an extremely influential article titled "On the Vedas, or Sacred Writings of the Hindus," in which he advanced his far-reaching notion that the Vedas—by which he means primarily the Upanishads—are the authentic, genuine Hindu scripture and that the goal of liberation from the world, or *moksha,* is the "real doctrine of the whole Indian scripture."[50] He was also one of the first to identify Shankara as the great and authentic commentator on the Vedas. In this same article, Colebrooke condemns the life-affirming theistic cults of Hinduism—as well as their scriptural sources, the Puranas—as inauthentic and deserving of being "rejected, as liable to much suspicion."[51] Here was the first major contribution to the construction of "neo-Vedantic Hinduism," which was soon to assume the status of canonical fact and seize the position of the authentic singular in most Western representations of Hinduism. The privileging of Shankara's Advaita Vedanta and its specific goal of *moksha* continued on throughout the nineteenth and twentieth centuries and is still very much with us today.

Paul Deussen and Max Muller, two writers deeply influenced by German idealism that defined philosophy as a study of the disjunction between appearance and reality, and perhaps the two most important Western interpreters of Indian thought in their day, both articulated this position with great enthusiasm.[52] Under their pens, Shankara's system came to represent the whole of Indian thought for Europeans in the late nineteenth century and early twentieth century. In his introduction to the Vedanta, Deussen assumes that Shankara's Advaita Vedanta represents the entirety of Vedanta and writes, "On the tree of Indian wisdom there is no fairer flower than the Upanishads, and no finer fruit than the Vedanta philosophy. This system grew out of the teachings of the Upanishads, and was brought to its consummate form by the great Shankara (born 788 A.D., exactly one thousand years before his spiritual kinsman Schopenhauer). Even to this day, Shankara's system represents the common belief of *nearly all thoughtful Hindus.*"[53] Along with the privileging of Shankara, *moksha*—understood to be liberation from the world experienced by the senses—came to be identified among a range of possibilities as the single goal of Hinduism. Andrew Tuck argues that during the nineteenth century it became "an established belief that *all Indian thought* was devoted to the attainment of *moksha,* or liberation from the 'earthly bondage' of perceived reality."[54] Thus under the influence of the Orientalist scholarship of this period, the rich and multifaceted vastness of Hindu religious culture was largely reduced to a singularity that either was in harmony with Christian ideals or was rendered so otherworldly that it became politically impotent. Specifically, what gets denied is the world-ordering temple cults that offered a variety of goals besides *moksha,* such as life blessings or a devotional rapture frequently defined in contrast to *moksha.*[55]

Through the politics of colonial scholarship, this portrait of Hinduism became the basis of early representations of Hinduism privileged in the Western academy. As Ronald Inden argues, "Whatever their interpretations of the Vedic ritual and Upanishadic philosophy, both the secularists and Christian idealists[,] on the one hand, and the philosophical idealists[,] on the other, have on the whole agreed that the monism embodied in Advaita Vedanta constituted the essence of Indian thought."[56] The resulting reductionistic view has caused many to overlook much that is important in Hindu religious culture, particularly its most popular features: temple beliefs and practices.

Before proceeding, I want to make clear the political agenda behind this reduction of Hinduism initiated in the nineteenth century. At the peak of the independence movement in 1935, Mulk Raj Anand published a novel titled *Untouchable*. In the novel Anand has a wise poet say:

> It is India's genius to accept all things. We have, throughout our long history, been realists believing in the stuff of this world, in the here and the now, in the flesh and the blood. Man is born and reborn, according to the *Upanishads*, in this world, and even when he becomes an immortal saint there is no release for him, because he forms the stuff of the cosmos and is born again. We don't believe in the other world, as these Europeans would have you believe we do. There has been only one man in India who believed this world to be illusory—Shankaracharya. But he was a consumptive and that made him neurotic. Early European scholars could not get hold of the original texts of the *Upanishads*. So they kept on interpreting Indian thought from the commentaries of Shankaracharya. The word *maya* does not mean illusion. . . . The Victorians misinterpreted us. It was as if, in order to give a philosophical background to their exploitation of India, they ingeniously concocted a nice little fairy story: "You don't believe in this world; to you all this is *maya*. Let us look after your country for you and you can dedicate yourself to achieving *Nirvana*."[57]

Regardless of the accuracy of this representation of Shankara, Anand has identified an important point regarding the political agenda of the privileging of Shankara's thought and the religious goal of *moksha*. The scholarly movement that reduces Hindu culture simultaneously justifies colonial rule. Inden argues a similar point. The implication of this reduction was that the "Indian mind requires an externally imported world-ordering rationality. This was important for the imperial project of the British as it appeared, piecemeal, in the course of the nineteenth century. Why? Because the theist creeds and sects, *activist and realist,*

were the world-ordering religions of precisely those in the Indian popu-
lace, among the Hindus, that the British themselves were in the process
of displacing as the rulers of India."[58]

In my own study of a well-publicized trial known as the Maharaj
Libel Case that took place in Bombay in 1862, I have demonstrated
how Orientalist representations of Hinduism were used to undermine
established religious authority in Indian societies associated with the
worship of Krishna.[59] During this libel case, much of Hinduism itself
was put on trial. The Oriental scholar and Christian missionary John
Wilson was brought into the court as the "expert" to determine the
authentic nature of Hinduism. He and the judges decreed together that
the world-affirming temple cults of Krishna devotionalism were ille-
gitimate forms of Hinduism; the true tradition was ancient, ascetic,
individualistic, transcendent, world-denying, and had the singular
goal of *moksha*. To the degree that the ruling had effect, the existing
culture of temple Hinduism, which involved the worship of embodied
forms of divinity and was very much focused on this world, lost all
legitimacy and its social leaders forfeited all authority. The undermining
of temple Hinduism, then, had not only a religious agenda but also a
political one: the leaders associated with temple Hinduism represented
a political challenge to the British Raj.

At this point the dominant claim of colonial scholarship on Hinduism
should be clear: the Vedas or Upanishads are the genuine Hindu scriptures, Shankara's ascetic interpretation of them is singularly correct,
and *moksha* is the true and only goal of pure Hinduism; the rites and
practices of temple Hinduism that engage the body, mind, and senses in
the worship of multiple forms of embodied divinity represent a popular
corruption of and even dangerous deviation from the authentic tradition.
Clearly, the world-affirming theologies associated with temple worship
have no place in this representation of Hinduism. Although the scholarship of the past two decades has done much to deconstruct this picture
of Hinduism and focus more attention on the types of Hinduism actually practiced by Hindus in India today, many dimensions of the earlier
representations of Hinduism are still with us. I have found this to be
particularly true in considerations of Hinduism found within ecological
literature. The authors of this literature would benefit greatly from a
study of recent scholarship on Hinduism.

Ironically, what is often missing in the oversimplified representation
of Hinduism constructed by Orientalist scholars during the colonial
period is its most common aspect: the theistic Hinduism present in the

temple cultures of India that focus on embodied forms of divinity, and which frequently promote a very positive view of the world. At this point an examination of the worldview expressed in the Bhagavad-gita would be advantageous for a number of reasons. First, this tremendously popular text gives representative access to theistic Hinduism. Second, the Gita was important for Gandhi, a key figure in many environmental movements in India and abroad, who regarded it "as the book *par excellence* for the knowledge of Truth," and who used it for daily meditations.[60] Through Gandhi the Gita had a deep influence on many involved in developing ecological philosophies in both India and the West. Arne Naess took the term *self-realization* from Gandhi, who in turn took it from the Gita.[61] One scholar remarks that self-realization "for Naess is not something new. For him, the view is expressed quite clearly in the *Bhagavad-gita*."[62] Indeed, Naess quotes the Gita himself to support his own view of self-realization.[63] Gandhi wrote in his commentary on the Gita that "self-realization is the subject of the Gita."[64] Moreover, Himalayan forest-defenders and other well-known environmental activists in India have organized readings of the Gita as part of their strategy for environmental protection, and some have used it to articulate a specifically Hindu ecological philosophy.[65] One can even find uses of the Gita in environmental publications such as *Down to Earth,* a periodical published by the Centre for Science and Environment in New Delhi: "Conserve ecology or perish—this, in short, is one of the messages of the *Gita,* one of the most important scriptures of the Vedic way of life now known as Hinduism." And: "It is time for another Hindu revival that restores the individual's link with the society and the environment, time for a fresh set of examples, a fresh set of heroes. This will have to take into account the scientific revolution that has changed the face of human civilization, for good or for bad. It is time for Hindus to re-read the *Bhagavad Gita.*"[66] Finally, the Gita introduces a theological framework for understanding the religious thought that informs much worship of the Yamuna River. The Gita is clearly at the heart of many ecological considerations in India.

The overdetermined presence of Shankara's Advaita Vedanta, however, still influences many scholars who explore the Gita with regard for ecological concerns. Two recent publications aptly demonstrate this point.[67] In an article titled "*Bhagavadgita*, Ecosophy T, and Deep Ecology," Knut Jacobsen examines the influence of Hinduism on the thought of Arne Naess and the development of deep ecology. He begins by correctly noting that many of the ideas central to environmental thinking

in Europe and North America—such as "non-injury (*ahimsa*), the oneness
of all living beings (*advaita*), and self- (*atman*) realization (*moksa*)"[68]—
come from the Hindu religious traditions, although this fact is rarely
acknowledged.[69] In a narrowing representational move, however, Jacobsen
identifies these influential Hindu concepts with the "monastic traditions"
of "ascetic Hinduism," which aim "to teach the realization of freedom
from the world." Moreover, he labels the Bhagavad-gita, which is the
product of the historically specific Bhagavata, or Vaishnava, tradition
that gives expression to a very particular theology, a nonsectarian text.[70]
This allows him to focus his greatest attention on Shankara's Advaita
Vedantic interpretation of the Gita. Jacobsen notes that for Shankara the
world of multiple appearances is ultimately not real. Since the world is
ultimately devalued in Advaita Vedanta, and the stated goal is to escape
from the illusory world, Jacobsen concludes that "Advaita Vedanta and
deep ecology have quite different intentions."[71] He points out that the
Gita according to Shankara teaches the cessation of the world, whereas
deep ecology teaches the celebration of the world, and thus he questions
any connection between the two. "There is therefore a great divergence
between *advaita* in Shankara and *advaita* in Ecosophy T [Naess's own
philosophy]."[72] Jacobsen seems to overlook the fact, however, that Naess
did not draw his ideas about *advaita* from Shankara.

Continuing in this reductionistic fashion, Jacobsen asserts, "The
monastic tradition of commentary [on the *Gita*] has continued up to
this day and will go on into the future. Its focus is liberation *from* the
world" (in contrast to liberation *in* the world).[73] If the primary meaning of the Gita necessarily implies a devaluation of the world, then
indeed it must be changed if it is to address ecological concerns in any
positive way. But is this true? Is this the only—or even primary—meaning
derived from the Gita for the variety of Hindu traditions? Assuming
that it is, Jacobsen argues that the change in positive political or ecological interpretations of the Gita was due to outside influences, suggesting that a socially conscious Christianity was foremost among these.
He concludes: "A comparison of the Hindu monastic with the political-
environmental interpretation of [the Bhagavad-gita] has shown that the
political-environmental interpretation in many ways is the opposite
of the monastic."[74] Although Jacobsen acknowledges that "for none
of the representatives of the monastic tradition was the *Bhagavad-gita*
their primary religious text," he seems unaware that Hindu traditions
with closer ties to the Bhagavad-gita offer interpretations of this text
that are directly opposed to the monastic interpretations.[75] Many of

these come from the Bhagavata or Vaishnava tradition that produced and maintained the Bhagavad-gita as a special sectarian text and that still has living representatives today. (It is this tradition that best enables an understanding of the religious world associated with the Yamuna.) It is not necessary, therefore, to argue for a radical transformation of interpretive possibilities for the Gita from the outside; interpretative traditions exist within Hindu religious philosophy that a figure like Gandhi might draw on, and which were more attractive to Naess and others committed to the perspective of deep ecology. Gandhi made it very clear in his autobiography, after all, that he was raised in the Vaishnava culture of northern India.[76]

Jacobsen contends that deep ecology "has *samsara,* the world of the natural processes of birth, flourishing of life, decay and death as its ultimate concern."[77] This leads him to highlight a huge difference between views expressed in the Gita and contemporary environmentalism. "Self-realization (*moksa*) for the Hindu monastic tradition meant freedom from *samsara,* while self-realization (*moksa*) for the environmental interpretation meant merging oneself with *samsara* and the preservation of *samsara.*"[78] Again, he assumes that the monastic interpretations of the Gita are the most authoritative and the most influential on Naess's teacher Gandhi. There is much to consider here. First we might question Jacobsen's use of the Sanskrit word *samsara* to refer to the manifest world of changing appearances. I contend that in the Gita *samsara* more correctly refers to the experience of alienation and suffering that results from ignorance about the true nature of the world. A more appropriate term for the world of multiple changing forms is *jagat,* most simply translated as the "world."[79] Escape from *samsara* is clearly part of the goal, according to the Bhagavad-gita, but not necessarily escape from the world (*jagat*). In fact, many have argued that the goal of the Gita is freedom *in* the world, not freedom *from* the world. Shankara and other ascetic thinkers may indeed see the world, or *jagat,* as an unreal illusion to be escaped, but the Vaishnava theologians who represent the Bhagavata tradition that produced the Gita differ from Shankara precisely on this point: in conscious opposition to Shankara, they insist that the world as *jagat* is real (*sat*). Drawing on the Gita and Upanishadic texts, the seventeenth-century Vaishnava philosopher Lallu Bhatta, for example, states in his *Prameya Ratnarnava:* "The world is not 'mayic' (illusory) nor is it different from the Lord. It is real."[80] The Gita itself identifies Krishna as the source of the *jagat* (7.6) and even goes so far as to state that the view that the *jagat* is unreal is demonic (16.8). The goal of *karma-yoga* as expressed in the Gita involves realizing freedom *in* the world, not freedom *from* the world.[81] Thus, it is the alienation of *samsara* that is negated in the liberation of *moksha,* not the world itself. As Richard Davis writes, "Moksa always involves leaving behind the sufferings and fetters that constitute our normal worldly existence, but it may lead one, according to which school one follows, to a merging with the godhead, to permanent service at the feet of the Lord, to autonomous and parallel divinity, or to some other final and ultimate state. The character of liberation was one of the major points of contention among the theological schools that developed during this period."[82]

The point I am trying to establish here is that the Gita does not simply relegate the world as *jagat* to an illusory realm; many Vaishnava Vedantic schools that follow it hold that the world is profoundly real. I am also highlighting the fact that there are multiple interpretive possibilities for the Gita, not simply that of Shankara. If we understand how deeply Gandhi was influenced by the Vaishnava schools of Vedanta, then we can avoid the philosophical acrobatics that Western scholars such as Fox and Jacobsen go through in representing Naess's attraction to Gandhi's teachings on *advaita* and self-realization.

Recognizing that Shankara's interpretation of the Gita is not the only one opens up the possibility for a deeper understanding of the particular Bhagavata theology expressed in the Gita and further developed by later Vaishnava thinkers. Important to this understanding is appreciation of conceptual terms used in the Gita to characterize the nature of the world.[83] Although the Gita recognizes a higher dimension of reality, it teaches that the world of multiple and manifest forms that we perceive with our senses is still very real. Indeed, the Gita identifies the world with an aspect of Krishna himself.[84] Thus, according to a Vaishnava interpretation of this text, the world is fully divine.

Once we acknowledge that Gandhi was raised in a world of Vaishnava culture, we can begin to make sense of statements such as this one from his commentary on the Gita, without turning to religious sources outside of Hinduism as Fox and others have done: "All embodied life is in reality an incarnation of God."[85] Gandhi identifies the goal of self-realization as *moksha,* which he defines as "seeing God face to face."[86] He views this realization as being dependent upon one's ability to identify compassionately with all of life: "To see the universal and all-pervading Spirit of Truth face to face[,] one must be able to love the meanest creation as oneself."[87] For Gandhi, loving compassion is rooted in the Vedantic vision of nonduality: "The rockbottom foundation of the technique for achieving the power of non-violence is belief in the essential oneness of all life."[88] Such an understanding leads Gandhi to endorse an all-inclusive and this-worldly form of religion: "My religion embraces all life. I want to realize brotherhood or identity not merely with the beings called human, but I want to realize identity with all life, even with such things as crawl upon earth. I want, if I don't give you a shock, to realize identity with even the crawling things upon earth, because we claim descent from the same God, and that being so, all life in whatever form it appears must be essentially one."[89] This position is clearly distinct from Shankara's negation of the manifest world and suggests a different source for Gandhi's understanding of the Gita: the Vaishnava schools of Vedanta encountered in his youth.

In an article published after Jacobsen's, Lance Nelson presents a reading of the Gita in close agreement with Jacobsen. After reviewing what he calls "ecological positives" in the Gita—mostly an "ethics of restraint" coming from ascetic ideals—he remarks, "The apparently ecofriendly images and practices cannot be isolated from the contexts in which they are embedded, especially from the underlying worldviews which give rise to them and condition their significance."[90] Nelson identifies the problematic worldview that he believes informs the Gita's vision: a dualistic perspective that sharply devalues the manifest world. Because of this, he, too, assumes the goal of the Gita to be liberation (*moksha*), defined as "escape *from* the world of nature."[91] With an interest in understanding how Hindus have "traditionally" read the Gita, Nelson follows the well-worn path that begins with an examination of Shankara's reading of the text. Nelson concludes that, according to the Gita, the real self has "nothing to do with nature," which it holds to be an "illusion."[92] Therefore, "the physical, including the empirical existence of other beings, does not matter."[93] He concludes his article by agreeing with Jacobsen, insisting that the Gita's "ideals are in many ways antithetical to ecological ethics as we know it. . . . If we are tempted to look to Asia for religious visions that give nature greater significance, however, the *Bhagavadgita* may not be the best place to start."[94]

Jacobsen and Nelson would have us believe, then, that the Gita expresses an ascetic worldview that greatly devalues the world by viewing it ultimately as a worthless illusion. Accordingly, it has little value for those with environmental concerns. There are two problems with this conclusion: First, it does not take into consideration the ethnographic fact that many in India today who would identify themselves as environmentalists claim to be following the teachings of the Gita.

Second, although there are clearly long-standing and influential ascetic traditions within Hinduism, by no means do they represent the majority of the tradition. Although they acknowledge other dimensions of Hinduism, Jacobsen and Nelson continue a long scholarly tradition in the West that tends to reduce the rich variety of Hinduism to Shankara's Advaita Vedanta. By assuming that the Gita is historically a nonsectarian text, they overlook the specific and sophisticated Bhagavata theology expressed in this text,[95] which informs a perspective that has challenged the very ascetic worldview that devalues the world of nature. Since this Bhagavata theology is precisely the one that informs the worldview of most worshippers of the Yamuna River, understanding it is extremely important.

Historically, the Bhagavad-gita is the product of the Bhagavata cult.[96] Introducing the philosophy of Pancaratra, an important branch of the Bhagavata tradition, Surendranath Dasgupta writes, "The Pancaratra doctrines are indeed very old and are associated with the *purusa-sukta* of the Rig-veda, which is, as it were, the foundation stone of all future Vaisnava philosophy."[97] Dasgupta further remarks, "The *bhedabheda* ['difference in nondifference'] interpretation of the *Brahma-sutra*s is in all probability earlier than the monistic interpretation introduced by Shankara. The *Bhagavad-gita,* which is regarded as the essence of the Upanishads, the older *Purana*s, and the *Pancaratra,* are more or less on the lines of *bhedabheda.* In fact the origin of this theory may be traced to the *Purusa-sukta.*"[98] Many scholars agree that the *Purusha Sukta* of the Rig Veda, which gives expression to the simultaneity of radical unity and diversity (*bhedabheda*), has played a significant role in the development of Bhagavata theology.[99] There is, therefore, no better place to begin an introductory understanding of Bhagavata theology than with the *Purusha Sukta* of the Rig Veda.

A thousand heads, a thousand eyes, and a thousand feet has Purusha. He pervaded the Earth on all sides and stretched beyond it by ten fingers. Purusha is this entire universe, all that has been and all that is to be. In the grand cosmic sacrifice that produced the world, Purusha became differentiated: three-quarters of Purusha rose upward to become the unchanging transcendent, while one-quarter remained behind, and from this portion came the sum total of all that we experience with our senses, animate and inanimate. The Purusha hymn of Rig Veda 10.90 is a cosmogonic myth that gives expression to the simultaneous transcendent and immanent quality of divinity. Jan Gonda, a historian of Indian religions, maintains that the "Purusasukta . . . is the first expression of the idea that creation is the self-limitation of the transcendent Person manifesting himself in the realm of our experience."[100] Although a majority of divinity is beyond the world of manifest forms, a significant portion of divinity is clearly identified with the world of manifest forms.

This central idea was elaborated further in Upanishadic texts, particularly in the *Brihadaranyaka Upanishad,* which became part of the *Satapatha Brahmana,* a text of considerable importance for Bhagavata theology.[101] The *Brihadaranyaka Upanishad* asserts that there are two aspects of ultimate reality, or Brahman: one is identified with all forms (*murta*), and the other is identified with the realm of the formless (*amurta*).[102] Brahman as all forms is everything that is manifest and transitory, whereas Brahman as the formless is unmanifest and unchanging. A good way to approach this nondual philosophical proposition is to reflect on the double meaning of the phrase: "Nothing ever remains the same." The world of concrete things is in constant flux and always changing; things never remain the same. On the other hand, the nothingness that is the source of all things is eternal and unchanging; it ever remains the same. It is important to remember in Vedantic thought, however, that these are not two separate realities, but different modes of the same unified reality.

Vedantic theological traditions frequently recognize a third dimension in the complex unity that is Brahman, for Brahman's nature is expressed as tripartite in much Vedantic literature. We read in the *Shvetasvatara Upanishad,* for example: "This whole world, which is the changing [*kshara*] and the unchanging [*akshara*], the manifest [*vyakta*] and the unmanifest [*avyakta*] combined, is supported by the Universal Lord [*vishvam isha*]."[103] This text identifies the three dimensions of the ultimate reality of Brahman as the manifest, the unmanifest, and the supreme lord upon whom it all depends. Although this text paints its theological picture in a specifically Shaivite hue, naming Rudra (a name of Shiva) as the "one God" (*deva eka*) identified with Purusha of the Rig Veda, it gives expression to a common feature of much Vedantic theological thinking current in the centuries just prior to the beginning of the first millennium of the common era.[104]

The language and concepts expressed in the earlier Upanishads are continued in that other important Vedantic text, the Bhagavad-gita. Three Sanskrit terms that characterize the nature of reality are introduced and defined in the opening verses of the eighth chapter of the Gita; these not only are indispensable for expressing the ultimate nature of

Krishna in this text but also become important later on for articulating much Yamuna theology.[105] The ever-changing and manifest dimension of reality (*kshara*) is identified with the Sanskrit term *adhibhuta;* the unchanging and unmanifest dimension (*akshara*) is labeled *adhyatma;* and the dimension that is said to be the source of, as well as higher than, the previous two dimensions is identified with Purusha and called *adhidaiva.*[106] The changing and the unchanging are also identified in this chapter with the manifest (*vyakta*) and unmanifest (*avyakta*), respectively. These dimensions of reality are regarded hierarchically. The fifteenth chapter of the Gita explains that there are two dimensions of Purusha in this world: the changing (*kshara*) and the unchanging (*akshara*). The changing is here identified with all beings, and the unchanging with the supreme spirit. This text asserts, however, that there is another dimension of reality higher than both of these. This dimension is identified as the Lord (Ishvara) who pervades and sustains the entire universe, and who is none other than Purusha of the Vedas. This latter and highest dimension of ultimate reality is also called Purushottama, the "Highest Person."[107] These three dimensions of reality are regarded in a hierarchical fashion, but, importantly, all three are aspects and expressions of divinity, namely Krishna. That is, while it is assumed to be only a portion of a much vaster and unmanifest reality, the manifest world of multiple forms that we perceive with our senses is fully divine. Vasudha Narayanan highlights the fact that "central to the *Bhagavadgita* is the vision of the universe as the body of Krishna."[108] This is not only an aspect of the Gita that is often missed by many Western scholars but also one that helps us understand the Vedantic teaching that informs Gandhi's claim that "all embodied life is in reality an incarnation of God."[109]

An interpretation of the Gita that focuses on these three Sanskrit terms and their resulting theological perspective would embrace a positive view of the world.[110] This is the position taken by most of the Bhagavata, or Vaishnava, schools of Vedanta that inform many of the theistic and temple traditions of Hindu India, and that certainly inform much of the theology associated with the Yamuna River. The goal of the Gita from this perspective, then, would be to escape the torments of alienated suffering (*samsara*), not the world (*jagat*) itself, which if viewed with proper knowledge is understood to be a manifestation of divinity. Again, the Gita very clearly affirms that the world is real, although many Westerners considering the Gita from a contemporary ecological perspective have missed this positive assertion. Living with a deluded or distorted understanding of the world leads to suffering, whereas living with a true understanding of the world leads to enjoyment. The world is a product of *maya* according to Vedantic thought. Since Krishna claims it as his own, the important Sanskrit term *maya* is perhaps best translated as "divine creative power," rather than as "illusion" or "delusive appearance," as Nelson translates it.[111] Jacobsen notes that, for Shankara, "the plural world is understood as *maya,* an appearance, created by the lower *brahman* (*saguna brahman, ishvar*a), which is not ultimately real."[112] This may be so for Shankara, but we have just seen that the Gita states that the highest reality is identified as Ishvara, the Lord who sustains the very real world. Scholars who have critically examined Shankara's commentary on the Gita and compared it to the commentaries of later Vaishnava theologians, such as Ramanuja, have concluded that Shankara had to stretch his interpretation of the text, since his position is farther from the expressed meaning of the Gita than that of the Vaishnava theologians.[113] This being so, it is perhaps better to approach the Gita with the interpretive aid of these commentaries, rather than relying heavily on that of Shankara, which has been the major tendency of Western scholars. If this were done, a new possible perspective would emerge with regard to the Gita and contemporary ecological concerns. In exploring possible resources within Hinduism for establishing deep interconnections and ecological health, Lina Gupta writes:

> The divine energy called the "Brahman" is immanent as well as transcendent. The world, with its infinite variety, is the manifestation of the divine principle. The world, with all its multiplicity and diversity, begins and ends in a cycle within the divine womb and therefore does not have any separate existence outside of the "Brahman." Being the manifestation of the same principle, all parts of the universe, human or nonhuman, mobile or immobile, organic or inorganic, are animated by the same life force. Being permeated by the same energy and essence, creation reflects kinship among all its facets. . . . Nature as seen in the Gita is clearly an example of divine expression in its varieties. Nature, being in the womb of God, is a living organism and as such is not to be treated as an "Other." If the One universal "Brahman" is revealing itself in the multiplicity of this planet, be it a river or a rock, all parts of this Nature have an intrinsic value; as such, all of Nature should be treated with dignity, kindness, and righteousness.[114]

The Bhagavata view of the nature of the world expressed in the Gita is further articulated in the *Bhagavata Purana,* the other major text of the Bhagavata schools. In the first chapter of the second book of the

Bhagavata Purana, the solid form of the Lord (*sthula rupa*), or the manifest portion of Purusha, is identified with the entire visible world.[115]
This form of the Lord is described in concrete detail. We are told, for
example, that the mountains are the bones of his body, the oceans are
his abdominal cavity, the trees are the hairs on his body, and the rivers
are his veins and arteries.[116] Whereas contemporary Christian eco-
theologians, such as Sallie McFague, creatively stretch Christian theology
to claim that the world is "metaphorically" the body of God, here such
a notion is stated without theological reservation.[117] Although the
Bhagavata traditions maintain that there is much to divinity beyond the
manifest world, they nonetheless acknowledge that the world we inhabit
is fully divine and must be understood as a manifestation of divinity, in
this case Krishna. This identification of the natural world with divinity is
pervasive in much Hindu theology and religious practice.[118]

Thus, knowledge of the Bhagavata perspective—which is shared by
many of the Hindu theistic traditions—leads one to expect that much
religious practice in India would be involved directly in the worship of
natural phenomena as embodied forms of divinity.[119] This is indeed the
case, as even the mildest form of ethnographic research demonstrates.
One need only travel about India to observe reverence toward natural
forms: the worship of mountains, forests, animals, trees, ponds, rocks,
plants, and rivers as natural forms of divinity is common in Hindu religious practice. Considering the Ganges, Diana Eck writes, "For the natural is the religious. Although the river has attracted abundant myth
and *mahatmya,* it is the river itself, nothing 'supernatural' ascribed to it,
that has been so significant for Hindus. The river does not stand for, or
point toward, anything greater, beyond itself; it is part of a living sacred
geography that Hindus hold in common."[120] Betty Heimann maintains
that this dimension of Hindu religious culture is informed by a "sacra-
mental natural ontology" and asserts, "In India the veneration of Nature
has never been discarded as outdated and primitive. On the contrary,
primitivity is here appreciated in its productive ambiguity and inex-
haustible potentialities. Nature cult is the fundament of the earliest
forms of Indian religions and remains the basis of even the highest and
most exalted speculations of Indian philosophy."[121] Whether or not this
characteristic makes Hinduism eco-friendly is another matter, but it is a
central and highly visible characteristic that reveals deep investment in
the world of nature. Importantly, the worship of natural forms in India
most certainly includes rivers.

Water is the very basis of all life. Around 75 percent of Earth's surface is covered by water, although only 3 percent of this is freshwater, with 2 percent frozen in ice. In recognizing that all life has come from water, modern science highlights water's significance; but because it is precious and life-sustaining, water has also evoked a religious response throughout humanity's history. "It seems natural that our ancestors should have regarded water as a living creature with the power to bestow the life force, health and energy," write Janet and Colin Bord.[122] The historian of religions Mircea Eliade claims that water has long been worshipped as the Universal Mother, since "water symbolizes the primal substance from which all forms come and to which they will return."[123] The worship of rivers as natural forms of divinity, usually goddesses, has been a significant feature of religious traditions in many parts of the world. In France, for example, there remains archaeological evidence of a temple for river worship at the source of the Seine River, which was sacred to the goddess Sequana.[124] The Nigerian river Oshun is worshipped as a life-blessing goddess by the same name not only in Africa but also in the African diaspora religions such as Candomble in Brazil and Santeria in Cuba. "Oshun is the symbol of river waters, without which life on the earth would be impossible. In the same manner, she controls all that makes life worth living, such as love and marriage, children, money, and pleasure."[125] The Nile was associated with the goddess Isis in ancient Egypt and the river Boyne was worshipped as a goddess by the Celts.[126] More specifically, rivers throughout the world have tended to be viewed as maternal presences. "The role of rivers as the sustainers of life and fertility is reflected in the myths and beliefs of a multitude of cultures. In many parts of the world rivers are referred to as 'mothers': Narmadai, 'Mother Narmada'; the Volga is Mat Rodnaya, 'Mother of the Land.' The Thai word for river, mae nan, translates literally as 'water mother.'"[127] What, we might ask, happens to the worlds of religious meaning associated with river worship as the rivers of the world become increasingly polluted?

Although river worship is found in many parts of the world, no religious culture has sustained river worship to the extent we find in Hindu India (figure 1). "India honors its rivers more than any other nation, seeing them as the manifest form of divine female powers sent to earth to assist humanity," writes Bill Aitken.[128] Although aesthetic appreciation is easily found in literature about rivers in the West, rivers are often regarded as something to negotiate, conquer, explore, fish, take recreation on, or exploit. Journeys to rivers in India are more typically

Figure 1. Scene along the banks of the Yamuna in Vrindaban.
The man in the foreground sings a song of praise to Yamuna
as others bathe in the river or gaze upon it. Photo by David
Haberman.

undertaken to honor, worship, or contact the river for spiritual benefits.
A poem well known in the region of Braj reads:

Having bowed to the water of Yamuna,
Drink the water of Yamuna.
Meditating continually on the water of Yamuna,
Bathe in the water of Yamuna.[129]

River worship has a long history in India. Archaeological evidence
links ancient pilgrimage activity with river worship,[130] and early religious

texts express a reverent attitude toward rivers. Many Rig Veda hymns celebrate water for its life-blessing qualities. Hymn 10.9, for example, reads:

Waters, you are the ones who bring us the life force.
Help us to find nourishment so that we may look upon
    great joy.

Let us share in the most delicious sap that you have,
    as if you were loving mothers.

Let us go straight to the house of the one for
    whom you waters give us life and give us birth.

For our well-being let the goddesses be an aid to us,
    the waters be for us to drink.
Let them cause well-being and health to flow over us.

Mistresses of all the things that are chosen, rulers over
    all peoples, the waters are the ones I beg for a cure.[131]

Bodies of water in general, and rivers in particular, are conceived of in Vedic hymns as feminine divine entities who are the source and support of abundant life; they are frequently referred to as "mothers of the world."[132] Although all rivers in India are praised for these qualities, seven are often identified in Rig Vedic hymns as being worthy of special attention because of their great powers.[133]

The celebration of rivers expressed in the Vedic period continues in the more sectarian literature of the Puranas, medieval scriptures full of references to river worship. In a summary statement the *Padma Purana* exclaims, "All rivers are holy."[134] Consideration of rivers in the Puranas, however, often involves a hierarchical ranking determined by the various sectarian traditions of different regions. Reflecting a northern perspective, the *Skanda Purana,* for example, states, "There are hundreds of rivers. All of them remove sins. All of them are bestowers of merit. Of all the rivers, those that fall into the sea are the most excellent. Of all those rivers[,] Ganga, Yamuna, Narmada and Sarasvati are the most excellent rivers. Among the rivers, O eminent sages, these four are highly meritorious."[135] Over time, the list of seven sacred rivers has varied, but the Yamuna has almost always appeared among the seven.[136]

We have seen that, in the *Bhagavata Purana,* a text of central importance for the Bhagavata tradition, the whole world is considered to be the body of God. As a playful youth, Krishna also appears in this text as an enjoyer of his own body, delighting in the beauty of nature.[137] Three embodied forms of divinity are marked for special attention in the sacred realm of Braj, a land identified with the body of Krishna and depicted as a vibrant world of nature.[138] Specifically, the *Bhagavata Purana* tells us that Krishna was particularly delighted by the forest (Vrindaban), the mountain (Govardhan), and most important for our concerns, the river (Yamuna).[139] For many of the surviving Bhagavata traditions, especially those observed in Braj, the Yamuna is considered to be the most sacred of all rivers.[140] According to these schools, the Yamuna has qualities possessed by no other river. It is regarded as a river of delights, viewed by many as the very source of all that is joyful in life. Yet today it is also a river with a great many troubles. To understand more about it, we must venture high in the Himalayan Mountains where its story begins.

CHAPTER 2

The Source

Mother of Life

Life would not be possible without water. Rivers bring us life
from the distant mountains. This is why we call them our
"Mother." We don't think of them as rivers. We think of
them as our Mother.

Baba Ramananda Giri

Drip. Drip. Drip. Drops of water fall steadily from the Yamunotri
glacier, perched on the southern face of Mount Kalinda about twenty
thousand feet above sea level, in the Garhwali region of the Himalayan
Mountains. Six miles to the east, majestic Bandarpunch Mountain
looms above the Yamunotri glacier. The mountain's name means
"Monkey's Tail," and it is associated with a story about Hanuman, the
heroic monkey devotee of the *Ramayana*'s epic hero, Rama. Prakash, a
rugged mountain man, recounted this story as we both looked up at the
glacier from his Yamunotri tea stall, where I sat sipping a cup of spicy
tea he had just made for me. When Hanuman leapt to the island of Sri
Lanka to search for Rama's abducted wife, Sita, he was captured by the
troops of the demon Ravana, who punished Hanuman by setting his tail
on fire. Powerful Hanuman escaped, however, and used this opportunity to incinerate the demon's city with his flaming tail. Then he jumped
far away, landing at this lofty place in the Himalayas, where he extin-
guished his fiery tail in the icy glacial water of the Yamuna.[1] "And that
is how it got its name," Prakash said, gesturing quickly in the direction
of the towering peak before turning to boil water in preparation for
another customer.

Two-thirds of the world's freshwater is contained in glaciers, the
residual remains of the last Ice Age or perhaps precursors of the next Ice
Age. Glaciers are formed from metamorphosed layers of melting and

refreezing snow that have been compressed into glacial ice. Mountain glaciers are sensitive indicators of climate change and are retreating worldwide. Glaciers are a vital source for water, an essential ingredient of all life. Photographs taken from space make it clear that we live on a watery planet: 75 percent of Earth's surface is covered with water, and about the same percentage of our own bodies consists of water. This life-sustaining liquid is primary; although water does not depend on living things, all living things depend on water. "The unique physical and chemical properties of water have allowed life to evolve in it. The following quote from Szent-Gyorgyi illustrates this point of view: 'That water functions in a variety of ways within a cell can not be disputed. Life originated in water, is thriving in water, water being the solvent and medium. It is the matrix of life.' All biological reactions occur in water, and it is the integrated system of biological metabolic reactions in an aqueous solution that is essential for maintenance of life."[2] Water is indeed the mother of all life, and this very fluid that supports all life is now threatened worldwide.

Still, the water coming from the Yamunotri glacier is as clean as any water on Earth; it is crystal clear—and powerful too. The pure water locked up in the glacier is melted by the sun (father of the river), producing a life-giving stream. Aquatic drops of nurturing love—as Yamuna's devotees here call them—untainted by the corruption and greed of the plains below, multiply rapidly to form the flowing stream and fill the icy lake of Saptarishi Kund located at the glacier's base. As the water gushes out of the lower end of Saptarishi Kund, it spills down the dark southern slope of Kalinda Mountain, forming a series of white cascading waterfalls and dropping a distance of more than eight thousand feet into Yamunotri, the "Mouth of the Yamuna." Here, at an elevation of around eleven thousand feet above sea level, it joins boiling water bubbling forth from hot springs, another source of the Yamuna River.

Some fifty million years ago, the Indian subcontinent collided with the Asian continent, and since then a significant portion of this landmass has been subducted under the Asian plate, pushing the latter upward and creating the highest mountain range in the world today. Yamunotri is located on the Himalayan boundary between the Indian-Australian and Eurasian lithospheric plates, where magmatic heat wells up from the Earth's mantle. Hot springs are one of the signatures of geothermal activity caused by shifting tectonic plates.[3] As water from deep reservoirs heats up, it ascends via vertical channels to emerge at the Earth's surface. Natural wells and springs have been worshipped worldwide as both purifiers and transmitters of spiritual power,[4] and they have been viewed as beneficial places at which to contact divinity. Religious hydrolatry seems to reach its zenith where fire and water combine in a natural hot spring. The dual sources of the glacial stream and the hot spring mingle in potent ways at Yamunotri.

The priests of Yamunotri provide a different account of how this life-giving force, known to them as the goddess Yamuna, came to be here.[5] Long ago, seven sages led by the great Jayamuni gathered at the place now known as Saptarishi Kund, the "Pond of the Seven Sages," high atop Kalinda Mountain, the mountain who had prayed to have the magnificent Yamuna descend upon his head from its celestial abode. For many years the sages practiced severe asceticism at this remote site, seeking to bring the heavenly river Yamuna down to Earth for the benefit of all humankind. The story of the descent of the Yamuna is similar to that of the Ganges,[6] except, as the Yamunotri priests point out, the yogi Bhagiratha brought the Ganges down for liberation (*mukti*) at death, whereas Jayamuni and the other sages brought Yamuna down to develop the devotional insight (*bhakti*) of the living.[7]

Yamuna is the daughter of Vivasvat, the "Brilliant One," later known as Surya, the "Sun." For this reason Yamuna is also known as Surya Putri, the "Daughter of the Sun." The brilliant solar source of all energy and light wished to marry and so approached Vishvakarma, the divine artist and architect. Vishvakarma offered his own daughter, Samjna, "Consciousness," to Vivasvat for marriage.[8] From this union came the divine twins, Yama, Lord of Death, and Yami, an early Vedic appellation for Yamuna. Yama was born first, making him the elder brother of the latter. Because she could no longer tolerate the sun's brilliance, Samjna produced a double of herself called Chaya, "Shadowy Replica," and left this shadow double behind to take her place. This union produced three offspring: Manu, the first human; the river Tapti; and Shani, the planet Saturn. The Rig Veda, an ancient collection of scriptural hymns, tells of a famous dialog between Yami and her elder brother, Yama.[9] Yami approached Yama with the desire for an amorous encounter. Yama refused her advance, saying that such a relationship was not proper between brother and sister. Yami argued that, since they had been together in their mother's womb, it would not be a sin to come together again. Unswayed, Yama again stressed the impropriety of the proposed union. The argument illustrates some fundamental and opposing characteristics of the divine twins. Yama represents righteousness, or dharma, to use the Sanskrit term. Indeed, he is later called Dharma Raja,

"King of Righteousness." Yami, on the other hand, represents passion, even passion that transgresses the bounds of social propriety. Although between the early Vedic period and the period represented in the Puranas Yamuna is transformed from seductress to river goddess of life-giving water, she retains an association with realms of passionate desire throughout her long history.

After gaining enormous power through their ascetic practices, the seven sages at last succeeded in their efforts to bring the life-giving waters of Yamuna to Earth. She came crashing onto the majestic peak of Mount Kalinda, spilling down its dark southern face in spectacular waterfalls. Some say that *Kalinda* means "dark shade" because the southern face of this mountain is covered with dense vegetation, causing it to absorb the maximum amount of sunlight.[10] Because Yamuna originates on Kalinda, she is also known as Kalindi, "She Who Comes from Kalinda." However, the place where Yamuna came down was a cold and isolated spot. Yamuna worried that very few people would be able to visit her at her source, and that those who did would experience great hardship. So she prayed to her father, the sun, to make the location of her origin on Earth more attractive and pleasant. In response, the sun gave her a gift: a single ray of his solar splendor. He hurled this intense ray of brilliant light so that it struck a rock face on the east side of the canyon at the base of the long waterfall, causing boiling hot water to burst forth. Thus, the Yamuna has a dual source: a cold stream and a hot spring. The two meet and become one in the bowl of Yamunotri. With the sun's gift of the hot spring, those who come to visit Yamuna at her source can experience being warmed year-round, cooking food without lighting a fire, and bathing pleasurably in naturally hot water. Yamuna also asked that whoever comes to her, bathes in her waters, and worships her at this spot will have a blessed life and will be spared the tortures of her brother, Yama, Lord of Death.

The act of bathing in and worshipping a river has a long history in India and is much discussed in Puranic literature. The Puranas—the term literally means "ancient"—are a group of early texts that date back to the beginning of the first millennium and give expression to religious thought and practices. These fluid and developing texts are compilations of multiple authors over long periods of time (thus making them difficult to date) and reflect oral and living traditions. The Puranas constitute the principal scriptures of theistic, temple-based Hinduism and are a treasure house for cultural practices that stretch over a period of some two thousand years. Ludo Rocher writes about them: "The

Puranas are, first, important documents for the study and reconstruction of the history of Hindu India. In a more practical way, they have contributed to the continuity of Hinduism through the ages, and are indispensable for a correct understanding of Hinduism today. As a matter of fact, every Hindu is influenced by the Puranas, and his activities are guided by them."[11] The Puranas are also used as an authoritative source for many of the narratives told at pilgrimage sites. This is particularly true of the *Skanda* and *Padma Puranas,* which deal specifically with the benefits derived from visiting pilgrimage sites. Within the Puranas there is much discussion of the sacredness of rivers and of ways to participate in their liquid power.

Today, many people visit and honor Yamuna at her origin. Thousands of pilgrims make the long trek up the steep slopes of the upper Yamuna valley to visit this natural shrine. Most pilgrims do so as part of a greater pilgrimage known as the Char Dham Yatra, the "Pilgrimage to the Four Sacred Abodes." During my four stays at Yamunotri, I met people from every major state of northern India but never encountered anyone performing solely the pilgrimage to Yamunotri. All intended to visit the three other sacred sites of the Char Dham pilgrimage, one of the most important pilgrimages for Hindus of northern India. Many whom I interviewed told me that as Hindus they believe they are to perform this pilgrimage at least once in their lifetime. Many identified it as the most important one they would ever undertake.

The four sites of the Char Dham Yatra are, in order, Yamunotri, Gangotri, Kedarnath, and Badrinath. All these sites are associated with the Ganges, since they are all located near the sources of rivers that eventually feed into the Ganges. Because of this, the religious culture of the Ganges—with its focus on the removal of sins in preparation for a good death—dominates much of the thinking about the entire Char Dham pilgrimage. Pilgrims on the Char Dham Yatra travel from west to east. The first two sites are located in the district of Uttarkashi, and the last two in the district of Chamoli, but the entire region is known as Garhwal and is identified by many Hindus as the *devata bhumi,* the "land of the gods." Significantly, all four sites are related to rivers. Yamunotri is the source of the Yamuna River, Gangotri is the source of the Bhagirathi River—considered to be the main branch of the Ganges— Kedarnath is near the source of the Mandakini River, and Badrinath is near the source of the Alaknanda River.[12] The Char Dham pilgrimage route follows these four great rivers. While the Yamuna merges with the Ganges far below on the plains, the latter three rivers are all major

Himalayan tributaries that make up the Ganges by joining together in
the mountains. The Alaknanda unites with other Himalayan tributaries
of the Ganges at Karnaprayag (the suffix *prayag* usually indicates the
confluence of two or more rivers); the Alaknanda and Mandakini
come together at Rudraprayag; these combined rivers—now called the
Alaknanda—merge with the Bhagirathi at Deoprayag. The combined
stream emerges from the mountains at Rishikesh and Haridwar as the
mighty Ganges.

Although work is under way to extend a jeep trail a few more miles,
for all practical purposes the footpath to Yamunotri begins at a place
called Hanuman Chatti, located at an elevation of about seventy-five
hundred feet. A *chatti* is a resting place typically featuring tea stalls,
shops selling necessary amenities, small outdoor restaurants, and even
beds for those who plan to sleep there for the night. This one is called
Hanuman Chatti because it is where the Yamuna absorbs a major
mountain tributary called the Hanuman Ganga. Pilgrimage buses typically clog the narrow road leading up to Hanuman Chatti; colorfully
dressed pilgrims from all regions of northern India throng the area.

Pilgrims leave Hanuman Chatti by crossing a bridge over the Hanuman
Ganga and taking the foot trail that begins on the east side of the
Yamuna River. The first three miles of the trail are carved into the wall
of a wide gorge formed by centuries of rushing water. The trail is not
exceptionally steep here, but during the rainy season this area is active
with falling rocks and landslides. During one of my visits, which coin-
cided with heavy rain, I witnessed a death from falling rocks. Mountain
pilgrimage in this region is hazardous.

A few miles up the trail lies the first of the terraced farms that take
advantage of the abundant water, and there is a small village consisting
of houses with stone walls and thick thatched roofs. In the warmer
months, small children stand in the wooden doorways and wave to the
pilgrims as they pass by. At this point the high snow-capped peaks to
the north become visible.

In September 1999, I trekked to Yamunotri with my wife, Sandy, and
two children, Meagan and Nathan, ages fourteen and four, respectively.
The weather was cool and rainy, making the trail slippery and dangerous; rocks were falling but our spirits were high. We broke our journey
at Janaki Chatti, taking two days to reach Yamunotri, where we stayed
an additional two days while I studied the site and interviewed pilgrims
and priests. Nathan rode a small pony the entire way. He turned out to
be a competent rider; but, ever mindful of stories I had heard of ponies

falling off the steep edges, I often ran alongside him, risking my own neck so that I could pull him from his mount if his pony slipped.

During the peak season of late May and early June, the trail is lined with pilgrims from all social backgrounds and all walks of life: old and young, poor and rich, businessmen and wandering mendicants. The bright red, yellow, pink, and green saris of the Rajasthani women add dazzling color to the zigzagging procession advancing up the mountain. Although walking is considered to be the most auspicious mode of transportation up the mountain, many pilgrims choose to ride horses, leaving behind a trail covered with slippery dung. Some even elect to make the journey in a wooden-seated litter carried by four men, and occasionally one can see a little old lady peering out of a large wicker basket as she is carried up the valley on the back of a sure-footed bearer. The most dedicated of all, however, are those who walk barefoot on the rocky eighteen-mile trail from Hanuman Chatti to Yamunotri and back. We encountered several elderly women doing just that. Regardless of how the traveler ascends the mountain, the trail offers magnificent views along the way, especially when one rounds the last bend and comes upon the Yamunotri complex and its stunning view of the glacier high above.

Temporary tea stalls set up along flatter portions of the trail tempt pilgrims to take a short break; these are often constructed of black plastic tarps stretched over frames made of wooden poles. I frequently stopped to rest and enjoy the scenery while talking with pilgrims over a cup of spicy tea. About three miles after the trail begins at Hanuman Chatti, it crosses over a high, narrow bridge and shifts to the western side of the river. From there the trail climbs sharply and then, at the end of the first five miles, levels off at the entrance to the village of Janaki Chatti. Many pilgrims stop here to rest and eat. There are several small hotels, and many pilgrims use Janaki Chatti as a base, walking the remaining four miles up to Yamunotri and back in a single day. I have always broken my journey here to allow time to converse with pilgrims at greater leisure than hiking allows. Across the river, on a plateau above its eastern bank, is the picturesque village of Kharsali, home of the Yamunotri priests. They spend the winter in stone houses covered by rough-hewn slate roofs supported by heavy wooden beams.

Janaki Chatti stretches along the trail for most of a mile. Above it, the trail becomes steep and passes through a thick stand of trees. Here the river roars loudly as it tumbles over huge boulders into waterfalls. The trail affords impressive views up the narrow gorge cut by the thundering water. Plumbeous redstarts, small dark birds with bright reddish brown tails, jump from boulder to boulder in the swift stream, continuously fanning their tails up and down as if ready to leap into the air with each motion. The tree cover is dense along the rugged sides of the valley above Janaki Chatti. Brown oaks and the evergreen Himalayan yew cling to the steep walls of the ravine; black crows perched in their branches caw raucously. Misty rain often falls in this region, and the plentiful water supports a diverse range of vegetation. The oaks are covered with lush moss and bright green ferns; beneath them, bamboo, shrubs, and flowering plants thrive.

The final two miles of the trail are arduous. After crossing another bridge over another roaring white tributary, the path shifts abruptly into a sharp ascent that consists of more than fifty switchbacks. These are necessary to climb the steep gorge, which rises several hundred yards between Janaki Chatti and Yamunotri. The trail in this section is frequently exposed, since it is carved into a vertical wall high above the riverbed. A fall here is almost always fatal. Clouds drift rapidly up the canyon, now concealing, now revealing the snowy peaks looming ahead. Here the beauty of the Yamuna is breathtaking. She is wild, free, and crystal clear when heavy rains are not falling on the glacier high overhead. Finally, when it seems impossible to endure one more switchback, the hiker rounds the last bend and is rewarded with the spectacular view of the bowl of Yamunotri—the "Mouth of Yamuna."

A series of long waterfalls plummets from the Yamunotri glacier down the face of Mount Kalinda into the box canyon of Yamunotri some eight thousand feet below. This is the location of the temple complex and the destination of this pilgrimage. The white, frothy appearance of the falling water has led many visitors and local residents to compare it to a stream of flowing milk.[13] The steep slopes immediately above the rocky Yamunotri bowl are covered with squat, dense trees, primarily brown oaks. Within a few hundred yards, the trees and shrubs give way to grassy hillsides. Above these, Kalinda Mountain becomes even steeper, and vegetation disappears altogether into rocky, snowy, icy terrain. Situated 19,200 feet above sea level, high up on a ridge near the summit of the mountain, is the Yamunotri glacier. On a clear day its shimmering ice is easily visible from the pilgrimage complex below. Above the glacier is the sharp peak of Mount Kalinda, covered with snow year-round.

As this magnificent scene captivates the eyes, one descends a narrow winding alley that leads to the temple site through a bazaar of a dozen or so shops constructed of wooden poles and black plastic tarps. These shops sell pictures of the goddess Yamuna mounted on a turtle, kits

Figure 2. The Yamunotri temple complex. The tall white building just below the waterfall is the main Yamuna temple. Photo by David Haberman.

designed to help the pilgrim worship this aquatic divinity, and the Indian version of vegetarian fast foods: samosas, chapatis, rice, lentil gravy, cooked vegetables, milk sweets, and tea. Unfortunately, trash from these shops, dung from the many mules, and even materials used for worshipping Yamuna and then discarded have accumulated on the ground near the river in Yamunotri. I recall the words of a temple priest downstream who told me, "It is a curse to be a place of pilgrimage."[14] Emerging from this small temporary shopping mall, which bustles with activity only during the pilgrimage season, pilgrims cross a bridge over deafening water to the east side of the river and enter the temple complex of Yamunotri (figure 2). Steamy fog hangs over the buildings where moist warm air from the hot springs mixes with the cool mountain breeze.

The sun's gift to his daughter Yamuna forms the major focus for many activities in Yamunotri. A rock face on the east side of the canyon blessed with the blast of the sun's fiery ray is called Divya Shila, the "Divine Stone." The face of this rock is reddish brown and is decorated with small ornaments presented to the goddess by pilgrims. The Sanskrit "Yamunotri Mahatmya" of the *Skanda Purana* is a major source for the Yamunotri priests' representation of this pilgrimage site.[15] They know this portion of the book well; several of them recited large sections of it to me during our conversations about the sacredness of Yamuna. This text claims that one can achieve spiritual liberation by merely touching the Divya Shila.[16] Many pilgrims touch it reverently while seeking contact with the goddess whose presence it indicates. Some distance from the source of the hot spring, a few holy men have carved cave residences into this rock wall. These are thermally heated year-round—one of the results of the sun's blessing to his daughter.

Boiling hot water emerges directly from a fissure in the rock wall. As it spurts out of the rock, it makes a continuous gurgling sound. One of the Yamunotri priests told me this is the voice of the sage Jayamuni—one of the seven sages—continually chanting "Kalindi namah" (All glory to Kalindi—another name for Yamuna) in praise of Yamuna.[17] The face of the rock where the boiling hot water gushes forth is now partially covered with white tiles, except for a square-shaped opening with a peak in the shape of an inverted V, which gives access to the bare rock and the water. In the Himalayan region, this is a common way of framing the divine or marking the presence of a goddess. Called Yamuna Mukharvind, the "Lotus Mouth of Yamuna," this stone mouth is the focal point for much of the worship that takes place in Yamunotri.

Most pilgrims worship the goddess Yamuna at the Divya Shila shrine with the aid of the Yamunotri priests. The "Yamunotri Mahatmya" states that even people without any virtues in the present age of decadence achieve their goal from a knowledgeable view of, and worship at this site of, Yamuna's origin.[18] The forms of worship conducted here range from minimal to complex: some pilgrims offer a simple prayer on their own, others prepare a more elaborate worship ritual by purchasing *puja* (worship) kits in the tented bazaar at the base of the temple complex. These kits contain items designed to please the goddess: a small red sari, a packet of *bindis* (red dots to ornament the forehead), decorative red *sindur* powder, a comb, a necklace, bracelets, nail polish, a mirror, incense, coconut, and candy sugar crystals. The pilgrims honor Yamuna by offering her these items with the aid of a priest, who provides fresh flowers and guides them through chants of Sanskrit mantras.

After watching the pilgrims at the Divya Shila, my son, Nathan, wanted to worship Yamuna where she emerges from the stone wall. I resisted, not wanting to get entangled with some of the more demanding priests tending the site that day. Nathan, however, quietly held onto his desire and, shortly before our departure down the mountain, asked if we could buy one of the red scarves on sale in the bazaar. Forgetting about his earlier request, I assumed that he wanted it as a souvenir for himself and bought one for him. After I handed it to him, he announced that he wanted to "offer it to Yamuna-ji." At first I thought he wanted to offer it to the river stream, but he insisted that we go back up to the temple complex and offer it at the Divya Shila. How could I resist his determined devotion? We retraced our steps, engaged a priest, and conducted a Yamuna *puja* at the mouth of the hot spring. In addition to the flowers, rice, red *sindur* powder, and incense that he supplied himself, the priest offered Nathan's red cloth while he chanted Sanskrit mantras. Nathan calmly imitated the clasped hands and bowed heads of those he had observed and grinned with pleasure as the *puja* finished. So did the officiating priest, who received a handsome fee for his services.

Immediately to the left of the Divya Shila is Surya Kund, the "Pond of the Sun," a low stone-and-cement tank measuring about four feet on each side, built to hold some of the boiling water as it emerges from the fissure in the rock. The steaming water in this tank is hot enough to quickly cook rice—another of the results of the sun's gift to his daughter. Pilgrims buy packets of rice in the nearby bazaar, tie them in cloth, and immerse the bundles in the boiling water by suspending them from an iron grate placed over the small tank for this purpose. When the rice is done, the pilgrims carry away the special *prasad*—grace in an edible form—of this place. One priest told me that, by eating the rice cooked in Surya Kund, one receives the blessings of Yamuna and her protection from her elder brother, Yama, Lord of Death.

Hot water flows from Surya Kund into another nearby tank, called either Tapta Kund, the "Hot Pond," or Yamuna Bai Kund, "Lady Yamuna's Pond." Here the water is mixed with enough water from the cold stream to make it agreeable for bathing. This stone-and-cement tank is a square structure that measures about twelve feet across and holds water approximately four feet deep. This is perhaps the most enjoyable of the effects of the sun's gift to his daughter Yamuna, for pleasurable it is to soak in the water of this natural hot tub on a cool mountain day while gazing at the snow-covered peaks sparkling high overhead. Bathing in this water is considered one of the most powerful ways to take advantage of Yamuna's blessings. The "Yamunotri Mahatmya" declares that one who bathes in this pond will be honored in the abode of the sun.[19]

Next to the Divya Shila shrine stands a temple dedicated to the goddess Yamuna Devi. This temple, called Ma Yamuna Mandir, "Mother Yamuna's Temple," was constructed in 1839 by Naresh Sundarshan Shah, then king of the Garhwali cultural center of Tehri. Pilgrims can directly worship the natural forms of Yamuna themselves, but all worship in the temple is conducted by the Yamunotri priests. There are more than one hundred hereditary priests who have the right to officiate in the Yamunotri temple, but at any given time only around a dozen are actively involved in the worship there and at the Divya Shila shrine. Although the river itself serves as the direct focus for worship in Yamunotri, and although nature worship is much older than temple worship, the Yamuna temple provides another kind of familiar forum for worship. Pilgrims visiting Yamunotri want to have *darshan,* or "visual communion," with the embodied form of the goddess Yamuna housed in the temple.

The temple opens at seven in the morning with the first "auspicious" waving of the ritual lamps (*mangal arati*), and it closes at seven in the evening with the bedtime waving of the ritual lamps (*shayan arati*). The most prominent figure in the temple is a black stone image of Yamuna Devi. She is approximately three feet tall and is usually dressed in a red sari and decorated with jewelry, a golden crown, and garlands of flowers. Because of her elaborate dress, I could not see her entire body, but several of the Yamunotri priests told me that in this temple Yamuna Devi sits on her turtle mount. This is certainly the way she is represented in pictorial form in Yamunotri. A white stone image of Ganga Devi, considered to be Yamuna's sister, stands to her left. This embodied form of the goddess Ganges is also decorated with beautiful ornaments. The primary recipient of the temple offerings is a silver form of Yamuna Devi about one foot tall. This form of the goddess has four arms and is also dressed in a red sari.

Yamuna is depicted at Yamunotri in a form typically portrayed in early Puranic literature. The twelfth-century *Agni Purana,* for example, describes Yamuna Devi as "mounted on a turtle, holding a pot in her hand, and of dark complexion."[20] All the pictures of Yamuna Devi sold in the bazaar at Yamunotri, as well as all the paintings of her on walls

Figure 3. The Goddess Yamuna as she is portrayed in Yamunotri. This print, available for purchase at the Yamunotri bazaar, is usually included in the kits sold to aid pilgrims as they worship Yamuna.

at this site, portray her seated on a lotus on the back of a turtle floating on a river, with high mountains in the background. She is dressed in a red sari and is decorated with gold jewelry and a golden crown. She is four-armed, holding a pot in her upper left hand, a lotus flower in her lower left hand, and a string of meditation beads in her lower right hand, and she displays the fear-not gesture with her upper right hand. (See figure 3.) The symbols of the bountiful pot and creative lotus make it evident that Yamuna Devi is a powerful goddess who manifests life-giving forces and blessings.

The natural phenomena of Yamunotri are worshipped continually by the few holy men who live here year-round in cave shelters heated by the hot spring, but the temple is open for only six of the warmest months of the year.[21] The priests close the temple during Dipawali, the "Festival of Lights," which occurs on the new moon in the middle of the lunar month of Kartik (which falls in late October or early November). The dark stone image of Yamuna resides here permanently, but the Yamunotri priests transport the silver one below by means of a palanquin wrapped in red cloth and decorated with flower garlands to their home village of Kharsali, located four miles down the trail on the eastern bank of the river just across from Janaki Chatti. The patron deity of this village is Shani, the god of Saturn and younger brother of Yamuna.

Kharsali is a picturesque village. The houses are constructed of stone secured with mud mortar; even the roofs consist of skillfully arranged slabs of stone. The wood used as support beams and columns to buttress the porches is intricately carved. The village walkways are paved with slabs of the abundant stone, and small productive gardens surround the homes. The temple of Shani is an old three-story stone structure, the top of which is reached by passing through small openings in the wooden floors. The steep ascent is made possible with the aid of logs cut in half lengthwise and carved with scooped footholds to form ladders. Shani resides on the uppermost floor. Embodied in a brass mask, he rests in a wooden palanquin.

Shani hosts his older sister, Yamuna, in this village for the six months of the winter season when deep snow covers most of the upper valley. During Dipawali, in late autumn, Yamuna arrives in Kharsali with great celebration as an honored guest. She returns to Yamunotri in spring, on the auspicious day of Akshaya Tritiya, the third day of the bright half of the lunar month of Vaishakh (which occurs in late April or early May). On this day the Yamunotri priests residing in Kharsali prepare a procession to accompany the silver form of Yamuna Devi back to the Yamunotri temple. Being a faithful brother, Shani, in the form of the brass mask, goes door to door in the village, announcing from his wooden palanquin that he is escorting Yamuna back to Yamunotri. Villagers gather together fruits and cloth to offer Yamuna at Yamunotri and join a procession up the mountain with accompanying drums, conch shells, and long copper horns. The goddess is once again transported in a decorated palanquin wrapped in red cloth, and Shani rides behind her in another ornate palanquin. Upon arriving in Yamunotri, Yamuna returns to her temple and Shani is bathed in the river to honor the direct form of his sister. The residents of Kharsali make their offerings and request Yamuna to fulfill some wish. Then they return to their own village with Shani; some weep as they leave Yamuna behind.

For most pilgrims the journey to Yamunotri is incomplete without a visit to the cold stream gushing forth at the base of the waterfall. I observed many pilgrims remove their shoes, approach the river, and touch the water with great reverence. Many brought this water in contact with their bodies, usually their heads, while the braver ones submerged themselves completely in a shallow pool of icy water. Some performed simple acts of worship on the edge of the river, such as offering sticks of incense while intoning a prayer. Others conducted more elaborate rituals, first offering flowers, red *sindur* powder, uncooked rice, and a coconut to the swiftly moving stream, and then honoring this direct form of Yamuna Devi by waving small flaming cotton-wick oil lamps before her on a brass plate. Regardless of the style of worship, it was clear from my conversations with the pilgrims that the most important form of Yamuna Devi here is the river itself.

When weather permits, some pilgrims choose to bathe in the cold pools just below the huge waterfall. The "Yamunotri Mahatmya" says that, merely by bathing in the Yamuna at Yamunotri, a person achieves perfection.[22] The bath is said to wash away all sins and insure that a person does not experience torture in the realm of death, the abode of Yamuna's elder brother, Yama. A primary characteristic of Yamuna's theology in Yamunotri is this ability to wash away sins and protect against untimely or painful death and later torment. This major theme regarding Yamuna's abilities is expressed again and again in the Puranas, and it remains important today. There is a common saying along the banks of the Yamuna: "Jaha Yamuna, waha Yama na," or "Where Yamuna is, there Yama [Death] is not."

Yama occupies a prominent place in this pilgrimage and in the ritual actions performed at Yamunotri. Today he is known as the terrifying god of death, but Yama has a long and varied history in Indian religious culture. During the early Vedic period, he was a celestial god who ruled over a blessed place in the highest heaven.[23] Worshippers prayed for a permanent stay in Yama's abode. Rig Veda 9.113.8, for example, reads, "Make me immortal in that realm where dwells the King, Vivasvan's Son."[24] In this early literature, Yama is represented as a kind and benevolent god. He granted longevity to the living, and happiness in his heavenly kingdom to the dead. Moreover, although Yama welcomed the dead into his enjoyable kingdom, he was not considered to be the cause of death.

During the Puranic period, however, all this changed. Residence in Yama's abode is now something not to be wished for, but to be greatly feared. Yama became the cause of death and the judge of the dead.

When people die, they are brought before Yama, who dispenses rewards and punishment in accordance with their deeds in life, tormenting the dead in a manner appropriate to their sins. Kusum Merh puts it this way: "Thus the region of Yama, which was the goal of all the dead and was conceived to be a place of enjoyment, where they lived under the loving care of Yama, has now become a most dreadful place with its gruesome methods of torturing the sinners."[25] Consequently, Yama is often called Dharma Raja, "King of Righteousness." As noted earlier, the Rig Veda (10.10) states that Yama displayed a high degree of propriety in the face of his sister Yami's excessive passion. The righteous but terrifying nature of Yama and the passionate but nurturing nature of Yamuna continue to be expressed today. In his *Shri Yamuna Mahima,* Nandalal Chaturvedi says this about Surya's divine twins: "The Sun's son is said to be Yama and his daughter is Yamuna. Yama is the harsh dryer [*shoshak*] and Yamuna is the nurturer [*poshak*], because the Sun is both a dryer and a nurturer. The Sun is able to fill a flower with nectar and it is also able to dry up a flower. The Sun gives life, but it also takes life; the Sun is both a destroyer and a life-giver. Therefore, it is said that Yama is the Sun's power of death and Yamuna is the Sun's power of life."[26]

In Puranic mythology, Yama is portrayed as a green-colored divinity. He wears red garments and is decorated with jewelry and a golden crown. He rides a black male buffalo and is accompanied by two fierce dogs. He holds a noose in one hand to capture his victims, and a mace or staff with the other to dispense punishment. It is the tortures of this Yama from which Yamuna protects those who come and worship her at her source. This is one of the most prominent characteristics of Yamuna as represented in Puranic literature and is still acted out at Yamunotri. The "Yamunotri Mahatmya" says, "One who bathes here in the Yamuna even once does not go to the realm of Yama, but achieves the highest goal."[27]

Bathing in a river is considered to be one of the most effective ways to honor and celebrate a river goddess and take advantage of the sacred gifts she offers. The religious benefits of chanting a river's name, seeing her, touching her, drinking her, and meditating on her are all recognized in the Puranas, but bathing is praised as the best of all practices for achieving the highest goal. Several river bathers told me that one should face the oncoming stream while bathing in a river, so as "to greet Mother face to face." A story narrated in the *Padma Purana* stresses the power of bathing in the Yamuna to destroy sins. It recounts the experiences of two brothers who lived fairly similar lives.[28] Both were killed on the

same day, one by a lion and the other by a snake. The elder brother was
taken to hell by the messengers of Yama, while the younger brother was
taken to Krishna's heavenly abode. The younger brother was confused
by this outcome, since in his mind the two had led identical lives. The
messenger of Death informed him that they had indeed led equal lives,
but with one exception. When the younger brother had lived in a jungle,
he had stayed for two months in an ashram located on the bank of the
Yamuna, in which he bathed daily. The messenger explained to him that
his dips in the Yamuna had washed away all his sins during the first
month, and that his Yamuna baths in the second month had made him
worthy of Krishna's heaven.

The *Padma Purana* contains a chapter titled the "Kalindi Tirtha"
that also extols the efficacy of bathing in Yamuna.[29] Here the sage
Narada explains that a bath in Yamuna insures that one does not meet
with misfortune but achieves a healthy, prosperous, and long life.
The water of Yamuna is declared to be especially efficacious for
"washing the mind of poverty, sins, and misfortune."[30] Narada tells
King Yudhishthira, "O King, he who with or without a desire bathes in
the water of Yamuna, does not see miseries here or in the next world."[31]
Yamuna's ability to purify a bather is emphasized: "All minor and major
sins are reduced to ashes by taking a bath in Yamuna."[32] We are also
told in this text that Krishna, the supreme Beloved of Yamuna, is satisfied when a person bathes in Yamuna's water: "Hari is not so much
pleased by means of vows, gifts or penance as he is pleased by means of
just a bath in Yamuna."[33] In fact, the *Padma Purana* goes on to declare,
"Those who are without a bath in Yamuna are born to die only like
bubbles on water."[34]

How is this river perceived? And who is Yamuna Devi according to
those who have such strong faith in her? Why do pilgrims make the
arduous trek to worship her at her source? Wanting to know how
those who worship Yamuna today conceptualize her, I sought to move
beyond textual sources and answer these questions through the conversations I had with pilgrims and priests I encountered on my visits
to Yamunotri. I began with the head priest of a small Narayana temple
in Barkot, the last town of any size on the upper end of the Yamuna
valley. This temple is the only place in the region where wandering
holy men can stay while on their way to the river's source. All the wandering holy men, or *baba*s, I met who were staying at the temple were on
a pilgrimage to Yamunotri, and they planned to travel next to Gangotri,
the source of the Ganges. Baba Ramananda Giri, a gregarious older

baba with long hair and beard who has traveled extensively throughout the Himalayas, had settled here to maintain the temple and assist his fellow mendicants.

I visited Baba on several occasions, during which we often discussed rivers as depicted in Hindu religious culture. On one visit, I asked him why people in India love rivers so much. "Because," he answered in Hindi, "they give us life. Life would not be possible without water. Rivers bring us life from the distant mountains. This is why we call them our 'Mother.' We don't think of them as rivers. We think of them as our Mother."[35] Here Baba Ramananda Giri articulates an idea expressed in much of Hindu literature from Vedic times to the present. The *Padma Purana,* for example, says, "All rivers are the mothers of the whole world."[36] Baba Ramananda Giri agrees with the religious literature on rivers in asserting that rivers provide a fluid essential for all life. As the *baba* says, life would be impossible without good water. Not only is water the very source of our life, but it continues to nurture our lives by supplying the fertile essence necessary for life to flourish. This is a key idea in Hindu river theology. C. Sivaramamurti writes, "The concept of the river in India is that of a sustaining mother. The stream of the river carries *payas*. The word *payas* stands for both water and milk. Appropriately this has been used in relation to the river as the stream that sustains the people, her children, with water, as a mother sustains her babies with milk."[37]

The seven sages brought the heavenly Yamuna to Earth for the benefit of humankind. As a nurturing mother, she came to give and sustain bountiful life; she is frequently addressed as Mother Yamuna. In this sense, Yamuna is a River of Life. Yamuna's sister, the Ganges, is viewed in similar terms, although an important distinction exists in the theology of these two sister rivers. The main reason the Ganges was called to Earth by the sage Bhagiratha was to purify his sixty thousand dead ancestors. By examining early myths and temple sculpture, Heinrich von Stietencron has shown that the Ganges is primarily a lunar river, and that "Ganga came down to earth as a river of the dead and for the purification of the dead."[38] In contrast, Yamuna is a solar river who bargains with her brother Death for her devotee's life. Although she too is associated with purification in preparation for death—especially in the Himalayan region, in which she is connected with the Char Dham pilgrimage—Yamuna is primarily concerned with the blessings of this life. There is an expression in northern India, "Ganga snan, Yamuna pan," or "Bathe in Ganga, drink Yamuna." This is usually interpreted to mean that one should drink the Yamuna to insure a fulfilling life, and bathe in the Ganges to prepare for death. While the Ganges is frequently associated with the yogic culture of the ascetics who seek release (*moksha*) from this life, the Yamuna is typically associated with the loving devotional traditions that seek enjoyment (*ananda*) in this life.[39] This becomes increasingly true downriver, especially in the religious culture associated with the region of Braj (see chap. 4). The difference in the theology of the two rivers is even reflected in the different bathing experiences possible at the sources of the two rivers. A bath at the source of the Ganges at Gomukh is austere, for it takes place in the icy waters of a swiftly moving glacial stream. A bath at the source of the Yamuna at Yamunotri, on the other hand, is a pleasant dip in a natural hot tub. Many people making the pilgrimage to Yamuna's source told me that they were doing it to get happiness and make their lives successful. They articulated a view of Yamuna as their nurturing Mother and said they were performing this journey to honor her as such.

How is Yamuna conceptualized specifically by the pilgrims who journey to her source? Although another *baba*, Vasishthagiri of Barkot, warned me to expect a plurality of conceptions, saying, "Yamuna is understood differently by different people in different regions," he also said: "She is Mother for us. From her comes all life."[40] When I asked other pilgrims who Yamuna was for them, the majority identified her simply as Mata-ji, a common Hindi word for "Mother." When I pressed them to articulate the characteristics of this mother, they generally responded that she is a nurturing Mother who purifies sins, sustains life, and protects her children from death. One young woman from Delhi told me, "She is our Mother. She gives us everything. So we come to worship her and thank her."[41]

Besides the identification of Yamuna as Mother, I also heard at Yamunotri that she is Surya Putri, the "Daughter of the Sun," Yama ki Bahan, the "Sister of Death," and Ganga ki Bahan, the "Sister of the Ganges." The priests of the Yamunotri temple describe her in similar terms. Almost all the people I talked with in Yamunotri characterized Yamuna in terms of her older Puranic portrait. They mentioned her connection with Krishna—of immense importance in Braj—only when I specifically asked them about this. When I brought up Yamuna's connection with Krishna, one of the Yamunotri priests told me that Yamunotri is Yamuna's father's village (*pihar*), whereas Braj is the residence of Yamuna's in-laws (*sasural*).[42] Two other temple priests listening to this claim added that Yamuna was Krishna's lover (*priya*), stressing that since no marriage was ever performed she never became Krishna's wife. They remarked that Yamuna was born in Yamunotri, where she did penance to win Krishna's attention, but she matured in Braj, where she experienced sweet union with Krishna. In fact, it is true that, in Braj, Yamuna theology is most elaborate, and Braj has the greatest concentration of Yamuna temples (see chap. 4).

Compared to the more complex theology developed in Braj, Yamuna's theology in Yamunotri as collectively expressed by priests and pilgrims is fairly simple. The Yamunotri priests seem to make their living on the promise that they can provide access to Yamuna as a life-giving, life-purifying, and life-protecting goddess. As noted earlier, people rarely make a pilgrimage to Yamunotri out of devotion to Yamuna alone—as they do in Braj. Instead they visit Yamunotri only as part of the larger Char Dham pilgrimage. Very few of the pilgrims I met in Yamunotri identified themselves chiefly as devotees of Yamuna: they come with a general devotion to all the sacred rivers of the central Himalayan region while clearly recognizing Yamuna as one of the most sacred rivers of northern India.

Beyond this general motivation, what specific reasons do pilgrims themselves give for their journey to Yamunotri? I heard a great variety of answers to this question during my interviews with many people performing this pilgrimage. The most common response was that they made this journey for purification. A man traveling in a group from the state of Madhya Pradesh told me, "This pilgrimage will take our sins away."[43] A party of pilgrims from the state of Gujarat identified Yamuna as the "sister of Ganga" and supplied a much longer list of answers to my question. They said they were performing this pilgrimage "to make our lives successful, to get happiness, to have sight of God [Bhagavan's darshan], to see the beauty of nature [prakriti], to satisfy the requirement that all Hindus must perform this pilgrimage at least once in a lifetime, and to gain heaven." "Really?" I prodded. "You can reach heaven by making this pilgrimage?" "Yes!" a couple in the group replied together. "And you too will get it by making this pilgrimage." Laughingly they quipped, "Come to heaven with us!" and continued on up the trail.[44]

The group from Gujarat mentioned that they were performing this pilgrimage to experience the beauty of nature. Others said the same. Three couples traveling together from Delhi explained that, instead of going to an ordinary hill station during the hot season, they had decided to combine an outing in the mountains with a religious pilgrimage.

Many others told me that a venture into the world of natural beauty, especially to mountainous rivers, had intrinsic religious value, and that they were here to experience it. The river valleys that drain the Himalayas are considered especially sacred by many Hindus in India today.

Several pilgrims I met said they were making this pilgrimage to expand their understanding of the world and to get "peace of mind." A young woman from Calcutta explained that she "desired to get out of the city and get peace of mind from nature."[45] A man from Rajasthan told me that he was conducting this pilgrimage "because the sages before us did this."[46] What he and others expressed was that they were following in the footsteps of previous divine models for nature worship. For them, the sages were paradigmatic nature worshippers; by imitating their behavior, the pilgrims were hoping to experience a realization similar to that acquired by the exemplary sages.

Another reason pilgrims gave for conducting this pilgrimage was that a trip to Yamunotri insures wide-ranging safety and protection. A man from Himachal Pradesh told me that he was completing this pilgrimage for "safety, that is, for Yamuna's protection as our Mother."[47] From Mother Yamuna, pilgrims seek general safety and protection (the trail itself is slippery and dangerous with falling rocks during the rains), but more specifically they seek protection against the torments of Yamuna's elder brother, Yama, Lord of Death. As we have already seen, this is an old and well-established Puranic theme. However, I frequently heard from both priests and pilgrims alike that, if people make the journey to Yamunotri and worship Yamuna there, they will not go to Yama's tortuous abode, thus adding ethnographic corroboration to the religious literature existing on the subject.

But pilgrims seek far more than protection against death: they also pursue ultimate goals. One of the temple priests of Yamunotri insisted that a person achieves either heaven (svarga) or spiritual liberation (moksha) by making this journey and worshipping Yamuna at her source.[48] The group from Gujarat said that, besides life blessings such as happiness and success, they were going to have darshan (sight, or visual communion) of Bhagavan, a common name for the supreme divinity. A man from Bihar told me that he was making this pilgrimage "to meet God. We want to meet God in this special place."[49] In his case, the divine encounter was expected to take place at the very source of the river. Another man told me that he came "to have darshan of Yamuna-ji where she begins."[50] As one holy man later explained to me, "Just by having darshan of Yamuna-ji, we get powerful energy. That is how we get energy; for example, just by seeing a person we get some of that person's energy."[51]

Many pilgrims perform this pilgrimage in hopes of fulfilling a wish. A sign painted in Hindi on a rock at the beginning of the foot trail near Hanuman Chatti reads, "May Mother Yamuna fulfill your wish!" Fulfillment is considered possible because Yamuna is said to be a kind, wish-granting mother. Another rock sign announces, "Mother Yamuna is a compassionate goddess." Other people told me, however, that they were not making this pilgrimage for any particular personal gain; rather, they were here simply to honor and show appreciation for Mother Yamuna. One middle-aged woman from Rajasthan I met on the trail said, "Yamuna-ji is my Mother. I am going to honor her."[52] A man from Uttar Pradesh remarked, "Mother Yamuna has given us so much. We should thank her for this."[53] Another man, from Haridwar, said, "I am performing this pilgrimage to increase my *bhava* [divine sentiment, or love for God]. The higher up the mountain I go, the higher my *bhava* goes."[54] Judging from the words of these men and women, the pilgrimage to the source of the river can be a means of getting in touch with a wider perspective on reality, one open to the natural gifts of life Yamuna offers, and it can be an opportunity to thank the very source of those gifts.

The Yamuna carves a valley through the mountains that stretches about one hundred miles from Yamunotri to the point where the river emerges onto the Indo-Gangetic plains at the town of Dakpathar. As the Yamuna flows from the high peaks toward the plains below, many changes take place. Below Hanuman Chatti are a few more stops for pilgrims, most notably Shayan Chatti, the "Resting Place." Until recent years this was as far as cars and buses could go, and it was used as a base camp for the foot journey to Yamunotri some fifteen miles above. The road between Hanuman Chatti and Shayan Chatti is steep, but it is now open to the vehicular traffic of the pilgrimage trade most of the time during the warm months of May through September. Below this point the Yamuna settles into a wider valley, and the water—although still forceful and turbulent—no longer rushes over huge boulders into waterfalls. When no rain is falling on the glacier high above, the water here is very clear. Small villages have sprung up where the valley widens, and the residents support themselves by farming rice, corn, wheat, and green vegetables in terraced gardens. During autumn preparations for the snowy winter, strings of yellow corn ears can be seen hanging from the edges of the stone houses and red peppers cover the rooftops, drying in the sun.

Another twenty miles downstream from Shayan Chatti is the town of Barkot. The only town of any size in the upper valley, it contains a Narayan temple that provides shelter for *baba*s on their way to Yamunotri and Gangotri. Fifteen miles below Barkot is the old village of Lakhanmandal. Weather here is less severe, and residents produce bountiful crops in walled gardens surrounding their picturesque stone houses. Local legend links this village to the epic *Mahabharata,* identifying it as the location of the lac (painted-wood) palace of Duryodhana, the eldest of the Kauravas, who had the palace built to incinerate his cousins, the Pandavas, with whom he struggled over who would rule their kingdom. The palace was burnt to the ground, but the wise Pandava brothers escaped through an underground tunnel. Although there is no remaining evidence of any palace, the residents of Lakhanmandal show visitors a doorway leading into an underground tunnel located in an old Shiva temple on a hill above the village.

As the Yamuna flows on down the valley, she displays a deep greenish blue color, especially in her deep pools. She sweeps gracefully around corners, leaving behind expansive deposits of white sand. On a sunny day, sparkling sun rays dance on the rippling surface of the swiftly moving stream as she rushes rapidly toward the plains.[55] Much of the valley is still forested with abundant deodar cedars. Colorful yellow flowers stand tall within the grass carpet at the feet of the trees. From here the Yamuna twists and turns freely as she carves the rock walls of the valley with her wild and unrestrained current.

At the site of Dakpathar, however, everything changes. Here Yamuna undergoes a dramatic transformation, for at this point the river leaves the untamed mountains and enters the plains of human civilization. She changes from the natural to the industrial, from pure water to increasingly polluted water. There is a shift from river worship to river management as she is transformed from a wild and free spirit into a tamed utilitarian channel. The great and energetic river is diminished as the majority of her water is removed from the riverbed and channeled off into controlled irrigation and utility canals. Here we witness a change from religious appreciation to functional demand with the first of the great human-made barrages that block her previously unimpeded flow.[56] Dakpathar is the site of the first of the big dams envisioned after independence by Prime Minister Jawaharlal Nehru, who personally laid the foundation stone for the Dakpathar Barrage. With great faith in modern industrial technology and considerable suspicion of theistic Hinduism, Nehru declared that dams were to be the temples of modern India.[57]

The huge, dark Dakpathar Barrage is an apt monument to modern industrialization.

P. C. Bhatta, the resident engineer of the barrage at Dakpathar, explained the entire system to me and provided me with governmental pamphlets on the project. The Dakpathar Barrage spans a distance of 1,703 feet (516.5 meters) and features twenty-five huge bays to control the river. By means of this obstruction, almost all the water from the river is diverted into a power channel used to generate electricity for the cities on the plains before most of it is returned to the riverbed, about ten miles downstream. "River Yamuna and its tributaries, specially [the] river Tons, have immense potential for development of Hydro power and irrigation," reports an Uttar Pradesh Irrigation Department publication.[58] The Dakpathar system generates 460 million kilowatts per hour. Since the completion of the Dakpathar Barrage, another hydroelectric dam has been built on the Tons about twenty miles upstream from where it joins the Yamuna. Finished in 1975, this system features an underground powerhouse. The average annual generation from this powerhouse is 900 million kilowatts per hour. The Uttar Pradesh state government is in the process of expanding both systems, adding to their capacity to generate electricity to meet the growing demands of the population living on the plains. About twenty miles downstream from Dakpathar, the Yamuna is dammed again, by the Tajewala Barrage. Here almost all the remaining water is diverted into the Eastern and Western Yamuna Canals for irrigation purposes. In fact, during certain months no water whatsoever is released from the Tajewala Barrage. The dams, in effect, break the river into disconnected segments. Clearly, dams have an enormous effect on the life of the river.

Although these dams have added to the government's ability to meet the increasing demand for electricity and irrigation on the plains, many people have questioned the wisdom of building them. In his study of large dams worldwide, Patrick McCully writes, "The damming of the world has brought a profound change to watersheds. Nothing alters a river as totally as a dam. A reservoir is the antithesis of a river—the essence of a river is that it flows, the essence of a reservoir that it is still. A wild river is dynamic, forever changing—eroding its bed, depositing silt, seeking a new course, bursting its banks, drying up. A dam is monumentally static; it tries to bring a river under control, to regulate its seasonal pattern of floods and low flows. A dam traps sediments and nutrients, alters the river's temperature and chemistry, and upsets the

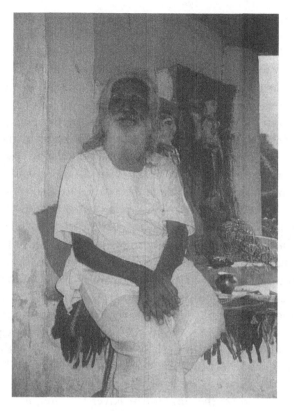

Figure 4. Sunderlal Bahuguna at his home in Tehri,
with a shrine to Ganga Devi in the background.
Photo by David Haberman.

geological processes of erosion and deposition through which the river
sculpts the surrounding land."[59]

There are also people within India strongly opposed to building large
dams on rivers. Arundhati Roy, for example, argues that large dam projects completely alter the ecology of an entire river basin and economically reward a privileged few at the expense of the common good.[60] In
addition to making such claims, Indian river activists often include religious reasons in their arguments against dams. One such person is
Sunderlal Bahuguna (figure 4), a founding pioneer of the modern Indian
environmental movement. Although it can safely be said that Bahuguna
is a major figure in this movement today, it is important to keep in mind
that the environmental movement has deep cultural roots in India.
While recognizing the Gandhian roots of modern environmentalism

in India, N. Patrick Peritore claims that "environmentalism is more firmly imbricated in India's heritage than in the West, where it is a recent and novel ideological addition."[61] Bahuguna has been a major spokesperson for the famous Chipko Movement, a "tree-hugging" movement that began in the central Himalaya in 1973, when peasants—mostly women—hugged trees to prevent them from being cut down. The Chipko Movement represented by Bahuguna has played a primary role in the modern Indian environmental movement and is, therefore, the source of another vitality flowing from the Himalayas. Two historians of Indian environmentalism write, "Indeed, the origins of the Indian environmental movement can be fairly ascribed to that most celebrated of forest conflicts, the Chipko movement of the central Himalaya."[62]

I met with Bahuguna on my way back from Yamunotri in June 2000. I had met him a few years earlier during a journey in which I rode a bicycle more than five hundred miles from Hanuman Chatti to Vrindaban with a group of international riders to study the Yamuna River and raise consciousness about its deteriorating condition. Because of an unwavering dedication to environmental protection that Bahuguna often articulates in religious terms, I have since come to regard him as an environmental saint. I looked forward to meeting with him again to discuss the current condition of Himalayan rivers. When I visited him in June 2000, Bahuguna was living in Tehri, a rapidly disintegrating town situated on the Bhagirathi River (the major branch of the Ganges) and scheduled to be flooded by the Tehri Dam, which was then under construction.[63] The Tehri Dam is currently the tallest dam in all of Asia.[64]

I found Bahuguna living in a small hut, which he called "Ganga Himalaya Kuti," that was perched tenuously on the bank of the Ganges at the base of the mammoth Tehri Dam. With the immense dam looming high in the background, Bahuguna's hut—made of stone and construction materials discarded from the dam project—looked tiny and fragile. One of the dozens of giant dump trucks hauling construction materials up the hillside behind it could have squashed it in seconds. And yet what a mighty presence this hut was. Bahuguna had stopped construction on the dam several times, almost single-handedly, by means of Gandhian fasts. When I met him, Bahuguna was wearing only a white cloth wrapped around his thin waist. His hair and beard were long and white. He was cooking his lunch of rice and vegetables with the aid of a solar cooker when I arrived. We sat and talked in the garden just out the door of his hut. A beautiful image of Ganga Devi, goddess of the Ganges, was housed in a small shrine at the center of the garden, around which he grew vegetables and flowers, creating an atmosphere of serenity in the midst of the raucous construction. Bahuguna has faced many hardships in his lifelong struggle for environmental justice, but during my interview with him he laughed easily and frequently.

Bahuguna joined Gandhi's freedom movement in 1940 at the age of thirteen and became well versed in the mahatma's teachings, which have sustained him throughout his long and active career. Ramachandra Guha points out that, although Gandhi himself cannot really be called an environmentalist, "Mahatma Gandhi has been the usually acknowledged and occasionally unacknowledged patron saint of the Indian environmental movement."[65] According to Bahuguna, Gandhi articulated a philosophy of life based on an Indian culture that had been "born and nourished in the forests" after Indian society had been seriously disrupted by the spread of Western materialism through British colonialism.[66] After independence, Bahuguna became involved with some of Gandhi's disciples who had begun to work for environmental protection in the Himalayan region, particularly those who saw a link between deforestation and the increasing degradation of rivers. This recognition led to new leadership among women living in the mountains, whose everyday labors—gathering food, fuel, and fodder—were intricately linked to the health of the forests and rivers. With this new leadership, the Chipko Movement was launched.[67]

The message of the United Nations Conference on Environment and Development held in Stockholm in June 1972 reached women struggling with these issues in the central Himalayas. In December 1972 a movement was initiated—one that called for community rights to the forests—by a group of women organized by Sarala Behn, an English disciple of Gandhi who worked with mountain women after Gandhi's assassination. Their first demonstration took place in the Yamuna valley, on the site where seventeen people had been killed in 1930 during a nonviolent struggle against the commercialization of forests.[68] In a forest near the site of this earlier tragedy, the government had recently allotted fifty ash trees to a sporting goods company, despite having refused the villagers a single tree to make yokes for plowing. In April 1973 the villagers decided to save the trees by hugging them, and a movement that was to become world famous was born.[69] It was called Chipko, which means "hugging" in the local language.

From these humble beginnings, the movement spread quickly from valley to valley throughout the central Himalayan region. What began as a movement to empower the mountain-dwelling villagers soon developed into a larger movement for wider environmental protection. In July 1977, the organization demanded a ban on the logging of live trees for a period of ten years in the catchment areas of Himalayan rivers. After much repression and political struggle, in April 1981 the government banned the cutting of live trees for commercial purposes above the elevation of thirty-three hundred feet (one thousand meters) in the central Himalayas, the place where Chipko was born.

Bahuguna organized a march in 1982 and another in 1983 to spread the message of the successful Chipko Movement throughout the entire Himalaya region—from Kashmir in the far west to Kohima in the far east. As a result of this and other Chipko efforts, forest health and river protection in the Himalaya region have become major political issues in India.

The Tehri Dam is yet another large dam project designed to supply electricity and irrigation to the plains. It was commissioned in 1972, but construction did not begin until 1978.[70] Although it had been dogged by environmental and safety concerns since its beginning, all scientific and socioeconomic arguments against it failed to stop its construction. The dam will flood scores of villages, destroy large tracts of forest, and submerge the town of Tehri, the ancient seat of Garhwali culture. It is also located in an active earthquake zone; if it breaks it will send a wall of water crashing down the mountains to the towns below, with disastrous results. Resistance to the dam began as soon as the project was proposed in 1949, but the real antidam movement came into existence in the 1980s, when the dangers to the environment and people living in the area became better known.

It is no accident that a Chipko leader like Bahuguna has become involved in the struggle against the dam in Tehri. Environmental historians Madhav Gadgil and Ramachandra Guha remark, "Having largely lost their forests to commercial exploitation, Himalayan peasants now face further suffering owing to external pressures on the other resource their hills are abundant in, water."[71] The general objections to the dam as formulated by the Tehri Baandh Virodhi Sangargh Samiti (Committee for the Struggle against the Tehri Dam) relate to "the seismic sensitivity of the fragile mountain chain (hence the possibility of a dam burst), the submergence of large areas of forest, agricultural land and the historic town of Tehri, and the threat to the life of the reservoir owing to deforestation in the river catchment."[72] But for Bahuguna, the threat of the dam is even graver than these points indicate.

Bahuguna has spent many years fighting this dam out of a sheer love for rivers in general, and for this river in particular as the goddess Ganga Devi. He argues that "materialistic civilization" is the result of human greed out of control. In agreement with many deep ecologists, he contends that worldwide industrial development has brought two basic changes in human thought: "Nature is a commodity over which human beings have a birth right of exploitation, and . . . society is only of human beings."[73] He contrasts this with India's forest culture, especially as represented by its sages who lived in the world of nature. "The close association with nature became the basis of a philosophy of life in which they realized . . . life in all creation—human beings and animals; trees and plants; rivers and mountains. They saw oneness in life. . . . They also developed a feeling of respect for all life and thus [a] worshipful attitude towards Nature. A life of austerity was highly regarded."[74]

This last principle calls for human restraint and for recognition of the need to live within limits. Bahuguna points to Buddha as an example of one who achieved peace, happiness, and fulfillment by curbing desires, and notes that, in contrast, modern people exist in a state of dissatisfaction as a result of trying to satisfy unending desires. He told me, "Everyone wants peace and happiness, and materialistic civilization says that affluence will get it for us. But our culture says that we need to seek fulfillment via inner peace. Materialistic civilization will bring only a small and temporary peace and happiness. True peace and happiness come from within, not from outside. . . . We have been followers of 'enough,' whereas materialistic civilization says 'more, more, and more!'"[75] Bahuguna is fond of quoting a statement by Gandhi: "Earth provides enough to satisfy every man's need but not for every man's greed." For him, the Tehri Dam is a monumental representation of an unbalanced society anxiously and dangerously chasing after limitless desires.

But there is more: Bahuguna truly loves the rivers of the Himalayas, and he believes that large dams kill them. I asked him why he worked so hard to save rivers. He got up and walked over to show me his shrine dedicated to the goddess Ganges and then replied, "I love rivers because they are God; they are our Mother. In our philosophy we see God in all nature: mountains, rivers, springs, and other natural forms. In the tenth chapter of the Bhagavad-gita, Krishna says, 'Among rivers I am the Ganges.' It is part of our religious culture to see God in all nature and to take dips in holy rivers. We go to pay our respects and to get inspiration at the birthplaces of our Mother, like Yamunotri and Gangotri."[76]

Rivers, for Bahuguna, are living forms of divinity. For him, failure to recognize the divinity of rivers is what distinguishes many modern viewpoints from Indian religious culture. He believes that the modern outlook is dangerously out of balance, with the result that both humans and the nonhuman world suffer. Restoring health to both depends on a return to a perspective in which the natural world is viewed as sacred. He sat down before the shrine, looked at the face of the goddess and then up at the clear blue sky before continuing:

> There is a basic difference between today's "civilization" and our culture. The basis of our culture is like mother's milk. The message of our culture is milk for us: that God is in all nature.
>
> We believe that our very existence and inner development of self are dependent on nature. Today there is much unbalance in our inner self and therefore also our outer self. The destruction of nature is due to a lack of inner balance.
>
> Living in the company of nature, one learns many things. This river here flows for others. It is a model of loving service [seva]. Have you ever seen a river drinking its own water? Thus, nature sets an example for us human beings, and says that, if you want real peace and happiness, be in close contact with me. Living rivers give us so much.

During our conversation I got the sense that Bahuguna fought the dam out of direct concern for the river herself, so I asked him, "What will this dam do to the river?"

"The dam will kill the river," he said.

A little shocked by this statement, I asked, "Really?"

"Yes," he replied, "the river will be killed by this dam. A river is living only when it is flowing freely in its natural course. Ganga is a goddess because like a mother she feeds everyone. She is always prepared to come for her children, but when you dam a river and change its course, you deny people and other beings access to their mother."

Pressing the theological point, I questioned him further: "Does this mean Ganga Devi will die?"

"Yes," he said, "the dam will kill the devi [goddess]." He elaborated: "The dam is a battleground between the gods and demons. Dams are the expression of demonic power. The dam will kill the goddess because the water will not be flowing. Only flowing water is alive; dammed water is not. The dam will take the energy out of the water. The dam will kill the shakti [divine life force] of the river."[77]

"This is the wrong direction," he concluded. "It is essential that we heal the wounds of Mother Earth."

Still a little startled by his proclamation of the death of the goddess, I asked, "What about the Yamuna, and the barrage at Dakpathar?" Without any hesitation, he declared, "The Yamuna is killed at Dakpathar."

For Bahuguna, a river is alive only when it is flowing freely in its natural course. Dams stop the natural flow and, in so doing, kill the river. In theological terms, they also kill the goddess who is the life-giving river. They take the energy out of the water, thereby destroying the *shakti* of the river.[78] *Shakti* is a technical Sanskrit term identified with goddesses in India. It means the "divine life force." "The Yamuna is killed at Dakpathar," declared Bahuguna; for him, it is a dead river after this point. A few residents of Dakpathar concurred with this, informing me that the barrage killed the Yamuna, that she is a living goddess only upstream from the barrage. Most people further downstream in the cultural region of Braj, however, would not readily accept this. But if not all agree that the Yamuna dies at the Dakpathar Barrage, many more certainly believe that it meets its death in the megatropolis that is the modern city of Delhi.

CHAPTER 3

River of Death

India has had a multi-millennial tradition of worshipping
rivers. Even though Hindu scholars will not get tired of
extolling the ecological elements of Hinduism, of which indeed
there are many, there is, nonetheless, disparity between the
word and the deed. Indians, including the river-worshipping
Hindus, do not think twice before polluting a river.

The Citizens' Fifth Report

Yamuna-ji is dying.

Krishna Gopal Shukla

Although no religious text refers to the Yamuna as the "River of
Death," I have taken the title of this chapter from journalistic and scientific environmental literature originating in Delhi. Professionals
within the media and environmental organizations of Delhi increasingly
refer to the Yamuna as a "dying" or even "dead" river. The *Hindustan
Times* ran an article at the close of 1999, for example, titled "Yamuna,
Victim of Criminal Neglect, Dying a Slow Death."[1] This newspaper
identified the source of the declining health of the river: "Long regarded
as lifeline of the Capital, river Yamuna is dying slowly—a victim of pollution emanating from industrial wastes and callousness of the millions
living around it." The *Times of India* went so far as to announce the
death of the river, reporting that the Yamuna, "once Delhi's lifeline, is
now 'dead' for a stretch of 32 KM around the capital."[2] This view is
corroborated by an editorial that appeared in the *Hindustan Times*
under the heading "A Hole in the Bucket": "The Yamuna is classified as
dead for a stretch of around 32 KM around Delhi."[3] *The Citizens' Fifth
Report,* published by Delhi's prestigious Centre for Science and Environment, concurred: "To say that Yamuna meets its Waterloo at Delhi

may be a bit dramatic. But in reality, the Yamuna is a dead river as it flows past Delhi."[4] The widely read bimonthly *India Today* printed an article on Indian rivers titled "The Rivers of Death."[5] In a startling reversal of traditional conceptions of rivers, the author reports that rivers in India today "symbolize not life but death."[6] The Yamuna features significantly in the article: "The Yamuna reaches Delhi abused. Water is drawn upstream primarily for agriculture; only 10 percent or less of its natural waters reach the capital. Yet its self-cleaning properties let life survive. Then wastes from 50,000 industries and sewage from its 8 million people tear the natural system asunder."[7]

Some publications originating in Delhi have gone so far as to suggest not only that the Yamuna herself is dead or dying but also that she who once nurtured others is now becoming a river that causes death. The *Earth Times News Service* published a story about the Yamuna in Delhi with the title "India's Sacred River Becomes Stream of Death."[8] The most complete nongovernmental report on the condition of the Yamuna consists of the third chapter of *Homicide by Pesticides,* published by the Centre for Science and Environment, titled "Yamuna: The River of Death."[9] As noted earlier, the religious literature and practices associated with Yamunotri demonstrate that Yamuna's attributes have long included life giving and life blessing. She also has a role as a protector from the torments of her brother, Yama, the Lord of Death. But in Delhi I encountered a twisted reversal of this portrayal. Rajat Banerji and Max Martin, the authors of "Yamuna: The River of Death" write, "Myth has it that the river Yamuna has been named after Yama, the god of death in the Indian pantheon. With alarming levels of pesticides, heavy metals and definite accumulations of carcinogenic chemicals like benzene hexachloride (BHC) in the waters, mythology could well have a touch of prophecy here."[10] In the year 2001 the Web site for the Delhi-based environmental group We for Yamuna read, "Mythology has it that the river Yamuna was named after the sister of Yamraj, the god of Death. Certainly not hard to imagine why! The Gods most certainly predicted her future. . . . Long regarded as the lifeline of the city of Delhi, the river is today dying a slow and painful death."[11] V. Subramanian, a professor at the School of Environmental Sciences at Jawaharlal Nehru University in Delhi who has conducted studies of the water quality of the Yamuna, began a conversation with me on a similar note, remarking, "Yamuna is the sister of Yama, and thus is a goddess of death."[12] These authors, who fairly well represent the scientific-environmental community in Delhi, seem relatively unaware that Yamuna has been viewed throughout her long history in the exact opposite terms—as a nurturing and life-enhancing goddess. Only in the last decade or two of the twentieth century has Yamuna been identified as a goddess of death. What could account for this radical change in Yamuna's theological portrait?

The answer, in brief, is the modern story of river pollution and exploitation. The Central Pollution Control Board (CPCB), which was established in response to India's environmental legislation of the 1970s (such as the Clean Water Act of 1974), and which is India's equivalent of the United States Environmental Protection Agency, has been monitoring the water quality of the Yamuna since 1974.[13] Reports published by the CPCB document the steady decline of water quality since serious pollution began to appear in the river in the late 1970s. According to the board's 2000 report, "The water quality of the river Yamuna has been gradually degraded during the past few decades. . . . The wastewater added from the urban centres have increased manifold[,] reducing the fresh water availability in many stretches of the river to zero [and] converting the river to merely a sewerline in Delhi, Mathura and Agra."[14] The consensus of such studies is that today the Yamuna is severely polluted. Dr. R. C. Trivedi, a senior scientist at the CPCB who has been monitoring water quality in the Yamuna for more than two decades, told me, "The Yamuna is the most polluted river in India, at least the five-hundred-kilometer stretch from Delhi to the Chambal confluence. There is no other river in India carrying this much pollution load."[15] When I asked him for his general assessment of the Yamuna at the beginning of the new millennium, he replied, "Yamuna is getting worse day by day, because the pollution load is growing with the population growth in the cities along its banks, particularly in Delhi."

Trouble begins as soon as the river meets the human presence now well established on the plains of northern India. Banerji and Martin write, "The water quality of the Yamuna deteriorates almost the moment it reaches the plains."[16] From this point on, the agricultural belt of Haryana and Uttar Pradesh and the industrial cities situated on the banks discharge significant amounts of toxic wastes into the river. Nonetheless, the metropolis of Delhi is by far the greatest contributor to Yamuna pollution. Although it covers only 2 percent of the river's length, Delhi produces more than 70 percent of the pollution load in the river.[17] The CPCB has identified three major causes for the degeneration of the water quality: unabated population growth resulting in increased domestic pollution loads, rapid industrialization resulting in greater discharge of industrial effluents, and a decrease in the flow of the river due to extensive extraction of water for irrigation.[18] By the time the Yamuna passes through Delhi, she is in serious trouble.

Moreover, today the Yamuna is a broken river trapped and divided by large barrages at three places; during some parts of the year, sections of the river are completely dry. According to the CPCB, "In the dry season [about nine months of the year; excess rain falls in the catchment area only in July, August, and September], the Yamuna cannot be designated as a continuous river, but [is] segregated into four independent segments due to the presence of three barrages[,] from where almost the entire water is being diverted for various human activities."[19] The three existing barrages are at Tajewala, located in the foothills 108 miles downstream from Yamunotri; Wazirabad, located in the National Capital Territory of Delhi 138 miles downstream from the Tajewala Barrage; and Okhla, also located in the National Capital Territory of Delhi, 14 miles downstream from the Wazirabad Barrage. Two more barrages are being added, at Gokul (construction completed in 2002) and Agra.

The Tajewala Barrage forms the headworks for the Western and Eastern Yamuna Canals. Water is extracted here and channeled into the two canals for agricultural use. During much of the year, no water is allowed to escape this barrage and flow downstream in the natural bed of the river. The Wazirabad Barrage forms a reservoir for the municipal water supply of Delhi, which gets more than 70 percent of its water from the Yamuna. At the Okhla Barrage, the river is totally blocked again and diverted to the Agra Canal, which channels it for irrigation. I visited the Okhla Barrage on the last day of the second millennium. Its twenty-seven large gates are imposing, stretching completely across the riverbed and funneling water into the Agra canal. On the day of my visit, the empty riverbed below the barrage was strewn with trash; a tiny stream of black sudsy water oozed through the garbage. A water quality report warns, "After the barrages at Wazirabad and Okhla[,] the river starts anew as an open drain of mostly domestic sewage and untreated industrial wastewater."[20]

Many people downstream are aware that the river that comes to them consists largely of sewage. A temple priest in Vrindaban, a pilgrimage town located about 100 miles downstream from Delhi, remarked, "Much of the year, the only water that reaches Vrindaban is that which passes either through a factory or a human body."[21] This fact poses a serious challenge to the religious practices of some Yamuna devotees. A pilgrimage guide in nearby Mathura told me, "Yamuna has become a sewer, and that is what we are worshipping. This makes us feel very bad."[22]

The complete blockage in the once-continuous river caused by these three barrages has led the Ministry of Environment and Forests to categorize the river into five segments according to these segments' characteristic hydrological and ecological conditions.[23] The Himalayan Segment flows from Yamunotri to the Tajewala Barrage (108 miles, 172 kilometers); the Upper Segment flows from the Tajewala Barrage to the Wazirabad Barrage (138 miles, 224 kilometers); the Delhi Segment flows from the Wazirabad Barrage to the Okhla Barrage (14 miles, 22 kilometers); the Eutrophicated Segment flows from the Okhla Barrage to the confluence with the Chambal River (303 miles, 490 kilometers); and the Diluted Segment flows from the Chambal confluence to the confluence with the Ganges in Allahabad (290 miles, 468 kilometers).

Government reports use the word *pristine* when speaking of the water of Yamuna in the Himalayan Segment.[24] The Centre for Science and Environment concurs: "Few industries are located along the Himalayan segment of the Yamuna[,] and modern agriculture with its props of pesticides and fertilizers is yet to make inroads here. As a result, the water quality in this segment is almost pristine."[25] During the summer months, when large amounts of inorganic sediment carried by runoff from melting snow cause high turbidity, the water in the Himalayan Segment runs brown. The remainder of the year, the water is generally clear, turning white where it rushes over huge boulders, and displaying dark shades of aqua blue and green where it forms deep pools in the mountain valley. The Himalayan Segment is thus characterized by the relatively uninhibited play of the aquatic goddess.

Deterioration of the Yamuna begins in a serious way at the Tajewala Barrage, where all water is diverted into two canals except during the rainy season of July through September. According to *The Citizens' Fifth Report*, "At the Tajewala barrage, 108 miles from its source, the two canals—the Western Yamuna Canal and the Eastern Yamuna Canal—divert all the Yamuna waters into Haryana and Uttar Pradesh for irrigation and other forms of consumption. This means that[,] for nine months in a year, the riverbed of the Yamuna immediately downstream of Tajewala, remains dry."[26] Water usage for irrigation is heavy in the Upper Segment, where only 4 percent of the water extracted is returned to the river. Although the massive irrigation projects that take water from the Yamuna have enabled the surrounding agricultural lands to experience a so-called green revolution, which has increased production yields and enabled India to feed its growing population (now above one billion), there are signs of increasing problems with this modern agricultural technique that depends on large amounts of water, pesticides, and chemical fertilizers. Vandana Shiva writes, "Wherever the 'miracle' seeds of the Green Revolution went, they created a new thirst for water. Intensive chemicals and intensive irrigation were two means used in Green Revolution agriculture to 'augment' land and improve soil fertility. Instead, they created land degradation and hence land scarcity, even while they created an addiction to pesticides, fertilizers and intensive water use."[27]

Two environmental scientists report that massive irrigation harms the soil in various ways: "Besides reducing the self-purification capacity of the rivers, flow regulation has resulted in water logging and increased salinity in the irrigated areas."[28] Salinity is a form of salt poisoning that results from irrigating arid regions. The ground contains a large amount of unleached salts in dry regions that are brought to the surface through intensive irrigation and left behind as a residue on the soil when the water evaporates. Waterlogging occurs when soils not accustomed to large amounts of water become excessively saturated and native plants drown because of insufficient oxygen for their roots. Soil salinity and waterlogging are two major agricultural problems that threaten to make previously productive land unproductive. Shiva concurs: "The intensive use of water also has major ecological impacts. The dramatic increase in water use with the Green Revolution has led to a total destabilisation of the water balance in the region. The water cycle can be destabilised by adding more water to an ecosystem than the natural drainage potential of that system. This leads to desertification through waterlogging and salinisation of the land."[29] Recent statistics show that the green revolution was a quick fix that gave immediate results, but which, in the long run, damages agricultural land and therefore decreases crop yields. Statistics show that the crop yields in the agriculturally rich state of Haryana are now in decline because of the excessive use of irrigation.

Furthermore, because of current farming practices, many agricultural pollutants find their way into the river. A report by the Central Water Commission notes, "Modern scientific agricultural practices involving application of chemical fertilisers, pesticides and insecticides are extensively developed in the Yamuna basin."[30] Thousands of tons of toxic pesticides are used every year in India. The agricultural state of Haryana alone has been using well over five thousand tons annually. Although the insecticide DDT has been banned in India for agricultural use, it is still

available for mosquito and disease-vector control as part of public
health programs. A study conducted by the Indian Agricultural Research
Institute found that insecticides, including DDT, aldrin, and heptachlor,
have been found in the Yamuna at levels exceeding World Health Organization guidelines. Others note that, "although phased out in the West,
persistent organochlorines are used in large quantities in India because
of their effectiveness and low cost."[31] Large quantities of the chemical
fertilizers used in green-revolution farming also find their way into the
Yamuna as it flows through the agricultural regions of northern India.
An Indian Agricultural Research Institute report notes that leaching from
agricultural fields contributes most of the non-point-source pollution in
the aquatic environment.[32]

Industrial activity on the Yamuna begins at Yamunanagar, a city
named after the river it now pollutes. Yamunanagar is home to many
manufacturers, distilleries, and sugar mills. Three other major industrial cities affect the quality of the Yamuna between Yamunanagar and
Delhi: Karnal, Panipat, and Sonepat. These heavy industrial cities are
home to highly polluting textile manufacturers. Although these cities
are located on the Western Yamuna Canal, and not directly on the river,
the industrial effluents they discharge into the canal find their way into
the river by means of major drains that connect the canal and the
riverbed. According to the Centre for Science and Environment, "Chloride
pollution in the Yamuna," for example, "is attributed to tanneries near
Sonepat that use huge amounts of chloride salts for processing leather."[33]
The untreated domestic sewage from these three cities also enters the
Yamuna via the drains that connect the canal with the river.[34] Alarmingly,
both the Western Yamuna Canal and the Yamuna River supply drinking
water to Delhi. The city's water treatment facilities remove general
contaminants, but "at no stage are pesticide traces or industrial toxins
removed."[35]

After all this abuse, the water in the Yamuna as it enters Delhi is still
in fair condition, at least according to the standards used to determine
pollution loads in India. The sampling station at Palla that tests water
quality for Delhi's water supply just upstream from the Wazirabad
Barrage reports that the dissolved oxygen generally is high enough and
the biochemical oxygen demand low enough for the river to sustain life.
Biochemical oxygen demand (BOD) and dissolved oxygen (DO) are
two ecological parameters used to determine biological pollution and
gauge the overall health of a river. Specifically, biochemical oxygen demand
is a measure of the amount of organic material that water contains.

Organic matter feeds aerobic bacteria, which require oxygen to biodegrade the organic pollutants. The greater the volume of organic matter, and the greater the number of bacteria, the greater will be the demand for oxygen dissolved in the water. BOD, then, indicates the organic pollution levels in a river. When BOD levels surpass the available DO in the water, oxygen depletion occurs and aquatic life suffers. Extreme oxygen depletion, known either as asphyxiation or eutrophication, leads to the death of a river. Although environmental activists in India have called for giving greater attention to other ecological indicators of river health—such as fecal coliform bacteria counts and the levels of heavy metals and chemical toxins—governmental officials have emphasized these two factors in determining water quality.

In terms of BOD and DO, the Yamuna is relatively healthy as it arrives at the outskirts of Delhi, but from Delhi on, as *India Today* reports, "a living river becomes a sewer."[36] A mid-1990s report states, "About 1800 million liters per day of untreated sewage winds its way through 18 notorious drains such as the Najafgarh, Sen Nursing Home and Power House nullahs and ends up into the river at various points along its 22 km stretch in Delhi. Though the length and basin area of the river in Delhi is only 2 per cent, it contributes 71 per cent of the wastewater and 55 per cent of the total BOD load discharge into the river every day."[37] And the amount of discharge is only becoming greater with the burgeoning of Delhi's population in the globalized twenty-first century. After the river enters the Delhi Segment at the Wazirabad Barrage, the dissolved oxygen necessary for sustaining life plummets to near zero and the biochemical oxygen demand skyrockets to levels far exceeding healthy limits. The Central Pollution Control Board reports that, in recent years, BOD levels of the Yamuna in Delhi have exceeded twenty milligrams per liter, whereas the limit for a healthy river is two milligrams per liter.[38] The board's Web site indicates that in the year 2000 the DO (which should be at least 4.0 milligrams per liter) was 5.20 milligrams per liter as the river entered Delhi at Palla, and that it fell to 0 milligrams per liter midway through the city, at the Nizamuddin Bridge.[39] What this means is that the Yamuna rapidly becomes asphyxiated in Delhi; it literally can no longer sustain life.

The poor quality of the water of the Yamuna as it passes through Delhi is clearly evident. The Old Yamuna Bridge connects the old part of Delhi, located on the western bank of the river, to newer developments on the eastern bank, just upstream from the center of the modern megalopolis; from this bridge the water is visibly very dark and dirty.

At the beginning of 1997, *India Today* commissioned the Shriram Institute for Industrial Research to collect and test the water of the Yamuna
as it entered the city at the Wazirabad Barrage; at two points partway
through the city, the Old Yamuna Bridge and Nizamuddin Bridge; and
at the Okhla Barrage, the point where it leaves the city.[40] Published
photos of beakers of the water collected at these points show that, by
the time the rather clear water that enters the city at the Wazirabad
Barrage reaches the Nizamuddin Bridge, it is the color of black oil.

Things were not always this bad; many longtime residents of Delhi
have fond memories of a river that no longer exists. Mohan Sharma, the
sixty-year-old owner of a hotel I frequent in Delhi, spoke with me about
the river one morning. With a twinkle of delight in his eye and a smile
on his face, he told me about swimming in the Yamuna in Delhi in the
early 1950s. He said he used to bicycle to the river with his brothers,
swim in the water, and then wrestle and play on the sandy shores. He
remembers clean water and clear skies. When I asked him about the
river now, his smile turned to a frown as he said with anger, "What
we have done to Yamuna is the shame of Delhi. I can't stand to go to the
river today. It is sickening to look at what we have done to her. My
grandchildren will never have the wonderful experiences I had." When
I asked him about the cause of the severe pollution, he replied, "No one
is managing the river. If I didn't manage my hotel, telling people to clean
this and that, it would become dirty very quickly. The government needs
to manage the river. But today all our politicians are corrupt. They just
don't care!"[41]

This sense of loss about the river is also described by Krishna Dutt,
an editor I worked with in Delhi, who reminisced with me about her
youth in Delhi. As a young girl growing up in the 1940s and 1950s, she
used to go to the banks of the Yamuna for picnics with her family. She
told me that her mother, a very religious woman, used to bathe in the
Yamuna in Delhi for religious purposes, particularly on special holy
days. She described a scene of great peace and beauty in which many
families living in Delhi would spend time enjoying leisurely swims in the
river. "And now?" I asked. "Ah," she responded with the wave of a
hand and a tone of sadness, "it is all gone."[42]

Other residents of Delhi described their shock at realizing how much
the river had changed during their lifetimes. Commander Sureshwar
Sinha, founder of Paani Morcha—a nongovernmental organization
dedicated to improving the water conditions of the Yamuna in Delhi,
was stationed in Delhi as a young naval officer from the late 1940s to

the early 1960s. At that time he was a member of the National Naval
Sailing Team, and he has fond memories of swimming in the Yamuna at
Okhla, in the southern part of Delhi. He recounts the beauty of the river
in those days, when he participated in races involving a large number of
colorful sailboats. "I can't tell you how clean and beautiful the river
was, even in the 1970s. Many Delhiites would bring picnics and spend
the day on the banks of the river." He told me that on one occasion his
boat capsized and he fell into the Yamuna, swallowing gulps of water as
he splashed about. He reported this as a "most enjoyable" experience:
"I was delighted to be in the water." The commander retired from the
navy and returned to Delhi in the mid-1980s to settle down. Soon after,
he joined the Defence Services Yachting Club, located near Okhla in
south Delhi, and began teaching schoolchildren how to sail. One day in
the late 1980s, Sinha testified, a boy capsized one of the boats during a
training maneuver, swallowed some water, and came out of the river
vomiting. The boy was so ill from his contact with Yamuna water that
he had to be taken to a hospital.[43] Another resident of Delhi told me,
"You see my pain is that I swam in the river as a child and my children
cannot swim in the river. It is now poison."[44]

Ironically, Delhi's location was chosen because of the attractive
nature of the Yamuna and the availability of freshwater. The Yamuna
has played a vital role in the city's development; almost all historical
accounts mention the beauty of the Yamuna as a major asset of Delhi.[45]
The causes of the present, massive pollution of the river as it flows through
Delhi are manifold, and they include rapid urbanization, industrialization,
heavy extraction, modern agricultural techniques, and some religious
and social practices.

The amount of urban development in India in recent decades has
been enormous. Delhi's growth rate has been greater than that of any
other city in India: the population has increased more than 50 percent
every decade since independence in 1947.[46] Delhi seems to have taken
the brunt of the globalization that has overwhelmed India since the
mid-1980s, growing even more rapidly in the past two decades. The
city's population doubled during this period and now stands at about
fifteen million, making Delhi the most densely populated city in India.[47]
By the mid-1990s over five hundred cars were being added to the streets
of Delhi every day, causing it to have more automobiles than any other
metropolitan center in the nation. The large number of automobiles
pollute Delhi's air and contaminate with gas and oil the city's runoff
that finds its way into the river. Established before the population

explosion took place, riverside cities did not plan for the problem of domestic sewage. As water came to be used more and more to remove human waste from settlements, Delhi began the practice of channeling untreated sewage directly into the river. With the sudden growth of population and consumerism, domestic waste increased sharply.

Industrialization has also expanded significantly in all the urban centers of India over the last few decades, but especially in Delhi, which became home to many multinational corporations toward the end of the 1980s, after the opening of India's economy to the global market. Effluents from new industries contain modern toxic chemicals and heavy metals; many of these flow directly into the Yamuna. At present, water treatment plants in India do not have the ability to remove heavy metals from drinking water. The industrial wastes are destructive to all life-forms, including human beings who get most of their drinking water from the river.

Extraction of water from the Yamuna for irrigation, industrial, and domestic purposes leaves almost no water in the riverbed around Delhi for much of the year. A minimum flow of freshwater in a river is necessary in order for it to cleanse itself and to maintain its own health, but the Yamuna's flow during the nine months from October to June is nowhere near the amount required to sustain ecological health. Maintaining a minimum flow of freshwater is a chief concern of many working to restore the river.

As already mentioned, agricultural techniques involving the application of chemical fertilizers and pesticides are now used extensively in the Yamuna basin. The runoff of these dangerous chemicals threatens the life of the Yamuna and all beings that depend on it as it flows through Delhi. This is particularly true during the monsoon period, when heavy rains flush the land. Farmers also bathe their water buffaloes in the Yamuna upstream from Delhi, and the fecal matter rinsed off the buffaloes increases the BOD and coliform load of the river. Moreover, carcasses of cows, buffalo, and other animals can be seen floating in the Yamuna, as this is an inexpensive way to dispose of them.

Although they are only relatively minor sources of pollution, several social and religious practices in and around Delhi contribute to the contamination of the Yamuna. An article that appeared in *Down to Earth,* a periodical published by the Centre for Science and Environment, titled "Pollution of Hinduism," emphasizes "defiling the sacred" on the part of Hindus. " 'Hindus have become champions at raping their own mother,' laments Swami Srivatsa [*sic*] Goswami, a Vrindaban based scholar. . . . The irony of ironies is that all the polluting rituals and festivals are carried out in the name of Hinduism, the inherent values of which stress keeping the environment clean and pure."[48] Ashes of human beings, and even unburned bodies, are placed in the Yamuna according to religious custom or as an economic way of getting rid of them. Flowers and other remnants from temple offerings are frequently thrown into the Yamuna, these days often in plastic bags. Festival images, now decorated with new chemical paints that contain chromium, mercury, and lead, are routinely immersed in the river once a festival is over. Huge religious gatherings on the banks of the Yamuna also contribute to the pollution. The Central Pollution Control Board reports that the fecal coliform organism count increased up to two hundred times the normal count as a result of the large Kumbha Mela gatherings on the banks of the Yamuna and Ganges.[49] This is especially true if soap is used in the mass bathings at these large gatherings. Washing clothes with detergents in the river also contributes both to organic and inorganic pollution.

Although the residents of Delhi might prefer to blame the many people residing upstream, Delhi is responsible for most of the pollution in the river. The Central Pollution Control Board makes it very clear that the city "is the largest contributor of pollution to Yamuna river."[50] Early in the twentieth century, perennial streams from the slopes of the Aravalli Hills northwest of Delhi flowed through this region to the Yamuna River, blessing Delhi with additional and abundant freshwater. One of these streams was called Shahibi Nadi, or the "Regal River." Today it is known by the less romantic name of Najafgarh Drain and is the biggest single contributor of pollution to the Yamuna. Around 45 percent of Delhi's total discharge, and around 42 percent of the BOD load in the river, comes from this drain—almost half of Delhi's river pollution. This formerly regal river is now nothing but an open sewage drain. About 85 percent of the pollution load in the Yamuna in Delhi is from domestic sources; the increasing discharge of both treated and untreated wastewater produced by a burgeoning urban population is the major cause of the rapidly deteriorating water quality in the Yamuna.

The government of Delhi has been trying to treat more of the sewage, yet hundreds of millions of gallons of untreated sewage are still dumped into the river every day. In the year 2000 the *Hindustan Times* reported, "A huge quantity of untreated sewage, all of 1,393 million liters, goes into the Yamuna every day through 19 major drains that flush sewage and industrial effluents from Delhi."[51] This figure represents over half of Delhi's total daily sewage output, all of which ends up in the Yamuna in some form or other.[52] The comptroller and auditor general of Delhi released a report at the end of 1999 that provided even higher figures for sewage output, stating "that, of the total estimated quantity of 2852 million litres per day (MLD) of sewage generated in the Capital, the Government is able to treat merely 886 MLD; 1966 MLD of sewage is being discharged in the river[,] causing serious pollution of the water."[53] The result is an alarmingly high count of fecal coliform bacteria, a major indicator of fecal discharge in water. A study conducted by the Shriram Institute for Industrial Research in 1996 reports that, whereas the upper limit for safety is 500 MPN (most probable number) fecal coliform bacteria per 100 milliliters, it found readings in Delhi as high as 43,000 MPN.[54] Since this organic matter drives up the demand for oxygen to biodegrade it, the dissolved oxygen in the river has been depleted. Not only has the river in Delhi assumed a foul smell and appearance, but also all life in it has suffocated. The result is that "Yamuna is on its death bed."[55]

The Central Pollution Control Board reports that there were ninety-three thousand industries in Delhi in 1993. Since then, many more have been added, with the result that industrial effluents flowing into the Yamuna have reached frightening levels. The infamous Najafgarh Drain is also the major contributor of micropollutants such as chemical toxins and heavy metals.[56] Scientists report that "the river bank soil throughout Delhi is contaminated with cadmium," and other heavy metals, such as zinc and aluminum, have been found at toxic levels in the river.[57] Due to the heavy industry in Delhi, scientists have found, "Yamuna River sediments are more enriched in metals than those of the Ganges and average Indian river sediments."[58] Although the chemical has never been manufactured or permitted in India, researchers from Jawaharlal Nehru University in Delhi have found high concentrations of PCBs in the Yamuna, as well as other cancer-causing agents, including DDT, hexachloro hydrocarbons, and cyclodiene.[59] The industrial toxins contribute both to the death of the river itself and to the life-threatening quality the Yamuna is taking on—thus transforming many cultural notions associated with the river for many people.

The Indraprastha Power Station is an enormous, coal-fired electrical generating plant located on the west bank of the Yamuna in south Delhi. This plant has been identified as another major source of river pollution. Belching clouds of smoke from its tall stacks into Delhi's air twenty-four hours a day, it has helped the city become one of the most polluted in the world. In 1989 it was producing about one thousand tons of coal ash every day. The coal ash from this power plant is mixed with river water, and the resulting slurry is pumped into ash settling basins. The turbid leachates from this are then discharged directly into the Yamuna. The gray, turbid appearance of the discharge indicates that the settling process is inefficient, and that the effluents contain particles laden with heavy metals, particularly aluminum.[60] Rivers have a natural ability to cleanse and regenerate themselves to a certain extent, and fresh flowing water dilutes the quantity and effects of pollutants. But for this to occur a river needs a minimum flow of freshwater.

For many years the operative ethos of policy makers and hydraulic engineers has been not to allow freshwater to be "wasted" by flowing unused into the sea. The flow of water in the Yamuna on the plains varies greatly throughout the year, since precipitation is confined mostly to the monsoon period of July through September. During many of the remaining dry months of the year, all of the freshwater is extracted from the Yamuna at the Tajewala Barrage for irrigation. This extraction has had the full support of state-level policy makers. These days, however, environmental scientists in India are arguing that a minimum flow is necessary to maintain a river's ecological health throughout its course. In this area too the Yamuna is in trouble. After telling me that the Yamuna is now the most polluted river in India, a senior CPCB scientist went on to say that "the situation is not improving, because the minimum flow is not enough. Since the minimum flow at present is way too low to maintain the ecological health of the river, all that leaves Delhi is sewage."[61]

According to river scientists, the pollution in the Yamuna cannot be remedied unless the required minimum flow of freshwater is restored. A committee established by India's Supreme Court to set the minimum flow for the Yamuna for a May 1999 ruling determined that the minimum flow of freshwater in the river should be ten cubic meters per second (10 cumecs). R. C. Trivedi of the CPCB contends, "The minimum flow requirement for any river should be at least 285 cum [cubic meters] per second. But the flow in Delhi drops to 5 cum per second during the summer months, and the river turns septic. Aquatic life, which needs a minimum flow of 10 cum per second, dies out. So even if we could somehow divert pollution from the river, it would not help unless the flow is maintained."[62] A CPCB report states that, for about 75 percent of the time, the downstream flow from the Tajewala and Okhla Barrages is less than 3 cubic meters per second, and that for a considerable period there is no flow at all.[63]

In early February the *Times of India* published an article titled "Is the Yamuna Getting Any Fresh Water at All?" The article recounts the ongoing difficulties related to minimum flow. "Despite the Supreme Court's and the Planning Commission's intervention to save the Yamuna during the lean season, the river is still full of filth and sewage. The Supreme Court had asked the Yamuna water sharing states to ensure that the river was getting a minimum fresh water flow. This was fixed at 10 cumecs per second of fresh water for the lean season to mitigate the effects of sewage which lies stagnant between various barrages in the city."[64] This article reports that, despite the Supreme Court's efforts, the freshwater is still not there. Sinha, secretary of Paani Morcha, informed me in December 2001 that the Supreme Court ruling was still not being enforced by the central and state governments.[65] The authorities in Delhi and Haryana claimed, however, that the river was receiving the flow determined by the Supreme Court, while acknowledging that it was still in serious trouble.

Dilip Biswas, chairman of the CPCB, has attempted to resolve these conflicting claims by marking the difference between the general minimum flow of the river and the minimum flow of *freshwater*. "What the states are maintaining," he says, "is the total flow, not the fresh water flow in the river. What we are talking about is 10 cumecs of fresh water, which is without waste water and also without treated municipal and industrial water."[66] Biswas argues that the ecological health of a river depends specifically upon the flow of freshwater, not simply the amount of any type of water. He also contends that the figure for freshwater flow should be increased because the government's calculations were done in the mid-1990s, when the population and pollution load were smaller than they are today. He claims that far too much freshwater is now being extracted from the river before it reaches Delhi.

The problem of water flow in and around Delhi is so severe that Sinha contends, "The Yamuna is undergoing a reverse flow, meaning the river is drawing from the aquifers instead of recharging the groundwater. This is happening because there is virtually no flow of water in the river."[67] As the growing population of Delhi requires more water, and as the farmers' irrigation demands increase, there can only be worsening conflicts between city planners, irrigation engineers, environmentalists, and religious devotees.

The problems do not end here. With ongoing deforestation, climate changes due to global warming, and increased pressure on the riverine environment, the sources of water in the upper Yamuna valley seem to be diminishing. Toward the end of 1999, the *Hindustan Times* reported that the Western Yamuna Canal Hydro Electric Project near Yamunanagar was forced to generate 50 percent less power due to a shortage of available water. "The inflow of water in the Yamuna river," notes the newspaper, "has decreased substantially due to the lack of rain and snow in its catchment area."[68] Although there has been no study of the health of the Yamunotri glacier, several recent reports have circulated that predict a rapidly approaching end of the glacier above Gangotri that feeds the Bhagirathi River, the major source of the Ganges. On September 27, 1999, for example, the *Hindustan Times* reported, "The Gangotri Conservation Project has recommended a monitoring station at Gangotri in view of the disturbing reports about the Bhagirathi river shrinking drastically." The article goes on to state that "'some experts feel that at this rate the river may disappear in ten years,' says Captain M. S. Kohli, Chairman of Gangotri Conservation Project and Himalayan Environment Trust."[69] Exponential growth in human consumption habits is clearly affecting the environment, even in the far reaches of the Himalayas, where the continued existence of glaciers is intimately linked to human behavior on the plains below, especially behavior in the major urban centers like Delhi, where the demands for water and for wood products, and the use of fossil fuels, are the greatest.

The second-most polluted stretch of the Yamuna is called the Eutrophicated Segment. Eutrophication results when a body of water is asphyxiated or is suffocating because of a high biochemical oxygen demand (BOD) and low dissolved oxygen (DO). This is the stretch of "water" measuring 303 miles (490 kilometers) that flows between Delhi and the river's confluence with the Chambal River, where cleaner water and a more plentiful flow revive the Yamuna somewhat. The CPCB has identified the Eutrophicated Segment as the "critical" section.[70] The water leaving Delhi is not in good shape. A CPCB report states that, after the Delhi barrages, "the river starts anew as an open drain of mostly domestic sewage and untreated industrial wastewater."[71] Here the water is reported to be "septic" and "eutrophic."[72] The results of this are obvious to the senses. The report notes the "severe odour problem and ugly look of the river, especially in the vicinity of Delhi, Mathura-Vrindavan, Bateshwar and World Heritage place Agra." As a result, says the CPCB, "the river Yamuna is losing its glory and significance, affecting the importance of these tourist places."[73] The CPCB states that the Yamuna from Delhi to the Chambal confluence does not meet its designated criteria, even during the monsoon season, when sufficient dilution is available.[74]

I have witnessed the rapid deterioration of the river in this section over the past couple of decades. I first saw the Yamuna River in early September 1981, when I arrived in Vrindaban to spend a year studying the religious practices of the Braj region. Looking across the Yamuna, I could barely see the opposite shore, so wide was the river. At that time it was full with monsoon rains, and the deep, powerful watercourse stretched for nearly a mile from shore to shore. It had been like this during the monsoon season for centuries. One nineteenth-century British observer wrote, "In the floods of the rainy season the river has a considerable breadth, swelling in places to several miles with a maximum depth of some 25 feet.... Religious reverence is due to the Yamuna from the Hindu."[75] When I saw it, I sensed immediately that this was a magnificent river. Over the course of that year, I grew fond of the Yamuna as I sat quietly on the massive stone steps that lined her banks in Vrindaban or as I walked along her shore. I watched huge turtles sun themselves on her sandy white beach and large silvery flat fish roll on the water's surface as they fed in the early morning and evening. I observed hunting kingfishers perform their acrobatic dives into the river during the bright light of day, and huge fruit bats chase bugs as dusk fell and the faint yellow light playing on the river's surface faded. During the winter months, Brahminy ducks, bar-headed geese, spoon-bills, and herons waded in the shallows of wide sandbars. I also had many occasions to observe people from all walks of life worshipping the Yamuna, especially at Keshi Ghat, the center of Yamuna worship in Vrindaban.

During May, June, and July, when temperatures can soar well above one hundred degrees Fahrenheit, I would pass my days sitting in front of a swamp cooler reading the Sanskrit texts I had come to study. As temperatures began to drop in the late afternoon, I would stroll down to Keshi Ghat to join a jubilant crowd of people, many of whom were children, swimming and playing in the cool water of the river. Naked young boys would run and jump off the sandstone meditation plat-forms that overlook the river at Keshi Ghat, landing with a splash and giggling as they surfaced. Others would float about the river using round clay pots turned upside down to trap air as a floatation device. Laughter and shouts of joy added a carnivalesque atmosphere to this delightful summertime scene on the Yamuna in Vrindaban. I often spent an hour or two in the deep water, coming out only after the priest at the Yamuna temple at the top of the steps waved the huge *arati* lamps above the river as an act of daily worship.

Today, little more than twenty years later, the Yamuna at Keshi Ghat has changed dramatically. Although bathing and worship do continue, the numbers of people playing in the water and bathing for long periods of time have noticeably decreased. During much of the year, the Yamuna here is reduced to a small, shallow stream barely forty feet wide in places. A drain pours large amounts of raw sewage into the river just fifty yards upstream from Keshi Ghat, turning the water—already seriously compromised by Delhi—black with its filth.[76] Plastic bags of garbage are strewn in large quantity on the banks, and the smell is not pleasant. It is not uncommon to see pigs rooting through garbage scattered on the riverbank just upstream from Keshi Ghat. Because of these conditions, I have not entered the water at Keshi Ghat for a long time. Many residents of Vrindaban report the same; several told me that they used to bathe in or even drink the water of the Yamuna daily but dare not anymore. The images of Krishna that stand in the numerous temples and home shrines in Vrindaban have for centuries been bathed with water drawn from the Yamuna River—the natural form of his lover. Today, many people use treated tap water in their home shrines, and some of the priests of the Vrindaban temples use water purchased at the market in plastic bottles to bathe the images of Krishna. Several residents of Mathura and Gokul downstream also reported to me that they no longer bathe in the river for religious purposes or use water from the river in their daily worship at temples and home shrines. Clearly, much is changing as a result of the river's pollution. And as the gates are dropped on the Gokul Barrage, things are becoming worse as the polluted water in Mathura grows more stagnant. As one resident of Mathura put it, "The Gokul Barrage is making the Yamuna a sewer tank!"[77] Echoing the title of this chapter, a pilgrimage priest from a well-established Vrindaban family told me, "The river is now very polluted. Yamuna-ji is dying."[78]

Aquatic life too is suffering. Not long ago it was common to see large turtles, the animal vehicle mounts of the goddess Yamuna, sunning themselves on her sandy shores. Today, only some small turtles recently released by the government can be seen; very few of the older large turtles have survived. Fish, also once abundant in the river, have been in sharp decline. According to *India Today*, "Fish have died by the millions. In the '70s there were more than 570 fishing villages along the Yamuna between Agra and Allahabad. Rare is the day that you now see a fishing boat on that stretch of the river, depleted of water and fouled. The fishermen now eke out a living driving cycle-rickshaws, toiling as daily

labour or simply begging."[79] Although few studies have been conducted, ornithologists fear that the bird populations which depend upon
the river for survival are seriously threatened. I have observed a decline
in birds over the years on my boat excursions down the river.

The contamination in this section is predominantly organic in nature.
To the huge amount of human waste originating in Delhi is added pollutants from the bathing of water buffaloes, from open defecation along
the riverbanks, and from the washing of clothes. I have seen corpses of
cows, buffalo, and dogs lying in the shallow water at the river's edge,
and have occasionally viewed the body of a human floating downstream. Open sewer drains flow directly into the river in both Mathura
and Vrindaban. Nonorganic waste is also added to the water here as
Delhi's industrial effluents are joined by wastewater from local industries. Even in Braj, the very center of Yamuna worship, large trash
dumps can be found along the bank of the river. All these factors add to
the rapid depletion of oxygen in the water. Consequently, all is not well
even here in the very center of Yamuna worship.

Downstream in Agra, the Yamuna passes below the famous Taj
Mahal, but the tourist who walks behind the monument is now met
with a narrow, unsightly river lined with garbage. After Yamuna reaches
Agra and receives the domestic and industrial waste from this city, "the
river condition becomes saprobic and the ecological condition resembles with the river stretch between Wazirabad to Okhla."[80] The city
of Agra, built on the bank of the river because of its beauty and life-
supporting liquid, also gets its drinking water from the Yamuna. The
editor of Agra's daily English newspaper remarked, "By the time it
reaches us, the Yamuna is reduced to a drain. We are made to drink the
dirt that the Delhiites throw out."[81] Fecal coliform bacteria in the Yamuna
at Agra has been recorded in extremely high amounts.[82] Waterworks
officials complain that they face the challenge of having to turn sewage
into drinking water. Treating the city's drinking water requires huge
amounts of chlorination, three or more times what Delhi requires.
One citizen of Agra quipped, "We survive because the chlorine is
adulterated."[83] The *Hindustan Times* reports, "The deteriorating quality of raw water arriving in Agra through [the] river Yamuna has resulted
in a shortage of water supply to the city area."[84] Two major causes for
this are the increasing amount of pollutants being added to the river and
the stagnancy of the water caused by the new Gokul Barrage.

Downstream from Agra, near the town of Etawah, the Chambal River
joins the Yamuna. Contributing five to ten times more water to the

Yamuna than now flows in the main channel during the dry season, the Chambal is the Yamuna's most important tributary on the plains. Its catchment area constitutes about 40 percent of the total Yamuna catchment area. Further downstream, the Sind, Betwa, and Ken also join the Yamuna from the west, so that by the time it reaches its confluence with the Ganges at Allahabad, the Yamuna is much bigger than her sister. With a new infusion of water, the Yamuna is greatly restored, and as a result, the 290-mile section downstream from the Chambal confluence is called the Diluted Segment. Although these tributaries are cleaner than the Yamuna, they bring their own pollution loads, especially fecal coliform bacteria. The CPCB summarizes the conditions of the river in this segment: "The stretch of Yamuna river after its confluence with Chambal river is termed as [a] diluted segment, as it receives significant dilution water. This segment after confluence with Chambal river regains its water quality up to some extent. . . . After [the] Chambal confluence Yamuna river restores its bacteriological quality to some extent, but even then is not suitable for its designated best use."[85]

At its confluence with the Ganges in Allahabad, the Yamuna is less turbid and has recovered some of its famous blue color. This is evident as it mingles with the chalky-white water of the Ganges and the two sisters flow on together past the holy city of Banaras (Varanasi). Although the Yamuna recovers some of its cleanliness from its convergence with the Chambal, the general conclusion of the Central Water Commission regarding the ecological health of the Yamuna is not hopeful: "It is found that during [the] lean flow period when the concentration of pollutants is high the Yamuna water is not fit for direct use for domestic, recreation and agricultural purposes. It is also found unfit for its direct application to textile and chemical industries."[86] This conclusion was announced over a decade ago; the consensus of governmental scientists these days seems to be that conditions have gotten so much worse that the above judgment now holds true even during the heavier flow period of the monsoon season. Even after taking into consideration all governmental efforts to lower pollution levels, most scientists conclude that the Yamuna lies on her deathbed, particularly in and downstream from Delhi. At the end of 2002, the last year I collected data on the conditions of the Yamuna, the *Hindustan Times* reported, "Despite the government pouring in lakhs of rupees into the second phase of the Ganga Action Plan, which envisioned restoring the Yamuna to its old pristine self, the pollution levels in the river remain very high. The ambitious plan to clean the river has clearly flopped. It was only when the Supreme Court intervened that the state government chalked out the plan, along with foreign agency. However, it failed to plan the thing through, with the result that today the river is actually more polluted."[87] Members of Paani Morcha sum up the conditions of the Yamuna and Ganges this way: "Clearly the rivers of hope have turned out to be rivers of despair. For their waters are polluted, not only by industrial wastes, but the wastes of the millions who populate their banks. The Ganga and Yamuna would not have been so desecrated had not dams upstream reduced the flow in them to such a drastic extent that it is unable to regenerate the river waters as was the case before these were constructed."[88]

What effect does such devastating pollution have on the religious culture associated with the Yamuna? This question can be answered with greater understanding after examining the religious culture of Braj, for ironically the most polluted section of the river runs through the area in which Yamuna theology and worship has been most fully developed. Although many Braj residents are aware of the rising levels of pollution, devotion to this river remains strong.

CHAPTER 4

Goddess of Love

We worship you, Shri Yamuna-ji.
We offer you a lamp of affectionate love
    that shines with the light of our souls.
You have a dark complexion, wear dark clothing,
    and are the Lover of the Beautiful Dark Lord.
You are Daughter of the Sun, Sister of the Lord of Death,
    and Princess of Mount Kalinda.
You flow on all sides of Vrindaban,
    arranging the love play of Radha and Krishna.
A pitcher of your pure water is the
    Chief Queen of the Lord of Dvaraka.
You satisfy the heart by fulfilling
    all goals of life.
All sins are destroyed merely by
    seeing or touching you.
I dedicate all to that drop of
    divine nectar on your feet.

                    Yamuna *arati* song

It is a beautiful spring morning. The sky is clear blue, and although the weather is warmer than during any previous April on record, reaching well into the nineties, a gentle breeze is blowing, making it a pleasant day. I arrive at Vishram Ghat in Mathura just after sunrise. The ancient stone steps leading down into the river are already lined with a crowd of colorfully dressed people gathered to worship Yamuna; many are standing in the water. A woman dressed in a beautiful green sari removes her sandals, approaches the river's edge, and squats to place a wicker basket containing a heap of red roses, a few sticks of incense, and a copper pot full of milk on the sandy shore. She scoops up some water from the river with her right hand, takes three sips, and sprinkles the remainder on top of her head. Next, she greets the river with joined hands, saying, "Shri Yamuna Maiya ki jaya"(Glory to Mother Yamuna). She then looks into the water and, with a loving smile, pours milk into the stream and places a few red rose blossoms on its surface. After this offering, she lights three sticks of incense, waves them before the river, and inserts them into the sand by her side. She bows her head to touch the moist sand at river's edge and then gets up to leave.

This simple *puja,* or act of worship, can be observed any day of the year on the bank of the Yamuna at Vishram Ghat. This day, however, was a special occasion, and much more elaborate *pujas* were being performed, for this day was Yamuna Chath. *Chath* means the sixth lunar day of the fortnight, and Yamuna Chath is celebrated on the sixth day of the bright half of the lunar month of Chaitra, which fell on April 10 in 2000. This festival, which is also called Yamuna Jayanti, is considered to be the celebration of Yamuna's birthday. Many people who gathered at Vishram Ghat on this morning told me that this day is "Yamuna-ji's Happy Birthday." Indeed, it is commemorated with much delight and happiness; I encountered one man who exclaimed with a huge grin on his face, "It is my mother's birthday today!"

The professional priests of Vishram Ghat were busy conducting more formal *pujas* for families and groups of pilgrims who had come to Mathura to worship Yamuna on this auspicious occasion (see figure 5). I neared the water and observed a family perform their worship. A man, woman, and their two children approached the river accompanied by a Chaube, or Chaturvedi priest. The Chaturvedi priests have been conducting Yamuna *pujas* here for centuries. They identify themselves as Yamuna *putra*s, or "sons of Yamuna," and greet one another with the words "Yamuna Maiya ki jaya" (Glory to Mother Yamuna). When the family reached the water with shoes removed, the priest instructed them to wash their hands as he poured river water from a copper vessel and sprinkled some of it over their heads. He then ordered them to hold a handful of the water in their cupped right hands and sip some of it. Next he had the four hold a coconut together while he placed red rose petals on it and chanted Sanskrit mantras requesting Yamuna to bless this family with abundance in life. The woman stepped forward to offer sweets, red *sindur* powder, and uncooked white rice, which she placed into the river. Finally, she offered a small red sari, a necklace, bangles, a comb, red decorative forehead dots (*bindis*), and a mirror to the goddess Yamuna, laying them on the sand

Figure 5. Yamuna worshippers conducting *puja* at
Vishram Ghat in Mathura. A priest standing in shallow
water helps a worshipper with the aid of items he holds
in his hand. Photo by David Haberman.

at the edge of the water. The priest retrieved these latter items and then
escorted the family up the stairs leading to the temple complex above
Vishram Ghat.

At this moment I heard a brass band approaching loudly. I first mis-
took it for a wedding band, since this was a common season for weddings. But I remembered that wedding celebrations take place primarily
at night, and so wandered downstream to investigate. I encountered a
colorful and festive sight, a glittery band leading a procession of about
a hundred and fifty Pushti Margiya Vaishnavas who had traveled here
from the southern state of Kerala. Most of them were dancing gaily;
some carried on their heads materials for a large *puja*. They brought
baskets containing red rose petals, uncooked rice, and red *sindur*

powder, as well as boxes of milk sweets, bundles of incense, packages of ornaments, and a large roll of colorful saris. Toward the front of the procession, a woman balanced a large copper pot of Yamuna water on her head; the pot was ringed with a flower garland and capped with a coconut.

This group had come to perform a special worship of Yamuna on the occasion of her birthday. When they reached the location that had been prepared for their *puja,* they settled down on the sandy shore under a multicolored patchwork cloth awning held up with stout bamboo poles embellished with banana stalks. To increase auspiciousness, strings of fresh *ashok* leaves were hung from the edges of the awning. Eight colorfully decorated wooden boats were docked before the *puja* site. The vessel containing the Yamuna water was placed on the moist sand at river's edge, where it became the focus of worship. An umbrella constructed of bright flowers on a bamboo pole was placed over it, and the materials carried to the site were offered to it along with Sanskrit mantras chanted by a presiding Chaturvedi priest. Once the offerings had been made, the priest led the group in singing a famous hymn to Yamuna, the "Yamunashtakam" (translated later in this chapter), written by the sixteenth-century founder saint of their Pushti Marga denomination, Vallabhacharya. They sang effortlessly, since everyone knew this hymn by heart. As they sang, a group of women slowly scattered heaps of red rose petals on the surface of the river, creating a beautiful crimson flow that swirled a great distance downstream.

After completing the hymn, everyone prepared to celebrate the climax of the birthday party: dressing the natural form of the river goddess in a sari that stretched from shore to shore (see figure 6). With the aid of the eight wooden boats, the huge roll of colorful saris was unwound onto the flowing surface of the river. One hundred and eight saris had been sewn together end to end, making one very long sari for Yamuna to wear for her birthday celebration. As this immense sari was unrolled, it was dipped into the water and then spread out between the boats in a zigzag fashion. Those gathered were visibly delighted by the string of colorful saris billowing gently in the breeze just above the water. Happy Birthday Yamuna-ji!

This elaborate *puja* was only one of many performed that day by local groups and those visiting Vishram Ghat from afar. Before I left the river around midmorning, I observed six such *pujas,* all culminating in the dressing of Yamuna with a string of one hundred and eight saris that undulated between the boats positioned from shore to shore as people

Figure 6. Worshippers wrapping Yamuna from shore to shore with 108 saris on the occasion of her birthday. Photo by David Haberman.

cried out "Jaya Yamune!" (Glory to You, O Yamuna) with celebratory joy. The ghats were also crowded with people who had come to Vishram Ghat, either individually or in small groups, to conduct simpler *pujas*. Overall the scene was spirited and festive. Special *pujas* were also taking place this day at other sacred sites in Braj. Why do all these people worship Yamuna? Who is Yamuna for those worshipping her in this region? In short, how do the people associated with the religious traditions of Braj conceive of the Yamuna River?

Braj is a distinctive cultural region located on the Yamuna River between Delhi and Agra that experienced a dynamic and wide-reaching cultural renaissance in the early sixteenth century.[1] This area is intimately associated with the playful lover Krishna; in fact, many view the entire land of Braj as an embodied form of Krishna. Here, the theology and worship of Yamuna as a goddess has reached its most sophisticated level. One of the priests at the Yamunotri temple in the Himalayas, who sometimes visited Vrindaban during the winter, told me that although Yamuna was born at Yamunotri she grew up in Braj. "Here in Yamunotri, Yamuna-ji is a small girl living in the house of her father, and in Braj she is a young woman who is the lover of Krishna." He related this to the fact that her theology became mature in Braj.[2] Although the entire stretch of the river is considered sacred, it is deemed to be especially so as it passes through Braj. The *Varaha Purana* states, "Yamuna joins Ganga at Prayaga known as Veni, but Yamuna is hundred times more sacred at Mathura."[3] There are three primary centers of Yamuna worship in Braj: Vishram Ghat in Mathura, Keshi Ghat in Vrindaban, and Thakurani Ghat in Gokul. These are fertile grounds for exploring the ideas and religious actions associated with Yamuna.

Vishram Ghat in Mathura is the most popular and elaborate of the three sites. Ghats are massive stone steps that descend to the river, designed to give pilgrims direct access to it. Vishram Ghat, which means "Place of Rest," is the central and most important of the beautiful sandstone ghats that line the waterfront of Mathura. One is often told that this is the place where Krishna bathed in the Yamuna and rested after killing the wicked demon king Kansa. But according to those immersed in Yamuna theology, it is the place where Yamuna as a young woman rested after rushing down from the mountains to meet her lover Krishna in Braj. The most prominent feature marking Vishram Ghat is a monumental stone arch that stands on the terrace just above the stone steps, and which has been ornately carved and painted a bright yellow with green and pink trim. The ornamental arch is surrounded by a compound open to the river on the east side and enclosed on the three remaining sides by a colorful variety of temples and shrines. The floor of the compound is paved with a checkerboard pattern of black and white marble squares. At the center of the Vishram Ghat complex is a small shrine housing Krishna and his elder brother, Balaram, who helped him defeat Kansa.

Among the surrounding temples, four are dedicated to Yamuna; all are associated with the Pushti Marga, a Vaishnava denomination in which Yamuna is regarded as the primary lover of Krishna.[4] One

Figure 7. Yamuna shrine at Vishram Ghat in Mathura. The taller of the two figures represents Yamuna; the shorter one is Giriraj, Krishna in the form of a stone from Mount Govardhan. Photo by David Haberman.

houses a beautiful brass image of the goddess Yamuna that is carried to the water's edge for special *pujas*. While I was present, on the evening of her birthday this image of Yamuna was brought to the river and placed on a boat inside a small temple made of flowers, where she was worshipped and entertained during the night with devotional songs. Another temple in the Vishram Ghat complex houses a blue image of the goddess Yamuna (see figure 7). Here she is called Shri Shyam Sundar Yamuna Maharani, "Dark Beautiful Queen Yamuna." *Shyam Sundar* (Dark Beauty) is an epithet that refers also to Krishna, indicating the theological connection of the two. To the right of this image of Yamuna is a sacred stone from Mount Govardhan, regarded to be a natural form of Krishna; it is dressed up as Krishna and called "Shri Govardhan Nath-ji" (Lord of Mount Govardhan). Here Yamuna is considered to be the lover of Krishna, particularly in his form as Govardhan Nath-ji. Residents of Braj typically worship two natural forms of divinity as a divine couple: the female river Yamuna, regarded as a liquid form (*dravi-bhuta*) of love, and the male mountain Govardhan, regarded as a condensed form (*ghani-bhuta*) of love. Individual and collective rites in the region of Braj celebrate the love affair between the river and the mountain.

Another temple in the Vishram Ghat complex houses the goddess Yamuna surrounded by Krishna, his brother Balaram, and their parents, Devaki and Vasudev, demonstrating Yamuna's centrality in the mythology of Braj. Close by is Bahan-Bhai Mandir, the "Sister-Brother Temple." This temple contains large black stone images of Yamuna and her twin brother, Yama, Lord of Death. While Krishna is always situated to the right of Yamuna, here Yama stands on her left. Together these temples constitute the largest concentration of Yamuna temples in the area of Braj, making it the major focus for religious activities related to Yamuna. However, these temples do not overshadow the importance of the river itself at Vishram Ghat; the most significant worship is directed at the physical form of the river. People can be seen worshipping the river here all day long. Every morning at five o'clock and every evening at seven-thirty an enthusiastic crowd gathers at Vishram Ghat to participate in a Yamuna *arati*. In this ceremony, an energetic priest stands under the stone arch and waves a huge, flaming brass lamp as an offering to the river; the worshippers gaze at the river, framed by the archway, through the flames of the *arati* lamp.

Keshi Ghat is the most important center for Yamuna worship in the town of Vrindaban. Some say it is named after the horse demon Keshi that Krishna is said to have killed on this spot before bathing in the Yamuna with his cowherd friends, whereas others say it is named after the hair (*kesha*) of the goddess Sati, whose hair fell here while she was being dismembered after death to keep her husband, Shiva, from destroying the world.[5] The massive sandstone steps of the ghat, and its ornate meditation platforms built above the water, stretch along the river's edge. Direct worship of the river is also common here, with many gathering daily for their ritual immersion and to worship the river at the base of the ghats. In a scene that can be observed almost any day, a young man wearing only a white loincloth came to the river as I watched. He fell to his knees and touched his forehead on the wet sand just below Keshi Ghat. He then entered the water and faced upstream to greet the oncoming river, immersing his body completely three times. Coming upright again, he sipped water from the palm of his right hand and then joined his hands together in a prayerful pose, addressing the approaching stream, "Jaya Yamuna Maiya!"

At the top of the sandstone steps that make up Keshi Ghat, a small temple dedicated to the goddess provides another focus for Yamuna worship. It houses an elegantly dressed brass image of Yamuna, along with Krishna in the form of a stone from Mount Govardhan. The priests of this temple are from the Nimbarki Vaishnava denomination. Every morning at sunrise and every evening at sunset, a priest conducts an *arati* here. He waves the ritual lamp with sacred flames before the temple image in the presence of an enthusiastic crowd, then turns to the river and waves the lamp directly above the water. One of the attendant priests told me that the worship of the physical river is the more important of the two acts.[6] While the lamps are waved, gongs are sounded and the assembled crowd sings songs. These songs, such as the one that forms the epigraph beginning this chapter, give voice to fundamental theological ideas about the river goddess.

Thakurani Ghat in Gokul is another vital center of Yamuna worship in Braj, especially for Pushti Margiya Vaishnavas, for it is connected with stories about Vallabhacharya, who founded this denomination in the sixteenth century. The *Chaurasi Baithak Charitra* narrates that Yamuna appeared here to Vallabhacharya in her divine form and facilitated revelations that transformed his life.[7] The tradition also maintains that it was here that Vallabhacharya composed his famous Sanskrit hymn praising Yamuna, the "Yamunashtakam," perhaps the most important of all theological texts on Yamuna.[8] There is a shrine commemorating this event at Thakurani Ghat, as well as a small temple dedicated to Yamuna, where worshippers gather every morning and evening to worship Yamuna and sing Vallabhacharya's "Yamunashtakam." The Yamuna temple houses a beautiful shiny black stone image of Yamuna standing beside a black stone image of her lover Krishna in his human form as Govardhan Nath-ji. This too is a popular site for ritual bathing and worship of the river.

Unlike those worshipping Yamuna at Yamunotri as part of the Char Dham pilgrimage, who tend to be devotees of the Himalayan rivers in general, Yamuna worshippers in Braj tend to be exclusive devotees of Yamuna. The latter hold a much more specific theological conception of Yamuna than the general view encountered among pilgrims visiting Yamunotri. Large numbers of people come daily to interact with the river at Vishram Ghat in Mathura, Keshi Ghat in Vrindaban, and Thakurani Ghat in Gokul, performing an assortment of acts of worship, bathing in a religious manner, reverently touching or sipping the water, meditating on Yamuna's divine form, or simply gazing at the aquatic form of their goddess and thereby experiencing a visual communion (*darshan*) with her. These worshippers of Yamuna are associated with all the Krishnaite denominations of the Braj region. However, Gaudiya Vaishnavas and Nimbarki Vaishnavas are the most numerous among those worshipping Yamuna at Keshi Ghat in Vrindaban, and Pushti Margiya Vaishnavas dominate the worship of the Yamuna at Thakurani Ghat in Gokul and Vishram Ghat in Mathura. Moreover, the Chaturvedi pilgrimage priests who conduct Yamuna worship at Vishram Ghat in Mathura have a long history of a devotional relationship with the Yamuna that predates the developments in the sixteenth century that produced many of the Braj Vaishnava traditions. Since these three sites are valuable sources for information about the theology of Yamuna in Braj, I spent many days visiting them, observing religious activities and talking with the numerous worshippers, including the daily bathers, temple priests, boatmen, and the pilgrims who came to visit these holy places. I sought to understand who Yamuna was for her worshippers here. What I discovered were lively and sophisticated theological traditions expressed in a variety of texts and religious acts; although differences exist among the diverse group of Yamuna worshippers in the Braj region, much is also shared.

ASPECTS OF YAMUNA

Almost everyone I talked with in Braj agreed that Yamuna the river and Yamuna the goddess are one and the same, therefore the conceptions of divinity that follow apply to both. First and foremost, I found that Yamuna is a goddess of exquisite love and compassion. In the pantheon of Hindu goddesses, it would be difficult to find one more representative of divine love than Yamuna. She is a goddess who experiences the deepest of all loves, and who, rather than holding onto that love for herself, shares it selflessly with all who approach her with an open heart. The theme of Yamuna's loving generosity is fundamental to her theology, and it ran throughout all the discussions I had with her worshippers in Braj. It is also a foundational idea expressed in the many hymns, poems, and theological treatises written about Yamuna.

Of all theological texts relating to Yamuna, the most important is the "Yamunashtakam" of Vallabhacharya, a Sanskrit hymn consisting of nine long verses.[9] Throughout Braj, one hears this hymn sung in a wide variety of contexts. Although it is not a lengthy text and it has its origins in a specific Vaishnava denomination, it has informed a great many other texts and poems. It was known by the temple priests of every Yamuna temple I visited.[10] In this hymn, Vallabhacharya describes Yamuna's physical body (*adhibhautika-rupa*) as being composed of her water, sandy banks, flora and fauna, and so forth. He defines her spiritual body (*adhyatmika-rupa*) as that which purifies one of sins and protects one from the torments of Death. And he describes her divine body (*adhidaivika-svarupa*) as that of the exquisite goddess who initiates souls into the world of divine love and nurtures their progress. Pushti Margiya Vaishnavas claim that the first two forms of Yamuna had been discussed in religious literature by previous saints, but that Vallabhacharya, in his "Yamunashtakam," was the first to reveal the highest form of the goddess. The commentaries on this text are especially important for gaining access to the more refined tenets of Yamuna theology; two of the most significant were written by Vallabhacharya's son Vitthalnath and his great-grandson Hariray. Many of the textual elements of the theological portrait that follows are drawn either directly or indirectly from Vallabhacharya's "Yamunashtakam." Thus I provide a translation of it here in its entirety.

[1]

Joyously I honor Yamuna, the source of all spiritual powers.
Her expansive sands shine as bright as the lotus feet
   of Krishna.
Her waters are fragrant with lovely flowers from the lush
   forests on her banks.
She bears the radiance of the Krishna, Father of Cupid,
Who is worshipped by both humble and assertive lovers.[11]

[2]

She shimmers as her abundant foamy water cascades down
   the peak of Mount Kalinda.
Playfully she descends the high rocky slopes, moving eagerly
   for love.

She flows as if riding in a swinging palanquin,
Dashing over uneven ground while singing songs of love.
All glory to Yamuna, Daughter of the Sun, who increases
    love for Krishna.

[3]

She came to Earth to purify all beings.
She is assisted by parrots, peacocks, swans, and other birds
    with loving sounds.
Her waves are her arms, her sands pearl-studded bracelets,
Her banks are her beautiful hips.
She is honored as the highest lover of Krishna.

[4]

Adorned with infinite qualities, she is praised by the gods
    Shiva and Brahma.
Her complexion is that of a dark rain cloud.
She always satisfies the desires of devotees such as Dhruva
    and Parashara.
The pure city of Mathura is located on her bank,
And she is surrounded by cowherd lovers.
She is joined with the ocean of compassion.
May this Yamuna always gladden my heart
    and mind.

[5]

Only after Ganges merged with her did Ganges become a
    lover of Krishna and able to grant worshippers
    all spiritual powers necessary for divine love.
If anyone can be compared to Yamuna, it is Lakshmi, who is
    like her cowife.
May Yamuna, Lover of Krishna, ever remain in my heart
    and mind.

[6]

All honor to you always, Yamuna,
For your greatness is most wonderful.
Those who drink your milklike water will never be
    tormented by Death.

For how could Death ever harm the children of his sister,
   even if they are bad?
From loving service to you, O Yamuna, one becomes a lover
   of Krishna, just like his cowherd lovers.

[7]

May my body be transformed by being in contact
   with you.
Then it will not be difficult to love Krishna, O Lover of
   Krishna.
This is why you are praised.
Ganges becomes supreme after her confluence with you.
Therefore grace-filled souls worship Ganges only after
   she has merged with you.

[8]

Who, O Lover, can fully praise you, cowife of Lakshmi?
When Lakshmi is worshipped in conjunction with Hari,
She can grant the satisfaction of liberation.
But you are even greater than this, since you flow with beads
   of sweat that come from the bodies of Krishna and his
   lovers as they make ecstatic love.[12]

[9]

O Daughter of the Sun, all sins are washed away and love
   for Krishna develops for one who recites this hymn of
   yours with joy daily.
Through you all spiritual powers are attained and Krishna
   is delighted.
You completely transform the nature of your devotees.
Thus says Vallabha, the lover of Shri Krishna.

I encountered in my conversations and textual readings in Braj culture
a number of related conceptual beads that are strung on the fundamental theological thread of Yamuna's ever-present loving generosity. Eight
seem especially prominent: Mother of the World, Highest Divinity,
Supreme Lover of God, Ultimate Giver, Perfecter of Love, Purifier of All,
Daughter of the Sun, and Sister of Death.

Mother of the World

An aspect of Yamuna's theology believed in both Yamunotri and Braj is that Yamuna is a "Mother." Devendra Sharma of Vrindaban told me, "All residents of Braj consider Yamuna as their own Mother."[13] Although this seems to be an important feature of her pan-Indian identity, it is understood in a particular way in Braj, where in addition to being seen as the Mother of life she is viewed more intimately as the Mother of the devotee.[14] Verse 6 of Vallabhacharya's "Yamunashtakam" indicates that devotees of Yamuna drink nurturing milk as they sip her water. Following the logic of this poetic assertion, Yamuna's devotees are her children and she is their Mother. Shyam Manohar Goswamy, a widely respected Pushti Margiya scholar and author of a contemporary Hindi commentary on this verse, writes, "In reality, then, since Shri Yamuna protects and nourishes those souls who take her shelter, she is the Mother of the surrendered souls, and the souls are the children of Shri Yamuna."[15]

This theme is repeated in a well-known Yamuna poem from a collection of forty-one poems sung daily by many Pushti Margiya Vaishnavas.[16] In it the poet Ganga Bai sings, "She cares for her people just like a mother cares for her son."[17] The view of Yamuna as a Mother is prevalent not only in the literature about Yamuna but also in the living culture of Braj. The greeting "Yamuna Maiya ki jaya" (Glory to Mother Yamuna) is common along the banks of the river. Yamuna is addressed as "Mother" (ma, mata, maiya) in many ritual settings. In almost all the arati hymns sung during her services, for example, she is addressed as "Mother Yamuna," and those who come to worship her daily greet her with the same epithet.

One beautiful spring morning, I met Lakshman Das while he was immersing himself in the river at Keshi Ghat in Vrindaban. He introduced himself as a sixty-five-year-old man who had lived in Vrindaban for more than forty years.[18] Shortly after arriving from his native Bengal, he had begun taking worshipful baths in Yamuna; he had continued this practice every day since. When I asked him who Yamuna is for him, he replied simply, "Ma" (Mother). Although I heard this from practically every one of the Yamuna worshippers I interviewed in Braj, I pressed Lakshman Das for further details: "What kind of mother is she?" He informed me that she is "a compassionate mother who looks after her children without them even asking. So Mother takes care of me. She is 'mother-hearted.' Therefore, I never approach her with any demands. I ask only for devotion. She knows everything I need without me asking."

When I questioned Mohanlal, acting priest of the Yamuna temple in Gokul, about the nature of Yamuna, he said, "Yamuna is Mother" (Yamuna Maiya hai). "I worship her with the feeling for a mother [maiya-bhava]. People worship her like a mother, for she takes care of everything for her children."[19] Giriraj, a holy man who lives in Gokul, also told me that Yamuna is "my Mother. She gives all things, but I don't ask for anything. Without asking she gives. Like a mother she takes care of me. She is not an ordinary river; she is Mother."[20]

"She is Mother," was a frequent response I received to my question "In your opinion, who is Yamuna-ji?" The conception of Yamuna as a compassionate Mother who takes care of those who are aware of her true nature and approach her with the appreciation of a devoted child is widespread throughout the Braj region. She is so loving to her children that she provides for their every need without them even asking. Some people I spoke with even used the conception of Yamuna as a compassionate mother to explain why a powerful goddess would allow her body to be polluted. One priest told me, "Most people look at her as a Mother, and as their Mother she forgives her children. She has a big heart, so she forgives all. Mother allows her children to be naughty."[21] (Others, however, as we shall see, fret about Yamuna's health as they would their mother's and worry about the limits of her ability to withstand the pollution. Still others are beginning to wonder if the pollution may change Yamuna's generous nature into something less forgiving.)

Yamuna is also considered by some to be the Mother of the entire world. Uddhava Bhai, a seventy-four-year-old Gujarati man I met on the bank of the Yamuna in Gokul, explained that, after retirement, he had come to live on the bank, where he wished to stay for the remainder of his life.[22] He told me that, for him, "Yamuna is the Mother of all existence." As such, she is both the producer of the world and its protector, at least for those who surrender to her. The author of the "Shri Yamuna Yasha Pachasa," a long poem composed in Vrindaban on the occasion of the new millennium, addresses Yamuna in the local Braj Bhasha language as both the "Mother of the world" (jag mata) and the "Mother who saves the world" (jag tarini maiya).[23] The poet Hariray writes, "Again and again she is declared to be the very essence [sar] of this world."[24]

Yamuna is identified as being both the creator of the world and as the world itself. Such notions connect Yamuna with the theology of other great goddesses in Hindu India who manifest the world out of their own bodies, and indeed, many simply refer to Yamuna as "Devi," a term often used to designate the goddess in general. Deepu Pandit, a young man living in Gokul who worships Yamuna at the Thakurani Ghat temple every day that he is in town, told me, "Yamuna-ji is another form of the goddess [Devi]. She is like Durga [a great and independent goddess often viewed as the ultimate divinity]."[25] Three technical and related Sanskrit terms used to express the theology of the great goddess in Hinduism are relevant here: *shakti, prakriti,* and *maya.*[26] *Shakti* means "power" or "energy"; it is the divine power inherent in all life. *Prakriti* means "nature" or "matter," the very material stuff of life. *Maya* is the "creative force" by which the world is manifested. These three terms have negative connotations in many of the philosophies informing the ascetic traditions that renounce the world as a dangerous illusion,[27] but in the goddess traditions that embrace all life as sacred they are seen as positive. David Kinsley says it well: "As *sakti, prakriti,* and *maya,* the Devi is portrayed as an overwhelming presence that overflows itself, spilling forth into creation, suffusing the world with vitality, energy, and power. When the Devi is identified with these three well-known philosophic ideas, then, a positive point is being made: the Devi creates the world, she is the world, and she enlivens the world with creative power. As *sakti, prakriti,* and *maya,* she is not understood so much as binding creatures to finite existence as being the very source and vitality of creatures. She is the source of creatures—their mother—and as such her awesome, vital power is revered."[28]

Thus the great goddess of Hinduism is the creator and protector of the world, and is the world itself. From this perspective the world is considered to be a divine gift from the goddess herself and is often regarded to be her own body. Identified with the great goddess in these terms, Yamuna is very much a "river of life." Associated with this deep philosophical tradition, the Yamuna River is both the source of life and a manifestation of life. Moreover, in a very specific way Yamuna is considered to be the highest form of divinity.

Highest Divinity

That Yamuna is the highest divinity, rather than some minor manifestation, is expressed repeatedly within Braj culture. In the *arati* song sung evenings at Keshi Ghat in Vrindaban, for example, Yamuna is addressed as the liquid form of the highest reality, Brahman (*brahma drava nadi*).[29] A lesser-known Sanskrit "Yamunashtakam" hymn composed by Iccharama Mishra in the early nineteenth century addresses Yamuna as Para-Brahma-Murti, "You whose form is the highest reality."[30] In response to my questions about who Yamuna is to her worshippers, several people told me simply, "She is Bhagavan." After he had just emerged from a dip in the Yamuna at Keshi Ghat, Brajendra Sharma of Vrindaban told me, "Ganga-ji came from Bhagavan's foot, but Yamuna-ji manifested directly from Bhagavan's heart. Therefore, she is a direct form [*sakshat-rupa*] of Bhagavan."[31] The word *Bhagavan* is a technical Sanskrit term with a long history in the Bhagavata or Vaishnava traditions represented in Braj. It is used to indicate the highest expression of divinity, and in the Bhagavata traditions is usually reserved for Krishna—but no matter, for Yamuna is also called "Krishnaa" because of her dark color.[32]

Yamuna's identification with the highest divinity, Krishna, is worked out in detail in the theological literature associated with her. One of the "Forty-One Yamuna Poems" recited daily by many Pushti Margiya Vaishnavas declares, "Being united with Dark Krishna [Shyam], Shri Yamuna herself is dark [*shyam*]."[33] The union mentioned here, however, refers to more than mere association; it means identity, for Yamuna and Krishna are understood to be essentially one. They are the female and male dimensions of the same divinity. A contemporary Hindi writer comments, "In this poem Shri Govindaswami-ji shows the sameness of the essential forms of Shri Yamuna and Shri Krishna. The color of Shri Yamuna's water is dark [*shyam*]. From this it is clear that Shri Krishna is dark, and Shri Yamuna is also dark, in the sense that darkness resides with darkness."[34] In fact, posters of Yamuna readily available in Braj portray her as dark blue like Krishna; she is even dressed in Krishna's clothing and wears his crown (see figure 8). Moreover, Mishra, the author of the "Shri Yamuna Yasha Pachasa," identifies Yamuna as the "essential form [*svarupa*] of Shyam [Krishna]," and the fourth name listed in the thousand names of Yamuna that appear in *Shri Yamuna Sahasra Nama* (Thousand Names of Shri Yamuna) is "she who is the form of Krishna [Krishna-rupa]."[35] In the words of the poet Krishnadas, "Yamuna's body is the color of Krishna; she has the qualities and character of Shri Krishna."[36] The assertion that Yamuna and Krishna are essentially identical is also found in later Vaishnava Puranas. The *Padma Purana*, for example, states that Yamuna and Krishna are nondifferent (*abhinna*).[37] Another way the identity of Yamuna and Krishna is expressed is by designating Yamuna as a liquid form of *rasa*, a term

Figure 8. The Goddess Yamuna as she is portrayed in
Braj. Here she is shown running to offer a garland of
love to Krishna. Common Braj poster.

used to characterize the "essence" of ultimate reality in the Upanishads
and later associated with divine bliss (*ananda*).[38]

These ideas are worked out in detail in the commentaries of
Vallabhacharya's "Yamunashtakam," a major source for much theological reflection on Yamuna within Braj Vaishnavism. Vallabhacharya
reveals in the fourth verse of the "Yamunashtakam" that Yamuna is
adorned with infinite qualities. In his commentary on this verse,
Vallabhacharya's son Vitthalnath declares this to mean that Yamuna
has the same nature (*dharma*) as Bhagavan Krishna. He explains that all
seven qualities that define the highest divinity of Bhagavan Krishna are

fully present in his lover Yamuna. The seventeenth-century commentator Hariray elaborates on this point, saying that the sevenfold nature of Bhagavan consists of six characteristics (*gunas*) plus his essential form (*svarupa*). He explains that the six characteristics are described in the "Venu Gita," the "Song of the Flute," found in the *Bhagavata Purana*.[39] He recognizes that the six characteristics are employed in this text to describe Krishna, but since Yamuna has the same nature, he maintains, they describe her as well. These six defining characteristics are greatness, potency, fame, supreme beauty, knowledge, and renunciation. Hariray comments that, although only these six are mentioned, Krishna and Yamuna's qualities are really infinite in number. The seventh characteristic of the highest divinity of Bhagavan is identified as *dharmi*, that is, the very source of all qualities (*dharmas*). Therefore, the sevenfold nature of Bhagavan—and by extension of Yamuna, since she is equal to him and shares in his nature—is composed of six ultimate *dharmas* plus the seventh, *svayam dharmi rupa,* the essential nature that is the source of all. This means no less than that Yamuna is a complete manifestation of the highest divinity; expressed in Sanskrit terminology, she is *svayam* Bhagavan.

The qualities of Krishna and Yamuna mentioned above, however, have a very specific meaning in the Bhagavata traditions of Braj. According to Pushti Margiya writers who have commented on Vallabhacharya's "Yamunashtakam," each of the seven phrases that make up the fourth verse of this hymn represents a particular characteristic considered to be a divine quality different from the ordinary quality identified by the same word. Moreover, the point is made that, by the rules of Sanskrit grammar, these phrases simultaneously refer to both Krishna and Yamuna.[40] According to Hariray, the first phrase indicates the first divine quality, "greatness" (*aishvarya*), meaning specifically that the qualities possessed by Bhagavan Krishna and Yamuna are infinite (*ananta-guna-bhushite*) because this blessed couple is free from the subjugation of time. Since Krishna and Yamuna are praised by the extremely potent gods Shiva and Brahma (*shiva-viranchi-deva-stute*), they are recognized to be the most potent. This phrase from the hymn, then, indicates the second divine quality, "potency" (*viryam*). Regarding the third quality, Hariray writes, "Just as a cloud gives life by giving its own essence—rainwater—so too do Shri Krishna and Shri Yamuna give life itself as well as their own essence in the form of bliss [*ghana-ghana-nibhe*]." Hariray maintains that the greatest fame of all belongs to the giver of gifts, and that the "fame" (*yasha*) of Yamuna and Krishna is indicated by this reference to the fact that they give the greatest gift of all: the highest bliss of divine love. The fourth divine quality, the "supreme beauty" (*shri*) of Yamuna and Krishna, draws great saints such as Dhruva and Parashara to them (*dhruva-parasabhishtate*). Hariray says that there is no greater purifier than true knowledge; since the city of Mathura is said to be pure because it is near to Krishna and situated on the bank of Yamuna (*vishuddha-mathura-tate*), this is an indication of the divine couple's "knowledge" (*jnana*), the fifth divine quality. Out of great compassion, Bhagavan Krishna gives his own self to those near him, and Yamuna gives herself to those who surround her (*sakala-gopa-gopi-vrite*). Hariray says that this infinite compassion and selfless giving define the sixth divine quality, "renunciation" (*vairagya*).

The seventh divine quality, *dharmi,* is really the source of all other divine qualities. Hariray articulates its meaning by explaining that all qualities of Bhagavan Krishna and Yamuna are considered to be eternal but are not always present or manifest. The loving kindness (*kripa*) of the divine couple, however, is their foundational quality, since it is manifest eternally and is present at all times and places. Therefore, loving kindness is declared to be the very essence of Bhagavan Krishna and Yamuna. Vitthalnath comments that Vallabhacharya reveals in his "Yamunashtakam" that Yamuna, as a result of this loving kindness, does not flow into the ocean like all other rivers, but rather merges with the ocean of Bhagavan's limitless compassion or loving kindness (*kripa-jaladhi-samshrite*).

Thus Yamuna Devi shares in all the infinite and eternal qualities of Bhagavan Krishna, the very measure of divinity in Braj religious culture, and their shared foundational quality is loving kindness. Following Hariray's commentary, Shyam Manohar Goswamy writes, "Since she is linked essentially to the highest divinity of Bhagavan of infinite loving kindness, this too reveals the essential nature of Shri Yamuna as infinite loving kindness."[41] Although they are two in form, Yamuna and Krishna are one in essence.

This asserts that Yamuna is identical in nature with Krishna and as such is a form of the highest divinity. In an article titled "Yamuna and the Environment," Devendra Sharma of Vrindaban writes, "Yamuna exists in Krishna, and Krishna exists in Yamuna-ji; the two of them are non-different. Because of this, Yamuna and Krishna are the same dark color."[42] Goswamy further elaborates: "Although Shri Krishna and Shri Yamuna are two, they are really just one. One is Purushottama and the other his most Beloved. Therefore, in both of them there is a sameness in all ways of form, qualities, and nature. . . . Between Shri Yamuna and Shri Krishna there is only a difference of form as lover and beloved. But in essence, the two are one. Shri Krishna and Shri Yamuna have an identical nature: they have six *dharma*s and are also *dharmi*."[43] This statement evokes the basic image of Hindu ontology first expressed in the early Upanishads, and which later became the basis of much theological thinking about divinity as a divine couple: In the beginning, ultimate reality was a single dimensionless point—called variously *atman, brahman, purusha*, or *bindu*—entirely alone. Looking around, it saw nothing other than itself. It had no delight, and therefore desired a second. Out of this desire for another, it split itself into a male and female, and from the interaction of these two came all of creation.[44] The interactive two, who are essentially one, are the god and goddess, who produce the world as well as play in the world.

The divine couple came to be identified as Radha and Krishna in later Vaishnava Puranas: "In the beginning, Krishna, the Supreme Reality, was filled with the desire to create. By his own will he assumed a twofold form. From the left arose the form of a woman, the right half became a man. The male figure was none other than Krishna himself; the female was the Goddess Primordial Nature, otherwise known as Radha."[45] Reality is accepted in the Braj Vaishnava schools to be *advaita,* or "nondual," but these schools also teach that for the purpose of dynamic love the one had to become two. The dynamics of love require a separation of the lover and beloved, as the taste of sweetness depends on the differentiation of the taster and tasted.

Many people in Braj identify Krishna's essential lover as Radha, but devotees of Yamuna often identify this female figure as Yamuna. *Shri Yamuna Sahasra Nama* lists Yamuna's sixth name as "she who is the left portion of Krishna" (*Krishna-vama-amsa-bhuta*), and the last of the "Forty-One Yamuna Poems" refers to her as "the other half of Krishna's body." Others emphasize a direct theological connection between Yamuna and Radha: "Like the main *swamini* Shri Radha, Shri Yamuna's situation is that of *nara-nari* (half man, half woman) like Shiva and Parvati. She is in all ways linked to Shri Krishna."[46] Some Vaishnava denominations of Braj, such as the Radhavallabhis, insist that Yamuna is a *sakhi* (girlfriend) serving the higher goddess Radha,[47] but many Yamuna devotees claim that there is no essential difference between Radha and Yamuna. This is evident in the *arati* song sung daily to Yamuna at Keshi Ghat in Vrindaban: "You appear in the eternal love play as a river who is a lover equal to Radha."[48] When I asked one elderly Bengali widow in Vrindaban who had been bathing in and worshipping Yamuna for nearly sixty years to tell me how she thought of Yamuna, she replied, "She is the same as Radha. Yamuna and Radha are the same; only their colors are different. Yamuna-ji is dark like Krishna, whereas Radha is golden."[49] Although the Bengali Gaudiya Vaishnavas of Vrindaban may more typically emphasize the similarities between Yamuna and Radha, I also heard this from Pushti Margiya Vaishnavas. B. C. Chaturvedi of Mathura told me on the steps of Vishram Ghat, "Yamuna is the only river that Krishna took as a *patarani* (lover). She is like Radha." In sum, a central point of Yamuna's theology in Braj is that, in essence, she is one with Krishna, though for the purpose of enhancing the taste of love she is different in form. Yamuna, then, is identified as the supreme lover of Krishna. And what a lover she is!

Supreme Lover of God

Although in essence Yamuna is "God Herself," she is also considered to be the supreme lover of God. In fact, she might be the Goddess of Love par excellence in the Hindu pantheon, and is often referred to as a river of love. She is said to flow literally with drops of love sweat or with the nectar of divine lovemaking.[50] A common designation for Yamuna is Patarani, meaning that she is the "Chief Lover" of Krishna. A temple priest told me, "She is like a mother for me. She is also the Chief Lover [Patarani] of Lord Krishna."[51] One of the most well-known poems in Braj, attributed to the famous poet Surdas, addresses Yamuna: "You are the Lover of Krishna, the Enchanter of Love, And are called his Chief Lover [Patarani]."[52] The term *patarani* can mean "main wife," and some intend that meaning, pointing out that, whereas Krishna eventually abandoned all his cowherd lovers (*gopis*)—including Radha—when he left Braj for Dvaraka, he took Yamuna with him as his wife Kalindi.[53] In Braj, however, Yamuna remains a lover of Krishna, and most people I interviewed used the appellation Patarani only to mean "Chief Lover," insisting that Yamuna and Krishna were never married in Braj.[54] This view is corroborated by Yamuna's pilgrims, priests, and daily worshippers and is also a primary theme in the theological literature about her.

The second verse of Vallabhacharya's "Yamunashtakam" describes Yamuna as she descends the peak of Kalinda Mountain. While Ganges is said to have sprung forth as purifying water from the foot of

Vishnu Narayana, Hariray informs us in his commentary on this verse that Yamuna manifested as the liquid form of love (*rasa*) from the very heart of Vishnu Narayana. Most of the commentaries state that Yamuna did not originate from the ordinary sun, but rather from the divinity situated inside the solar disk: that is, from the blissful, golden, supreme Vishnu Narayana located within the sun. Hariray explains that this is the divinity described in the ancient scriptures, and that Krishna himself originated from this Vishnu Narayana as he manifested in the house of Nanda as Purushottama, the highest personal reality, in the complete form of condensed love (*rasa*).[55] Similarly, Yamuna overflowed from the blissful heart of Vishnu Narayana as Purushottama in the complete form of liquid love (*rasa*) and spilled onto the top of Mount Kalinda. The love affair between Yamuna and Krishna, then, is the love affair between liquid and condensed *rasa*, the mixing and mingling of these two forms of love.[56]

Like her beloved Krishna, Yamuna is dark blue in color, but Vallabhacharya tells us in this verse that she becomes bright with foam as she rushes eagerly down the mountainside on her journey to meet her lover in Braj. In her excitement she dashes quickly over the huge boulders in the upper valley, bobbing up and down as she goes. Filled with anticipation, she sways attractively as she hurries over uneven ground, making much noise. Hariray comments that the sounds of the babbling stream are her love songs as she moves excitedly toward Braj. Yamuna travels as a passionate lover anxious to meet the beloved in a lovers' tryst. The waters that carry her divine form are like a palanquin designed to take a bride to the bridegroom's house. Because of the double meaning of a term in the original Sanskrit, Hariray explains, this verse can also mean that, impatient with the slowness of the palanquin, Yamuna has dismounted and is running on foot. In fact, all images of her in Braj picture her in a running posture (see figure 8). I asked several temple priests in Braj why, in her temples there, Yamuna is not sitting on a turtle as she is in Yamunotri. They replied that the turtle is far too slow for the anxious lover of Krishna. So in addition to being the love songs she sings while approaching Krishna in Braj, the sounds of the rushing river are interpreted as the jingling of anklets on her running feet. Yamuna is thus portrayed as an excited lover, hurrying eagerly and impatiently to meet her beloved. Her love knows no bounds, and no one surpasses the depth of Yamuna's love for Krishna.

Yamuna's eager love is the subject of many of the "Forty-One Yamuna Poems." The poet Govindaswami writes, "She is like a young lover who is so restless that she cannot remain in her own home. . . . She comes to him like a new bride."[57] According to the Vaishnavas of Braj, then, Yamuna rushes down from the mountains out of her immense love for Krishna. So great is Yamuna's love for Krishna that she cannot bear being away from him, even for a moment. Exclaims Govindaswami, "She cannot live for a single second without her Lord."[58]

Yamuna's love is so exceedingly powerful that even Krishna, the ultimate divine playboy, cannot resist it. According to one poet, "When Krishna makes music with his flute, The women of Braj hear it and lose consciousness of their bodies. Chaturbhujadas says: But Krishna, the youthful Holder of the Mountain, sways with bliss in the ocean of Shri Yamuna's love."[59] Poets declare that Krishna too cannot bear being separated from Yamuna, even for a moment. "Chitaswami's Lord, Shri Vitthal, Holder of the Mountain, cannot tolerate a single second without her," writes the poet Chitaswami about Yamuna.[60] Referring to the winding nature of the river, Hariray uses his poetic voice to say, "Her course is twisted and she enchants her beloved. He cannot live without her for a single second."[61] Moreover, Yamuna's love is so strong that she is able to hold sway over Krishna, lord of the entire universe. The *arati* song recited every evening at Keshi Ghat sings to Yamuna, "Krishna is charmed by each and every one of your drops of water."[62] The author of the "Shri Yamuna Chalisa" exclaims, "You are the true love of Madan Mohan [Krishna] and completely control Murari [Krishna] in many powerful ways."[63] Krishna is the charmer of the whole world, but Yamuna's love is so irresistible that even he falls under its spell: that is, the enchanter of the entire world is himself enchanted by Yamuna's love. The poet Ganga Bai sings, "Who is able to describe Shri Yamuna-ji? Krishna, the beloved Enchanter, enchants the mind of everyone, but she steals his mind. Krishna, the Wealth of the Soul, cannot remain without her for a single second. She is so blessed that she provides bliss for the heart of Krishna, the Moon of Braj."[64] According to much Yamuna theology in Braj, Krishna, the very Lord of Life, is completely captivated by Yamuna. Paramanandadas celebrates this point.

Shri Yamuna, you have the beloved Krishna under
   your control.
You captured him with the snare of love and keep him close
   to you.
You have managed to purchase this priceless jewel.
He always runs wherever you send him.

He is soaked in the nectar of your love.
Paramanandadas says: I have now found Krishna, the Moon
   of Braj.
Shri Yamuna is so generous that she gave him to me as
   a gift.[65]

Yamuna, then, is considered to be the Supreme Lover of God; the
power of her love is surpassed by none. The fifth verse of Vallabhacharya's hymn "Yamunashtakam" compares Yamuna to Lakshmi,
the other well-known consort of Krishna Vishnu: "If anyone can be
compared to Yamuna it is Lakshmi, who is *like* her cowife" (emphasis
added). Commentators from Vitthalnath on make much of the fact that
Vallabhacharya says Yamuna is "like" (*iva*) a wife, and not actually
one. In fact, they all emphasize that she is a lover (*priya*) of Krishna and
not a wife (*patni*), asserting that, because a lover's passion is more
intense than a wife's, Yamuna is superior to Lakshmi. Vallabhacharya
himself uses the term *priya* (lover) to refer to Yamuna in the fifth and
eighth verses of his famous hymn, and many cite this as the authoritative view of Yamuna's position.

Yamuna's superiority over the wife of Vishnu, the goddess Lakshmi,
is expressed in many ways.[66] Vitthalnath explains that worshipping
solely Lakshmi can result only in material well-being. According to Vallabhacharya's hymn, when Lakshmi is worshipped together with
Vishnu, she has the ability to grant even *moksha*, "spiritual liberation."
She does not, however, have the ability to grant the highest bliss, divine
love. Only Yamuna among the goddesses can grant this ultimate gift,
since she is nondifferent from Krishna and is understood to be the liquid
form of the nectar (*rasa*) of divine love itself.[67]

Commentaries on Vallabhacharya's "Yamunashtakam" identify
another important difference between the goddesses Yamuna and
Lakshmi: as the wife of Bhagavan, Lakshmi enjoys amorous union with
him, but she neither allows the privilege of this experience nor gives the
happiness of her own union to her devotees. Lakshmi keeps this privileged position and its joy for herself. She might be able to grant *moksha*,
but devotees of Braj Vaishnavism want much more than this: they want
the bliss of divine love, which is declared to be far superior to the more
limited joy of *moksha*.

Yamuna, on the other hand, receives much pleasure from the loving
union of Krishna with her devotees and gives freely the limitless joy
of supreme love. Rupa Gosvamin celebrates this aspect of Yamuna's

disposition in his "Yamunashtakam": "She is delighted by the union of Krishna and her devotees."[68] Goswamy writes, "Lakshmi experiences the bliss of being with Bhagavan for her own self, but Yamuna holds this bliss for her devotees. Shri Yamuna acts on behalf of others, whereas Lakshmi is concerned with her own self. Regarding the inconceivable greatness of giving up one's own bliss to one's devotees, Lakshmi lags far behind Shri Yamuna."[69]

This is another key point of Yamuna's theology in Braj: whereas Lakshmi, the majestic wife of Lord Vishnu, keeps the Beloved for herself, Yamuna gives him lovingly as the ultimate gift to those who approach her respectfully. The last line in the poem by Paramanandadas cited earlier states that Yamuna is so generous that she gives as a gift Krishna, the Moon of Braj. From the denominational perspective of Pushti Margiya Vaishnavas, Yamuna is the most generous of all the goddesses because she alone rises above all selfishness and freely gives the ultimate gift of divine love.

Ultimate Giver

Since she gives the ultimate gift of divine love, Yamuna's worshippers say that there is no one nobler than her; she is the Ultimate Giver. To be sure, Yamuna is approached by worshippers hoping to receive life blessings, particularly related to marriage, children, health, and other domestic concerns. One of her worshippers told me, "People believe that if they have diseases, then by taking a bath in Yamuna the disease will go away. There are plenty of cases where even doctors could not cure a sick person, but worship of Yamuna made the disease go away."[70] Yamuna is also recognized as the giver of all happiness (sukha-deni) and the remover of all sorrows (dukha-harani). However, her greatest power lies in granting access to the supreme lover, the very source of divine love. The poet Chitaswami writes, "Blessed Shri Yamuna gives the divine treasure."[71] Hindi commentator Hariprasad Sharma explains that the divine treasure referred to in this poem is the obtainment of Krishna, the very source of all bliss.[72] The poet Govindaswami further elaborates on this: "There is no greater giver than Shri Yamuna. She instantly gives union with Lord Krishna to the person who takes refuge with her."[73] The author of the "Shri Yamuna Chalisa" claims, "Whoever performs loving service [seva] to you, O Yamuna, is united with the young King of Braj [Krishna]."[74] Yamuna, moreover, has the ability to change Krishna himself; whereas he normally grants only liberation (*moksha*) to devotees, she prompts him to give devotional love (*bhakti*) to her devotees.[75] Thus, not only does Yamuna give the bliss of her own love, but she also introduces her devotees to the Ultimate Lover and initiates them into the divine love affair.

Yamuna's desire to give is so remarkable that she has taken a vow to give her devotees whatever they ask for. The poet Kumbandas sings, "How can one even speak of the greatness of the bliss she gives? Whatever the devotee asks for, she gives in a second. Acting in this way she carries out her vow."[76] In another poem Kumbandas exclaims, "Bow your head to Shri Yamuna, the treasure house of divine love. She gives all bliss to those devotees who know her greatness. They receive whatever they ask for."[77] The devotee's greatest desire is for the experience of a loving encounter with the very source of love, Krishna, and Yamuna knows this without being told. "Shri Yamuna-ji fulfills the devotee's wish. She gives what is best without even being asked," sings Kumbandas.[78] Hariprasad Sharma comments, "Usually the gods give people what they ask for, but Shri Yamuna-ji has such grace that she gives to her devotees whatever is good for them without them asking. She gives the devotees unlimited love. . . . Shri Yamuna-ji has such love for her devotees that she gives them the best of all without them even asking."[79] The best, of course, refers to the love of Krishna. This poetic view was confirmed by many of the Yamuna devotees I interviewed in Braj. Giriraj of Gokul told me, "Yamuna-ji gives all things, but I don't ask for anything. Without asking she gives."[80] Narayan Das of Mathura exclaimed, "I don't ask Yamuna-ji for anything. I don't have to; she gives everything without asking."[81] Both of these devotees made it clear to me that the gift Yamuna gives is divine love.

Yamuna knows no jealousy in the realm of love. On the contrary, as the goddess of love par excellence, she experiences great happiness when others experience the joy of her ultimate love. As we have seen, she not only gives others union with the Lord but also shares with them her own bliss, which by definition is the most intense of all. The poet Hariray writes, "Full of love, she plays with her beloved. She signals her beloved to give her bliss to everyone. Her heart is overjoyed when he says he will do this."[82] It is said that, when something very good has just happened, a woman's left arm quivers as a sign of delight. Yamuna experiences this as she runs excited to her beloved when a soul is initiated into a relationship with him. Hariray celebrates this in another poem: "Her left arm quivers when a soul is initiated into the divine relationship. She runs noisily while going to her beloved. She becomes delighted as her

heart is filled with great bliss."[83] Her excitement over her devotee's new
love affair is another reason Yamuna is depicted in a running pose in the
artwork of Braj. The poet Nandadas writes, "Knowing completely the
state of the devotees' hearts, she ran here quickly."[84]

Yamuna's display of loving kindness and generosity is continual, said
to be uninterrupted like the flow of oil. The poet Krishnadas informs us,
"Shri Yamuna does not remain for a single second without doing good
for her devotees."[85] Remarkably, this holds true even when she is
absorbed in the bliss of her own love play with her beloved. The poet
Ganga Bai reveals, "She plays with Krishna, Holder of the Mountain,
but does not forget her devotees even for a second."[86] That she not only
gives her devotees access to her own Beloved but also gives them the
bliss of her own love for her Beloved makes Yamuna the very pinnacle
of selfless love. She generously initiates one into the world of divine
love, in which one has direct access to the Beloved; this initiation involves
perfecting the soul's ability to love in preparation for the ultimate
encounter.

Perfecter of Love

After observing a young man emerge from a reverent dip in the river, I
asked him about the benefits of bathing in the Yamuna. "She increases
love," he said as he made a squeezing motion at his heart with his right
hand.[87] Although Yamuna is considered useful for finding love within
ordinary marriage, the more important love she nurtures is the love
affair with God.[88] "She safeguards refuge and increases love for
Gopala," sings the poet Krishnadas.[89] Vishuddhananda, priest of a
Hanuman temple on the bank of the Yamuna in Vrindaban, explained
to me that Yamuna came from the heavenly realm of Goloka to engage
in love play with Krishna, and added that "she came before Krishna to
prepare the playground of love."[90] A Yamuna *arati* declares, "Your
water turns a wild jungle into Vrindaban, the forest of love."[91] In a
sense, Yamuna's presence is considered to be essential for the development of Krishna's love: she enables him to enjoy love. Braj Vaishnavas
also believe that Yamuna came to Earth to prepare her devotees for divine
love. Commenting on the last line of the second verse of Vallabhacharya's
"Yamunashtakam," Vitthalnath declares that Yamuna became manifest
on Earth in order to awaken and nourish love for Krishna, and the third
verse of Rupa Gosvamin's "Yamunashtakam" states, "She increases the
stream of loving devotion for Krishna, Son of Nanda."[92] As the one who

initiates the soul into the world of divine love, she is considered to be essential for the development of the devotee's love.[93]

Among all the river goddesses, Yamuna's devotees claim, only she possesses this ability. In the fifth verse of his "Yamunashtakam," Vallabhacharya suggests that, by herself, Ganges, who is associated more with the ascetic cultures of northern India, can bestow liberation (*moksha*) but not the exquisite love of devotion (*bhakti*). Only after she merges with Yamuna at her confluence in Allahabad does Ganges become a lover of Krishna herself and acquire this ability. The poet Krishnadas concurs: "Ganges obtained Krishna from merging with Yamuna, and she became filled with the power to grant all spiritual powers."[94] Yamuna's devotees regard her as superior to Ganges because Yamuna alone can grant, nurture, and perfect devotional love without the aid of another. Accordingly, many Pushti Margiya Vaishnavas claim that they do not worship Ganges upstream from Allahabad, but only downstream from this confluence, where she merges with Yamuna. Competitive claims of the superiority of Yamuna over Ganges are evident in Braj, where only Yamuna is regarded as capable of cultivating the highest love. A sign at Keshi Ghat in Vrindaban reads, "A single sip of Yamuna water here gives one more spiritual benefits than one hundred baths in the Ganges."

A young man who lives in Mathura and comes to honor Yamuna daily told me, "I worship Yamuna-ji because she gives love and love everywhere. This is what I get from Yamuna-ji. The whole world gets love from Yamuna-ji."[95] The last lines of the sixth verse and the first lines of the seventh verse of Vallabhacharya's "Yamunashtakam," translated earlier in this chapter, establish that Yamuna is the generator of divine love, "From loving service to you, O Yamuna, one becomes a lover of Krishna, just like his cowherd lovers. May my body be transformed by being in contact with you. Then it will not be difficult to love Krishna, O Lover of Krishna."

Both the young man and Vallabhacharya's hymn express the notion that Yamuna prepares the devotee to acquire a new perspective and have a loving encounter with the ultimate. This was first spelled out explicitly in the commentaries on the first verse of Vallabhacharya's "Yamunashtakam." Vitthalnath, and all commentators who follow him, explained that each of the eight verses of the hymn represents one of the eight special qualities of Yamuna, and that each quality helps her perfect the devotee's love for Krishna. Her first quality is that she grants all spiritual powers or abilities (*siddhi*s). Although the concept of spiritual abilities has been prevalent in yogic culture for centuries, in this context they have a particular meaning. Vitthalnath identifies the first four of the eight spiritual abilities: (1) attaining a body suitable for direct loving service (*seva*) to the Lord, (2) having direct sight of His love play (*lila*), (3) experiencing Him and His loving essence (*rasa*) with one's own senses, (4) and being emotionally aware (*bhava*) that everything is the Lord. Hariray spells out the other four. They are similar to the first four but apply to separation: (5) attaining a body that is totally engrossed in the Lord, even in separation, (6) seeing the Lord's *lila*s directly inside, even when the eyes are turned away from Him, (7) experiencing His *rasa* and His essential self by means of one's own essential emotion, and (8) sensing that He is everywhere, even during times of separation. All these spiritual powers are deemed useful for experiencing the ultimate love affair.

Yamuna's second special quality is that she increases the love for the Lord. The opening line of the "Shri Yamuna Chalisa" reads, "One who sings 'Shri Yamuna! Yamuna!' is flooded with love for the feet of Hari [Krishna]."[96] Many people I interviewed told me that increased love for Krishna is a major benefit of worshipping Yamuna.[97] Lakshman Das of Vrindaban, who has been bathing in the Yamuna daily for more than forty years, explained to me, "By bathing in Yamuna I get more loving devotion [*bhakti*] for Krishna."[98] Many others believe that this benefit comes especially from contact with the Yamuna in Braj. This is corroborated with statements that appear in the Puranas. The *Padma Purana,* for example, states, "At other places Yamuna is holy and removes great sins, but in contact with Mathura the deity [i.e., Yamuna] gives devotion for Vishnu."[99]

Yamuna's third special quality is that she purifies the soul to make it fit for union with the Lord. Since she has the same nature as the Lord, she can easily perfect the devotee's relationship with him; this is her fourth special quality. The fifth involves her ability to remove all sins that stand as a barrier to the ultimate relationship. Her sixth special quality is that she gives her devotee the extremely attractive nature of a lover of the Lord. The seventh allows her to make the devotee a lover of the Lord. And finally, her eighth special quality is that she enables her devotee to achieve a newness of body. The transformative quality of the Yamuna is expressed in numerous narratives in the region of Braj; two stand out as particularly noteworthy.

The first narrative illustrates how Yamuna transforms a lusty love into a form more suitable for a relationship with Krishna. One day, when he was a passionate young man, the poet Nandadas caught sight of a beautiful young woman living in the desert in northwest India who had just finished a bath and was drying her hair. He fell hopelessly in love with her and declared that every day he would not eat or drink anything until he had sight of the woman's face. When the woman's husband discovered what was going on, he confronted Nandadas, but the latter silenced him by threatening to commit suicide. In desperation the husband decided to move his family to Gokul, the home of his guru, Vitthalnath. Nandadas followed the family to Gokul, refusing to give up the object of his desire. When the family reached the Yamuna at Gokul, the husband bribed the ferryman not to take Nandadas across the river to the other shore. Later in the day, Vitthalnath asked the husband what was to be done with the man they had left on the other side of the Yamuna. Vitthalnath then explained to the couple that Nandadas was a worthy soul whose lust for the woman had been transformed into an ecstatic love for Krishna the moment he saw Yamuna. Meanwhile, Nandadas sat on the bank of the Yamuna composing his first poem: "For love, first I came to you, Shri Yamuna, for you know all about the condition of your devotee's mind."[100]

The second story represents Yamuna's ability to transform a devotee's body and nature in preparation for a loving encounter with Krishna. When Krishna sounded his flute to summon his cowherd lovers to the enchanting forest of Vrindaban, the mighty ascetic god Shiva was meditating high atop Mount Kailash, his Himalayan retreat. Shiva is typically portrayed as a prototypical hardened ascetic who has turned his back on the world of emotion, and is, accordingly, the patron deity of many ash-smeared ascetics striving to achieve liberation from the world. In Braj, however, Shiva is portrayed as an ardent devotee of Krishna. Hearing the irresistible notes from Krishna's flute, Shiva experienced an overwhelming desire to join in the love dance taking place in Vrindaban. He hurried to Braj but, no matter how hard he tried, was unable to cross the Yamuna and enter the forest of Vrindaban. Eventually he worshiped Yamuna and sought her aid. She appeared before him as a beautiful goddess and informed him that he could not enter Vrindaban in the form of a male ascetic. She then instructed him to bathe in her water. Shiva did so and emerged from the Yamuna as an attractive young woman. Shiva—now transformed into a passionate lover through reverent contact with Yamuna—was able to enter the forest of Vrindaban and engage in love play with Krishna.[101]

The poet Nandadas composed a few lines that aptly express the transformative powers of Yamuna.

Shri Yamuna showers amazing grace upon her devotees.
She leaves her own abode and comes to Earth
To reveal to her devotees the divine love play.
She fulfills the highest aim of all her devotees,
Giving them a very wonderful body.[102]

The body referred to in this poem is frequently understood to be a special form (*svarupa*)—similar to the bodies of the cowherd lovers of Krishna—suitable for participating in Krishna's love play.[103] Thus, Nandadas's poem and the two stories above depict Yamuna's ability to perfect a person's love and change that person into a passionate devotee of Krishna. Much of this work requires purification.

Purifier of All

The theme of purification is an important one in the theology of Yamuna, and as noted in chapter 2, it is common in much of the Puranic literature. The *Padma Purana*, for example, declares that "all minor and major sins are reduced to ashes by taking a bath in Yamuna."[104] Although the theme of purification seems to be more common in Yamunotri, it is shared by many of Yamuna's devotees in Braj. Brajendra Sharma of Vrindaban said, "All sins are destroyed merely by looking upon Yamuna-ji."[105] Many of the pilgrims and worshippers I interviewed along the river mentioned that they bathed in it to be purified of their sins. Kinkiniwala Chaube of Mathura told me, "My soul is washed clean by bathing in the Yamuna."[106] A Braj text, the "Shri Yamuna Yasha Pachasa," states, "All sins are destroyed by bathing in Yamuna."[107] The theme of purification also appears in the Sanskrit hymns addressed to Yamuna. In his "Yamunashtakam," for example, the Gaudiya Vaishnava theologian Rupa Gosvamin writes, "She eradicates the evil consequences of former births for the person who touches but a few drops of her water," and he closes each of his eight verses with the refrain "May the Daughter of the Sun always purify me."[108] A verse in the "Yamunashtakam" attributed to Shankaracharya reads, "She destroys the sins of all beings who come in contact with her shining waves," and each verse ends with the refrain, "May Yamuna, Daughter of Kalinda, always remove the impurities of our minds."[109]

Yamuna's purificatory capabilities include ridding a person of physical diseases. The second *arati* song in the appendix says to Yamuna, "You remove all misfortune and disease." The other declares, "Sickness, poverty, and death never come near your water." I met several people who reported having been cured of sickness by bathing in Yamuna, and many others who bathed daily in Yamuna to protect themselves from incurring disease. Additional religious texts agree that Yamuna can do this: Rupa Gosvamin celebrates in his "Yamunashtakam" Yamuna's ability to destroy all disease and sickness in those who bathe in her, and the "Shri Yamuna Yasha Pachasa" declares that "all afflictions are destroyed by sipping her water."[110] Yamuna, then, is a riverine goddess whose powers include the ability to protect from illness those who drink or bathe in her water. One might wonder: what will happen as she who protects from disease herself becomes a possible source of disease through pollution?

In the opening line of the third verse of his "Yamunashtakam," Vallabhacharya declares that Yamuna came into this world in order to purify it (bhuvana-pavanim). Hariray explains in his commentary on this verse that, for Pushti Margiyas, this means Yamuna comes to purify the world in all ways, but most specifically she comes to purify the devotee's body so that it is fit for loving service (seva) and the devotee's heart so that it can love more perfectly. Pushti Margiyas employ the terminology of the three forms of Yamuna to explain her different purificatory abilities. With her physical form (adhibhautika-rupa), Yamuna cleanses the body; with her pervasive spiritual form (adhyatmika-rupa), she cleanses the soul; and with her essential divine form (adhidaivika-svarupa), she prepares the soul for a divine love affair. Pushti Margiya Vaishnavas maintain that the first two forms of Yamuna (celebrated also at Yamunotri) were revealed early in the Puranas, but the third form (celebrated only in Braj)—which initiates one into the divine love affair—was not revealed until Vallabhacharya did so in his "Yamunashtakam."[111] Thus, many devotees of Yamuna in Braj claim that the highest reason for the manifestation of Yamuna is to purify the soul so as to awaken and increase love for Krishna. Once again, we see Yamuna functioning as a gracious goddess who prepares souls for the ultimate loving union with the divine.

Daughter of the Sun

Although Yamuna comes to Braj from Mount Kalinda in the Himalayas, her true origin is understood to be the sun, the origin of all. One of Yamuna's most common appellations is Daughter of the Sun.[112] Textual references to this name appeared more than three thousand years ago in the Rig Veda, where Yamuna's father is identified as Vivasvat, god of the Sun. This designation continues to be used through Puranic texts to the present day. Her connection with the sun is evident in the story of her origin told at Yamunotri (see chap. 2), and she is addressed as the sun's daughter in many of the devotional poems recited in Braj. The opening line of the "Shri Yamuna Yasha Pachasa," for example, reads, "All glory to Yamuna! All glory to the Daughter of the Sun!"[113] This text also declares, "You know how the sun manifested the world; for this reason you are considered to be the Daughter of the Sun."[114] The "Shri Yamuna Chalisa" identifies Krishna's lover as "the Daughter of the Sun" and "darling of the mighty sun king."[115] Devotees of Yamuna living in Braj are fond of saying that, although Ganges comes from the foot of Narayana, Yamuna manifested out of the very heart of Narayana, the primeval source of all that is identified with the sun. For this reason too she is called the Daughter of the Sun. The commentaries on the second verse of Vallabhacharya's "Yamunashtakam" indicate that this verse reveals the manner in which Yamuna manifested. Vitthalnath remarks that she fell from the disk of the sun onto the top of Mount Kalinda, thus producing her white foamy color. Hariray elaborates on this point by saying that Yamuna manifested from the blissful heart of Narayana, the divinity that resides deep within the ordinary disk of the sun. According to Hariray, this shows that Yamuna shares in the essential form of the highest divinity that is the very foundation of all that is ultimate.

Sister of Death

As noted in chapter 2, Yamuna's identity as the twin sister of Yama, the Lord of Death, is one of her oldest. The earliest textual references to the affectionate relationship between Yamuna and her twin brother, Yama, appeared several millennia ago in the Rig Veda. In this text she is often called Yami and is always associated with Yama.[116] Yamuna's connection with the Lord of Death remains a common theme in the literature produced in Braj. The sixth verse of Vallabhacharya's "Yamunashtakam" declares that those who drink from Yamuna's milklike waters will not suffer the torments of Yama. This verse goes on to ask, How can Yama kill his younger sister's children even if they are bad? That is, as children of Yamuna her devotees become the nieces and nephews of Yama, who as their uncle is obliged to protect them. The "Shri Yamuna Chalisa" states, "There is no greater means than you for one seeking refuge from the terror of Death [Yama]. . . . One who bathes in your water will never

Figure 9. Vishram Ghat in Mathura on the occasion of Bhai Duj. Photo by David Haberman.

experience Death's noose."[117] The "Shri Yamuna Yasha Pachasa" confirms this special quality of Yamuna: "The messengers of Death [Yama] do not come near the person who sings about the magnificence of Yamuna."[118] For her devotees, Yamuna is a powerful goddess who will protect them from the torments of dying and death administered by her brother Yama. A common Hindi saying in Braj states, "Where Yamuna is, there Yama is not."[119]

The relationship between Yamuna, her devotees, and her brother Yama is acted out in a celebration that occurs each autumn in Braj, and which falls on the second day of the bright half of the lunar month of Kartik (figure 9). This celebration is known either as Yama Dvitiya, "Second Day of Yama," or Bhai Duj, "Brother's Day." The "Shri Yamuna Yasha Pachasa" explains it this way: "On Bhai Duj, sister Yamuna adorns her brother Yama Raja with all decorations. After applying an honorific mark [tilak] on his forehead, Yamuna feeds her brother Yama. He rewards his sister with presents and kind words. Brothers and sisters who come together on the second day of the bright half of the lunar month of Kartik and bathe in Yamuna's water have the sins of lifetime after lifetime destroyed. Those who bathe in Yamuna on Bhai Duj never approach the door of Yama."[120]

Early references to celebrations of Bhai Duj are found in the Puranas. Since Bhai Duj occurs two days after Dipawali, which takes place on the night of the new moon in the lunar month of Kartik, the *Padma Purana* discusses it in a section describing the Dipawali festival of lights. Here Yama's celebration is called Yama Dvitiya, the veneration of Yama on the day he was fed and honored by his sister, Yamuna, in her home. This text explains how a brother should go to his sister's house on this day, honor her with gifts, and receive a meal cooked by her. As a result, the brother and sister will avoid unpleasant contact with Yama and will be blessed with bountiful life.[121]

Although the *Padma Purana* makes no reference to bathing in the Yamuna, such practice is central to the celebration of Bhai Duj or Yama Dvitiya in Mathura. I visited Mathura's Vishram Ghat on Bhai Duj of 1999 to observe the annual celebration and acquired a pamphlet distributed there describing the story that informs the festival.[122] The story is narrated by Lord Brahma to the wandering sage Narada, who had asked to be told the means by which humans can avoid suffering. Brahma tells him that this can be accomplished by celebrating Yama Dvitiya. On this day a man is to honor Yama, bathe in Yamuna, and go to his sister's house. Brahma says an ancient account explains why this is so.

Long ago Yamuna frequently approached her brother and requested that he come to her house to eat. Because he was so busy with the business of death, Yama put her off again and again, promising that he would come tomorrow and, if not tomorrow, then certainly the following day. Yama, however, never managed to find the time to pay his sister a visit. One day Yamuna went to him and insisted that she was not leaving without him. Seeing his sister's determination, Yama accompanied her to her house, where she honored him by dressing him in elaborate clothing and ornamentation, draping him with a flower garland, and feeding him wonderful foods. Yama was so pleased with the loving attention of his sister that he showered her with gifts and asked her to make a request, promising to grant anything she desired. Yamuna asked Yama to visit her house every year on this particular day and to grant happiness and freedom from the sorrows of hell to any man who travels on this day to his sister's house to eat her food and give her gifts. Yama promised that any brother-and-sister couple that engages in these activities together and worships and bathes in Yamuna on this day would never see the gates of hell.

It was close to noon by the time my bicycle rickshaw left me off at Mathura's Holy Gate, one of the remaining arched entrances to the ancient city. I wound my way through the crowds in the lanes of the old bazaar and headed toward the river. The banks of the Yamuna at Vishram Ghat were crowded with boisterous activities; more than five thousand people were bathing in the river as a loudspeaker blared announcements punctuated with "Yamuna Maiya ki jaya!" (Glory to Mother Yamuna!). I hired a boat to take me out to the middle of the river, where I could better observe the activities of the day. Everywhere around me were brothers and sisters of all ages dipping into the water together and splashing each other with peals of laughter. Some joined hands in circles of three or four couples of alternating brothers and sisters. A number of people around me sipped handfuls of water and smeared their bodies with muddy sand scraped up from the bottom of the river. Back on the sandy shoreline, couples established altar spaces by drawing *svasitka*s (symbols of well-being) with red *sindur* powder and offered coconuts, flowers, rice, milk, money, and incense to Yamuna. Some used the services of local priests, others performed the worship themselves. The collective mood was joyous; delight in Yamuna was palpable. The exquisite goddess of love seemed fully present.

But what about the pollution? When I asked one young woman from Gujarat if she was aware that the river was polluted, she said with a beguiling smile, "Yes, the river is polluted. But today our hearts are unpolluted, so there is no problem." Her smile was infectious, the day was beautiful, and for a while I too forgot about the pollution. Perhaps Yamuna was indeed watching over those bathing in her water, but all the charm of these celebrations did not succeed in making the pollution disappear.

CULTURAL VIEWS OF POLLUTION

The conception of the Yamuna River presented in this chapter has been evident in Braj culture since long before the Yamuna became polluted. Yet, as explained in chapter 3, the river is now seriously polluted, especially downstream from Delhi. How do those invested in a deep religious relationship with Yamuna view this modern problem? And how is the pollution affecting the religious culture associated with the river? Before answering these questions, we must address a preliminary question: Just what is meant by the term *pollution*?

Like most notions, "pollution" is a cultural concept viewed differently in different cultures. In the religious discourse regarding the Yamuna are two sets of terms that might define *purity* and *pollution*. The first set has to do with the physical condition of the river; many understand that material pollutants in the river contribute to its "dirtiness" (*gandagi*). In this context there is a recognized difference between being clean (*saph* or *svaccha*) and being dirty (*ganda* or *asvaccha*). Dirtiness labeled *gandagi* is caused by human beings. This view of pollution is roughly tantamount to a Western scientific view of pollution, "the defilement of the natural environment by a pollutant."[123] Now current in Indian discourse is the word *pradushan,* a Hindi version of the English word *pollution* that is roughly analogous to *gandagi.*

The second set of terms has more to do with the spiritual nature of the river; though the spiritual dimension may include the physical world, it need not. This set of terms contrasts a spiritually powerful state of purity (*pavitra* or *shuddha*) and a spiritually dangerous state of impurity (*apavitra* or *ashuddha*). This view tends to focus more attention on a transcendental quality of a river. What is important to keep in mind is that a river in Hindu India can be dirty (*gandi*) and polluted (*pradushit*) but still pure (*pavitra*).[124] This being the case, we must be careful not to reduce the condition of the Yamuna to one of scientific pollution.

In his famous work on caste in India, the sociologist Louis Dumont warns against confusing Hindu notions of purity and impurity with Western notions of hygiene.[125] Water may be pure by Western scientific standards but deemed impure in India because of its contact with the wrong person or thing.[126] And water may be impure by Western scientific standards but deemed pure because of some inherent property. Before Dumont, the sociologist Mysore N. Srinivas had noted a difference between ritual purity and cleanliness: "It is necessary to stress that ritual purity is fundamentally different from cleanliness, *though they overlap frequently.* A simple association of ritual purity with cleanliness and ritual impurity with dirtiness would be a neat arrangement but it would falsify the facts. One comes across ritually pure robes which are very dirty, and snow-white clothes which are ritually impure."[127] So too with rivers in India. The Yamuna is almost always considered pure (*pavitra*), even by those who clearly recognize her polluted condition. This means that the Yamuna may become dirty but never impure. As Srinivas insists, however, overlaps do exist. Bodily eliminations, especially human waste matter, are considered polluting by both Western scientific standards of hygiene and Hindu standards of religious purity. With such substances coming down the Yamuna to Braj in increasingly large amounts, a wide range of observers have recognized polluting materials as being present in the river.

How do Yamuna's devotees in Braj view modern pollution, and how does the presence of polluting substances in the river affect devotees' religious perspective and practice?[128] Answers to these questions are necessarily complex. Lance Nelson, who warns against thinking too simplistically about the connections between religion and ecology, highlights the fact that the very act of sacralizing some aspect of nature can both motivate people to protect it and obscure a need to protect it.[129] I received roughly three types of responses to my inquiries. Some denied that the pollution has any real effect on the river goddess or on living beings dependent on her; some acknowledged that the pollution harms living beings who come in contact with the water but does not affect the river goddess herself; and some contended that the pollution is having a harmful effect on beings who come in contact with the water as well as on the river goddess herself. I have observed that the latter group—and to some extent the second group—is much more inclined than the first group to engage in activities that the West would label as "environmental activism."

Bhagavan Devi, the elderly mother of my milkman in Vrindaban, fairly well represents the first type. For more than sixty years, she had walked barefoot to the Yamuna every day at four in the morning to bathe, regardless of weather conditions. She believed that Yamuna protected her, and she attributed her good health and life blessings to her daily baths. When I asked her if the Yamuna was polluted (pradushit), she responded emphatically, "No! Not at all!" (Na! Kachu nai!).[130] She told me that "even if sewage goes into the river, the river is still not polluted." To prove her point she asked her son to fetch a large mature tulsi plant. Showing it off, she explained that she waters this plant with Yamuna water every day. Whereas other plants she had watered with tap water had died, this one had thrived. She told me that the Yamuna is the "direct form" (sakshat svarupa) of Krishna, and that as such the river goddess's spiritual power (shakti) is very strong (bahut zyada). Unwilling to accept that Bhagavan Devi saw no sign of pollution in the river, I asked her about the pollutants entering the Yamuna from the sewage pipes. She said, "Yamuna makes the dirty water from Vrindaban completely pure [shuddha]. For this reason cows can drink it safely." Still not satisfied that I had understood, I pushed on, inquiring about the plastic bags of garbage in the river. "Yamuna takes all garbage—even plastic bags—and turns it all into dirt, just like she does with the remains of a person cremated on the bank of the river."

According to Bhagavan Devi, the Yamuna possesses a power that makes all lasting pollution impossible. She is not alone in this view.

On the river one afternoon, I asked my boatman if the river was polluted. "Yamuna-ji is never polluted," he insisted. "Her water is pure
[*shuddha*]."[131] To demonstrate his point, he picked up a drinking pot,
filled it with water from the Yamuna, and proceeded to gulp down half
of the pot. "It tastes great!" he exclaimed, and then offered the remainder of the pot to me. (I declined.) A number of people expressed similar
views. A man I met during evening worship at the Yamuna temple at
Keshi Ghat in Vrindaban insisted that the Yamuna could never be polluted (*pradushit*) or even dirty (*gandi*). Needless to say, such people
have little concern for cleaning the river.

In her study of differing cultural views of the pollution of the Ganges
in Banaras, the anthropologist Kelly Alley found that the pilgrimage
priests at Dasashvamedha Ghat—who benefit economically from maintaining such views—emphasize a transcendent dimension of the river
that is unaffected by any pollution. She writes, "For Brahman pilgrim
priests (*purohit* or *panda*) who live and work on Dasashvamedha in
Banaras, the river Ganga is a goddess who possesses the power to
absorb and absolve human and worldly impurities."[132] Although some
priests do speak of limits to her cleansing power, many contend that the
Ganges has the ability to handle all the pollutants humans send her
way; they also insist that pollutants cannot alter the Ganges's divine
power to purify souls or grant liberation. This representation of the
Ganges rests on a feminine theology that views the river as a good
mother who "cleans up the messes her children make and forgives them
lovingly. In this way, she cleans up other kinds of dirtiness people bring
to her and excuses dirty behavior with maternal kindness. Ganga is forgiving rather than angry about human dirtiness."[133] Thus, the Ganges
as a mother goddess takes all abuse in a gracefully loving manner; she
can purify all pollution without becoming impure herself. Alley argues
that conceptualizing riverine power in feminine terms—"based on the
Mother's self-negation, her ability to endure privations for the family, to
nurture and give sustenance, no matter what the sacrifice, with no thought
of her own needs"—may actually undermine efforts for environmental
protection and cleanup.[134]

A similar view is found among some of the pilgrimage priests at
Vishram Ghat in Mathura who direct rituals worshipping the Yamuna.
Kameshvar Chaturvedi, for example, told me as he pressed me to hire
him to perform a ritual, "Yamuna-ji is not polluted [*pradushit*] in any
way. She can never be polluted."[135] And many Yamuna devotees told
me that she too is like a mother who takes care of everything for her

children. Mohanlal, an elderly priest at the Yamuna temple at Thakurani Ghat in Gokul, said, "People look at her as Mother, and as Mother she forgives her children. She has a big heart, so she forgives all. Mother allows her children to be naughty."[136] With such attitudes in mind, Rajmohan Gandhi published an editorial in the *Hindustan Times* that supports Alley's conclusion:

> In India, rivers and mountains are gods and goddesses to us. This sounds wonderful, and even an improvement on the idea of living in and living with nature. Yet our attitude contains a fatal flaw. For gods are self-sufficient. They have miraculous powers. They will cleanse themselves and their surroundings. We don't have to keep them clean. It is they who will clean us and purify us. Meanwhile, we can pour and spread our waste onto them. . . .
>
> So what is the solution? It is to make our mountains, seas, rivers, cows, and even Mother India herself a little less divine. To see them as human, vulnerable and in need of help, so that they arouse our pity and our care.[137]

Alley has demonstrated that many of the Dasashvamedha priests promote a highly transcendent view of the Ganges, effectively removing the river goddess from any realm that pollution can affect. "This interest in distancing their approach to Ganga from worldly pursuits is connected to their lack of interest in protecting, saving or cleansing Ganga."[138] Alley argues that, for many of those she interviewed, "Ganga's purity has lapsed into a fixed transcendent state."[139] Extreme transcendentalism obstructs efforts to promote environmental health. "More broadly, the essentialism of Mother undermines the efficacy of scientific and governmental statements about pollution and weakens activist discourses on environmentalism."[140] What Alley says about the Ganges is also true of the Yamuna, but the picture is far more complex than this. David Kinsley writes, "Pious Hindus, it might be argued, are encouraged by their tradition to discern the mystical dimensions of the landscape, but this may obscure their perception of its physical, natural features."[141] This assertion is correct—spiritual notions about the river may cause Yamuna's worshippers to overlook her pollution—but as Kinsley himself argues, the rich mythological traditions also provide possible resources to motivate people to care for the physical river too. Alley deftly highlights the environmental position of those deeply invested in a radically transcendent view of a river goddess, but there is a significant population of river worshippers in India invested in a different view of river goddesses.

The second type of Yamuna devotees I encountered were willing to recognize that pollution poses a serious problem, though they too usually insisted that the pollution does not affect Yamuna herself. Vishuddhananda, head priest of a small Hanuman temple at Keshi Ghat in Vrindaban, represents this type. Every morning around five, he bathed in the Yamuna. One morning after his bath, I asked him if the Yamuna was polluted. "Yes, city people are polluting her," he complained. "Fifty years ago, she was not polluted. I used to drink directly from the river every day, but I don't anymore. It's dangerous. There are bad things in the water now."[142] But when I asked him whether Yamuna the goddess was polluted, he insisted, "No! Yamuna Devi is not polluted. She can never be polluted. She is always pure [pavitra]." Brajesh Kumar Shukla, a priest of the Yamuna temple at Keshi Ghat, told me, "Yamuna-ji is completely pure [shuddha], but people put impure [ashuddha] things into her. However, she herself as a goddess [devi] is not polluted."[143] These are fairly common responses. Many people maintained that the pollution was adversely affecting human life, but claimed that it had no effect on Yamuna Devi herself. A young priest in Vrindaban explained, "Mother Yamuna gives us back whatever we give her. If we give her good things, we get back good things. If we give her bad things, then she gives us back bad things. Therefore, for our sake we should stop polluting her."[144] Vasishthagiri, who spends his life wandering along the Yamuna, put it this way: "There are two sides to reality—to Yamuna-ji. One side is supernatural [alaukik] and one side is natural [laukik]. Pollution cannot affect the supernatural. For those who can see this, Yamuna-ji is a pure goddess. She cannot be polluted. But we are not supernatural. We are natural. Therefore, it is us who will suffer from the pollution."[145] He went on to repeat what I heard many times, that there is a difference between "purity" (pavitra) and "cleanliness" (svacchata). He said that the river can become dirty (gandi), but it will never lose its purity (pavitra).

Triloki Sharma of Gokul phrased this notion in a slightly different form: "Yamuna-ji is not polluted. There is no difference between the river and the goddess, but there is pollution in the water. The water is like a murti [embodied form or sacred image worshipped in a temple]. When a murti is broken in a temple, God is not affected by this, but our bhava [spiritual feeling] is affected. In this way the pollution harms us."[146] Divinity is resident in an embodied form, according to this view, but not reducible to it. Deepu Pandit of Gokul agreed, "It is like the murti being broken in a temple; God is not affected by this, but our bhava is affected. We cannot approach God without a murti. Here water is like the physical murti."[147] Moreover, people like Deepu Pandit are beginning to consider limits to Yamuna's forgiveness: "The people polluting Yamuna-ji do not see her real nature. The people polluting her will be punished. She will punish those people with diseases caused by the pollution. Just as karma takes time to come to fruition, so too people are beginning to break the limits, and we will see the effects of this in the near future. It will take some time, but we will be punished for what we are doing to Yamuna-ji." Perhaps this is the beginning of the transformation of a cool and forgiving goddess into a hot, angry, and punishing one.

Although the second type of devotee stopped short of believing that pollution harmed Yamuna directly, the third type was willing to go further and even claim that pollution is affecting Yamuna herself. Although they share in the theological perspective of Yamuna as a divine mother, some of her worshippers are beginning to view her as a vulnerable and ailing mother in need of care. Maternal theology, then, can now work both ways, evoking either a self-nurturing presence or a presence in need of care herself. It is not uncommon these days for Yamuna devotees to speak of her as sick or even dying.[148] When I asked Lakshman Das of Vrindaban whether Yamuna was polluted (pradushit), he said, "Yes. And I am anguished because of this. Mother is sick now, but still I can't leave her."[149] This statement signals an emerging and significant shift in Yamuna theology. Previously she was viewed as a powerful Mother, the source of life, filled with spiritual vitality. She nurtured and blessed the lives of her devotees, removing their faults and illnesses with loving grace when necessary. No problem was too great for her to take care of, for she was the very essence of divinity that imparts life's highest gifts. But here she becomes an ill mother in serious need of help.

Lakshman Das is not alone in these expressions. A Nimbarki priest tending a small shrine dedicated to Krishna as a Mount Govardhan stone had an even graver prognosis: "Yes, Yamuna Devi is polluted. The river is dying. I used to bathe in the river with faith when she was alive, but now she is dying. In my view the river and the goddess are the same. Therefore, if the river is dying, the goddess is dying. When the river is finished, life will no longer be possible for human beings."[150] In a similar vein, a man in Gokul wondered, "If Mother dies, how can her children survive?"[151] When I asked my friend Krishna Gopal Shukla, whose family serves as priests in the Yamuna temple at Keshi Ghat in Vrindaban, whether the river is polluted, he said, "Yes! Of course!" I pressed the theological point and he responded, "Yes, the goddess [devi] is polluted. She must be. The river and the goddess are the same. Yamuna-ji is slowly dying. The sewage drains are Kaliya Nag [a poisonous serpent defeated by Krishna in local lore] and the poison has returned to Yamuna-ji. She is dying, and the religious culture surrounding Yamuna is also dying."[152]

While all of Yamuna's devotees share the general riverine Mother theology noted by Alley, I found that this theology was understood and applied differently by the three groups mentioned above. For the first, Yamuna is an all-powerful Mother who is not affected by the pollution and who takes care of her children no matter how naughty they are. The second group agrees that she is an all-powerful Mother unaffected by pollution, but posits limits to her forgiveness, suggesting that she will not protect those polluting her, and that she may even punish them with the horrible diseases caused by the human-generated pollutants themselves. The third group views Yamuna as an ailing Mother who is herself affected by the pollution and who is in need of the loving care of her devotees. Alley may be correct in asserting that the first and older view may actually undermine efforts for environmental protection. In the next chapter, I discuss how the emerging third view may actually promote such environmental work as devotional service to Mother Yamuna.

Many people echoed the notion that the religious culture associated with the Yamuna is increasingly threatened as the pollution in the river becomes more serious: the pollution of the river has certainly brought about significant changes in the religious practices of Braj. Yamuna water has been used for centuries in many different ways in Braj culture. People gain access to Yamuna's powers by ritually sipping (achaman), bathing in (snan), and worshipping (puja) Yamuna. She is approached for many life blessings, especially in women's rituals on the occasions of weddings and births. The deities housed in home shrines are bathed daily with Yamuna water, and small amounts of Yamuna water are drunk as a form of liquid grace. All the famous Krishna temples in Braj use Yamuna water in their services. The large Shri Vaishnava Rangaji temple in Vrindaban sends a procession to the river every morning before sunrise to ceremoniously fetch a pot of Yamuna water to be used in temple rituals.[153] Trucks routinely carry Yamuna water to Krishna temples associated with Braj in Rajasthan.[154] As Krishna is bathed with Yamuna water, the Lord meets and mingles with his riverine lover.

But all this is changing. Many told me with great sadness that they are no longer willing to bathe in the Yamuna for fear of catching some disease. Triloki Sharma of Gokul informed me, "I used to bathe daily in Yamuna, but now I only come for sight [darshan] because of the pollution."[155] Prakash Sharma of Mathura said, "Ten years ago I used to bathe in Yamuna-ji every day and bring her water to my house to bathe my Thakur-ji [embodied form of Krishna]. But no more! The smell and sight of the garbage in the river is very bad [bahut kharab]. It is so dirty [gandi] that I no longer do this. This is a very sad thing."[156] Even more people have stopped the practice of ritually sipping Yamuna's water for fear of getting sick. An elderly woman I met one day at Keshi Ghat in Vrindaban told me, "I used to sip Yamuna-ji's water as a way of honoring her. But I can't do this now. How can I drink the bodily waste of those in Delhi?"[157] One man went so far as to say, "These days I can't even touch the water, let alone sip it or bathe in it,"[158] illustrating a shift from the understanding of Yamuna as a protector from disease to seeing her as a possible source of disease. Other changes in religious traditions also evidence this shift. One day Shrivatsa Goswami, a respected priest of the famous Radharaman temple in Vrindaban, told me with great agitation, "Today I have broken with Yamuna-ji."[159] Surprised, I asked him what he meant. "Ever since I was a small boy, I have bathed in Yamuna on the day of a family funeral, but today [his aunt had just died] I could not do it." With a turned-up nose he explained, "The water was too disgusting." This priestly family's five-hundred-year tradition had just changed as a result of pollution in the river. Many images of Krishna in both home shrines and temples are now bathed with water sold in the bazaar in sealed plastic bottles. This transformation has been marked as both drastic and significant by many of the temple priests I spoke with in Vrindaban. The love affair ritually celebrated in the shrines and temples of Braj has been seriously altered with the substitution of bottled water for the liquid love of Yamuna.

People who view Yamuna herself as sick or even dying tend to closely identify Yamuna as river with Yamuna as goddess; that is, they emphasize divine immanence over divine transcendence. During a conversation with a Vrindaban holy man living near the Yamuna, I explained that some people believe the goddess is separate from the river, and that we can destroy the river without harming the goddess. "They're foolish!" he exclaimed. "If you destroy the river, Yamuna-ji is finished! The river is the real goddess, not some lady sitting on a turtle. That is just a symbol. The river is the main thing, the main form of Yamuna. Those people who say the physical river is not important are foolish people. They are the ones shitting in the river. They don't know what life is, what this world is. They are so busy trying to get things for themselves that they don't have time to think about the nature of the world."[160]

In Alley's study of the transcendental theology of the pilgrimage priests of Banaras who denied that pollution was in any way harmful to the Ganges, she notes that such views can undermine efforts to restore environmental health and can even foster further abuse of a river.[161] While I too heard such ideas expressed by some river devotees, I found the picture to be far more complex, particularly among those who emphasized more immanent views of river goddesses. A view quite different from the one articulated by Alley is suggested by the river environmental activist M. C. Mehta, "If we believe that Ganga is our mother, how can we let our mother not be clean?"[162] A cultural transformation seems to be under way in which devotees are beginning to perceive limits to a river goddess's ability to cleanse herself. In increasing numbers, Yamuna's devotees are seeing her as a sick, possibly even dying, mother who herself is need of help. Says Krishna Gopal Shukla, "Now Mother Yamuna is sick. We need to help her, not abuse her anymore."[163]

This seems to support the suggestion made by Lynn White and others that radically transcendent theologies tend to devalue any real concern for environmental degradation and exploitation, whereas immanent theologies tend to foster more positive attitudes and behavior toward the environment. All those I met who were actively engaged in protecting the Yamuna subscribed to an immanent theology (even though they might hold some transcendent views of Yamuna) that links the goddess Yamuna closely to the physical river and recognizes the harmful effects of modern pollution on the goddess herself.

Gopeshwar Nath Chaturvedi of Mathura is one such person. He recognized that "Mother is sick," which not only made him tremendously sad but also prompted him to call for urgent action. "When Mother is sick," he declared, "one cannot throw her out of the house. We must help her."[164]

CHAPTER 5

Signs of Hope

Mother Yamuna has given much.
Now Yamuna asks for loving service [*seva*].

Popular Sign Posted in Hindi along the Yamuna in Braj

Something is happening. People are becoming more and more
aware; there are signs of hope.

M. C. Mehta

On the morning of January 1, 2000, a line of several thousand people
stretched through the streets of Vrindaban. After demonstrating soli-
darity by linking hands in a continuous chain for several minutes, the
people marched in procession through a light mist to the stone-walled
compound of the imposing Shri Vaishnava Rangaji temple on Vrindaban's
east side. Among the crowd were hundreds of enthusiastic school children, many carrying hand-painted signs and some of them wearing
yellow paper bills on their foreheads that read in large green Hindi letters:
"Loving Service to Yamuna, Environmental Protection" (Yamuna Seva,
Paryavaran Surakha; see figure 10). Dozens of large cloth banners lined
the walls of the compound featuring slogans designed to inspire environmental awareness and action: "Make a campaign in each and every
house to make Mother Yamuna clean"; "It says in all the holy scriptures
that there is no well-being without clean Yamuna water"; "Yamuna is
the grandeur of India, and cleanliness is her life"; and "Mother Yamuna
has given much. Now Yamuna asks for loving service [*seva*]."[1]

A stage had been erected in front of the area reserved to seat the
crowd. A large picture of Goddess Yamuna draped with fresh flower
garlands formed the backdrop to the stage. A banner on the stage
announced that this gathering was the "Celebration of Loving Service
to Yamuna" (Yamuna Seva Karyakram). Its purpose, on the occasion of

Figure 10. Schoolchildren in Vrindaban demonstrating
against the pollution of the Yamuna. The uppermost sign
can be translated as: "Yamuna is crying out from pollution.
Let her be a stream of pure Yamuna water!" Photo by
David Haberman.

the beginning of a new millennium, was to celebrate Yamuna, recognize
environmental achievements to date, and generate new efforts to rid the
river of pollution.

Seven public officials assembled on the stage to deliver speeches.
Anup Sharma, head of the World Wide Fund for Nature in Vrindaban,
acted as master of ceremonies for the event. After praising Mother
Yamuna, he began by acknowledging that the work accomplished so
far in reducing the pollution of the river in Braj was due primarily to

Figure 11. Gopeshwar Nath Chaturvedi at Vishram
Ghat in Mathura. Photo by David Haberman.

public interest litigation (PIL) filed in the High Court of Allahabad by
Gopeshwar Nath Chaturvedi of Mathura (figure 11) with the aid of the
celebrated environmental lawyer M. C. Mehta and implemented by
R. D. Paliwal, who was assigned by the court to the position of Additional District Magistrate of Mathura District. Both Chaturvedi and
Paliwal were present on stage. As a result of Chaturvedi's PIL, the court
had imposed a ban on the release of untreated effluents into the Yamuna
by the end of December 1999. Today's program was designed to mark
major achievements of this sort.

I had first met Chaturvedi a month earlier at the college in Mathura
where he worked as a professor of economics. A stocky middle-age man,
he was dressed in a traditional white *dhoti* (a long waist cloth), a white
shirt, and a brown wool vest. The name *Chaturvedi* identifies him as

belonging to a priestly family of traditional ritual specialists who cater to the religious needs of those who visit this Krishnaite pilgrimage center. I asked him to explain the relationship between the Yamuna and the Chaturvedi priests. "We are all Yamuna-*putra* [sons of Yamuna]," he told me.[2] "I am proud of this," he continued. "Yamuna is my Mother, and love for her is in my blood." He went on to explain that the Chaturvedis also celebrate Yamuna as a loving goddess, specifically as the Chief Lover (*patarani*) of Krishna. He informed me that all of the festivals of the Chaturvedis, both religious and social (e.g., weddings), begin with a dip in and worship of Yamuna. He said that the Chaturvedis worship Yamuna on many different occasions to express their appreciation. They immerse themselves in Yamuna regularly or respectfully sip her water if they do not bathe in her. Overall, he stressed that the Chaturvedis of Mathura have an intimate relationship with Yamuna. Even the upper left-hand corner of his professional card features a picture of the goddess Yamuna, with the words "Jaya Shri Yamuna."

Because of such sentiments toward Yamuna, Chaturvedi and others he associates with all experience much pain in confronting the massive pollution load the Yamuna now carries. He reported, "When people come to Mathura and see the condition of the Yamuna, it hurts them and they leave with a broken heart." Chaturvedi easily articulates his own anguish at the condition of the river, but his religious convictions are only strengthened by his resolve to clean the Yamuna. "When Mother is sick," he told me, "one cannot throw her out of the house. We must help her. Therefore, I do Yamuna *seva*." *Seva* (loving service) is a word I would hear many, many times throughout my interviews with river worshippers and activists. Chaturvedi represents his environmental activism with this religious term, as do many others in India. For him, restoring the river is a deeply religious act.

Chaturvedi's involvement with efforts to clean the Yamuna began one September day in 1985 when he guided a group of pilgrims to Vishram Ghat, the main place in Mathura for worshipping Yamuna. Red and green dyes were visible in the river and dead fish were floating on its surface. Dogs and crows had gathered on the bank to eat the lifeless carcasses. Viewing this scene with his pilgrim charges, Chaturvedi was horrified. He realized that Yamuna was in serious trouble and decided then and there to act.

And active he has been. Chaturvedi investigated the pollution of the river and, through his investigations, learned a great deal. In 1985 there were several hundred industries operating in the Mathura-Vrindaban area that were discharging harmful effluents into the river. In addition, all domestic sewage from Mathura and Vrindaban was going untreated directly into the river. Chaturvedi also learned that not one drop of unsullied Yamuna water was released from the barrages in Delhi from October to June. "This meant that all the water coming to Mathura was sewage water," he complained. "And this is what we are worshipping. This makes me feel bad!" Chaturvedi started to organize and act, first gaining leadership and recognition in his own community by becoming president of the Mathur Chaturvedi Parishad, a society for the Chaturvedi priests. He began to educate people in Mathura and organized demonstrations to protest the conditions of the Yamuna. Initially, government officials in Mathura labeled him a "public enemy" and threatened to invoke the National Security Act against him because he had called for strikes and street demonstrations to protest the condition of the Yamuna. Chaturvedi, however, would not be silenced. For many years he worked without much support. He complained, "It is horrible that the residents of Vrindaban and Mathura collect so much money from the pilgrims, and yet they will not give any money to help clean and protect the Yamuna."

Things began to change the day Chaturvedi met M. C. Mehta, who added legal muscle to Chaturvedi's religious dedication. The two met at a workshop in Vrindaban organized by Mehta, who had come to this holy center on January 1, 1998, to launch his National River Conservation Campaign on the bank of the Yamuna on behalf of the Indian Council for Enviro-Legal Action. I was introduced to Mehta myself on this occasion and made arrangements to visit him in his New Delhi home after interviewing Chaturvedi about his environmental work.

Mehta's first environmental case involved the famed Taj Mahal. At a social gathering in 1983, someone said to him that lawyers were making a lot of money but were doing nothing for the country. This person told Mehta that the marble of the Taj Mahal was being destroyed by air pollution and suggested that he do something about it. Mehta accepted the challenge and began investigating the harm being done to the famous monument. What he learned about was acid rain and its destructive effects on marble. He also discovered something that concerned him much more: that acid rain is a leading cause of lung cancer and even more damaging to human health. Thus, in 1984 Mehta filed his first environmental case to protect the Taj Mahal. He has since become what some have called the "world's most effective environmental attorney,"[3] and in 1996 he received the Goldman Environmental Prize, an international award given each year to an individual with a distinguished record in protecting the environment. He is certainly the most effective and well-known environmental lawyer in India. He told me, "It was God's wish that I begin this work."[4]

Mehta's involvement with river protection began early in his new-found career as an environmental lawyer. In 1985 the Ganges caught fire near the sacred pilgrimage center of Haridwar. Toxic effluents released into the water from just two factories were so flammable that a stretch of the river about a mile long exploded in flames. Outraged, Mehta filed a petition in the Supreme Court against these two factories. The case eventually expanded to include all the industries and munici-palities in the entire river basin. More than one hundred thousand industries were affected by Mehta's petition, making it the largest such case in the history of the world. As a result of his action, the Court ordered thousands of factories to install air and water pollution control devices, and it shut down many that would not comply.

Mehta expressed the motivation driving his legal work in religious terms. "I have a love for Ganga," he told me. "While visiting Haridwar, I came to realize the religious meaning this river has. Whatever Lord Krishna said about Yamuna, or the sages said about Ganga, is based on truth. Those people had the vision of the true nature of these rivers. They could also see what was ahead. To protect the rivers, they said, we need to limit our intake to save this for future generations. . . . Ganga and Yamuna have a deep spiritual significance. On the banks of these rivers, our whole civilization has prospered. Our whole spiritual growth has taken place on the banks of these rivers. The sages have done tapasya [spiritual practices] on the banks of the rivers. We should respect the places where the sages have done their spiritual practices. The difference between the West and India is that we love and worship rivers." Mehta referred to his own environmental awakening: "In 1983 I was a totally different person. Now I understand that all life is sacred, and that we cannot survive without the other life-forms. I don't want to harm any living being. We are like one family. We are all interdepen-dent. When I talk about rivers, I see rivers as nucleuses. When I talk about Yamuna, I am also talking about the catchment area. The whole area then needs to be protected for the river. The whole ecology is linked to the river. The river is a way to approach the whole."

Mehta believes that India is experiencing the same environmental degradation happening around the world because "India is copying the West. By copying the West we have forgotten our own heritage. We should not copy the Western world! Western materialism is like a whirlpool. Look what we have achieved in the last decades by copying the West. When I visit America I see hollowness in the eyes of Americans. I feel sorry for them. They want something they don't have." The solution, he said, is "to return to traditional Indian culture. We don't need outside models when we already have all the models we need." According to Mehta, the task before India is to engage in an honest assessment of what has been lost and what has been gained by following the West. "The duty of leadership is for proper introspection. We need to ask frankly what we have achieved and what we have lost. We have the people who can do this, but no one will listen to them. What if we were to stop developing for one year and just think about what we are doing?"

Mehta believes that India does not need to make new environmental laws but rather to enforce the ones already on the books. He explained that the Water Pollution Control Act of 1974 makes it illegal to pollute any river, stream, well, or lake. According to this legislation one is not to change the character of any body of water. "If this law would have been enforced," he says, "there would have been no need for GAP and YAP."[5] But still the rivers are being polluted. Mehta attributes the lack of implementation and enforcement to the organized lobbying power of industry and to governmental corruption.

Was he hopeful? "Yes, I am quite optimistic. In 1983 I was considered a crazy lawyer, but today there is great change in people's thinking. Letters of support are increasing day by day. Something is happening. People are becoming more and more aware; there are signs of hope." Mehta also had a strong opinion about the role religion is to play in all this: "Religion has a major role to play in environmentalism in India. People listen to religious leaders, and these leaders have access to the traditions that worship rivers as goddesses, for example."

Mehta's presence and workshop in Vrindaban was a catalyst for legal environmental work in Braj. As a result of meeting Mehta, Chaturvedi filed a PIL in the Allahabad High Court in 1997 with Mehta as his advocate. The petition addressed the problems of minimum flow in the river and of industrial waste and domestic sewage entering the Yamuna, primarily from Mathura and Vrindaban. The ensuing case has been remarkably successful. In 1998 the High Court ordered closure of all industries in the Mathura District that were releasing untreated effluents into the Yamuna; those that remained open had to install functioning effluent-treatment plants. The court also ordered the Uttar Pradesh government to insure that more water was released from Okhla Barrage in Delhi to maintain a healthier minimum flow. In addition to this, the court recommended that government funds be used to install sewage lines and treatment plants in Mathura and Vrindaban. To insure the implementation of its orders, the court recommended the placement of an Additional District Magistrate in the Mathura District. By mid-2001, all four new sewage treatment plants were operational in Vrindaban and Mathura. Chaturvedi helped organize the boatmen of Mathura and Vrindaban who make their living rowing pilgrims on the river to be watchdogs for local pollution, and he arranged to have slogans painted on the sides of their boats to raise awareness about the pollution. He also established a shore patrol to walk the banks of the river and stop local pollution and the dumping of rubbish into the river. These people carry whistles and wear T-shirts or chest banners that read "Protector of Yamuna Shore" (Yamuna Tat Rakshak). Moreover, he helped educate schoolchildren in Mathura and Vrindaban about the condition of the Yamuna. When asked why he has been so successful, Chaturvedi said with a smile, "Yamuna Ma is supporting me."

Shortly after my meeting with Chaturvedi, I arranged to meet R. D. Paliwal, the man assigned in 1998 as Additional District Magistrate to oversee implementation of the court's order that industries and municipalities stop polluting the Yamuna in the region of Braj. An energetic young civil servant, he was smartly dressed in Western clothing and sported a fine mustache. Under the Yamuna Action Plan (YAP) of 1993, Mathura and Vrindaban were to receive funds for the construction of sewage treatment plants, but because of a complete lack of coordination nothing had been done. "The officials ate all the money," one boatman in Vrindaban told me.[6] A common joke in the Braj region was that there had been a lot of YAP-ping about cleaning the Yamuna, but no action.

Paliwal told me that, since his placement in the Mathura District, everything had changed. Under YAP, all drains carrying sewage and domestic waste into the Yamuna were to be tapped and pumped to sewage treatment plants, so that no untreated waste went into the river. The treated sewage water would be used for irrigation. During our meeting in Mathura on December 14, 1999, Paliwal told me that one treatment plant was already operational in Mathura and another was due for completion in March of 2000; in Vrindaban one treatment plant was operational and another scheduled to be operational by the end of the year.[7] He claimed further that most of the drains leading into the Yamuna in Mathura and Vrindaban had already been tapped, and that all remaining untapped drains would be tapped by the end of the year. He did admit, however, that the systems—whose success depended upon the drains remaining open, and the supply of electricity for the pumps being uninterrupted—would be difficult for the municipalities to maintain with their limited resources. Other than that, he was quite optimistic about his success and had helped organize Vrindaban's "Celebration of Loving Service to Yamuna" on January 1, 2000, in part to commemorate the achievements in Mathura and Vrindaban.

Although a civil servant by profession, Paliwal saw religion as a vital component in ongoing efforts to stop the pollution of the Yamuna. He said that the government would not be successful without the full support of the people, but in order for that to happen there had to be a reawakening of the peoples' environmental consciousness so that they lived more eco-friendly lives. Religion could make a major contribution toward this end. "Our religion is basically nature-loving," he explained. "But these days, we are not alive to this sentiment. Yamuna is a source of life and spiritual solace, always benevolent and providing us with everything. We have always worshipped such natural forms, but now people don't treat her as a pious river. Still the concept is there. This concept has to be utilized to achieve environmental health. When people see Yamuna as a *devi* [goddess] once again, they will stop polluting her and clean her."

Paliwal believed that materialism and other things have undermined the concept of Yamuna as a goddess. He looked to the leaders of the religious communities in Braj to revitalize this concept and approached many for this purpose. Overall, Paliwal was optimistic, contending that these changes will happen because we have little choice if we are to survive. "We have to succeed in cleaning our rivers, because if we fail, then it will be the failure of all human beings."

Paliwal was onstage for the "Celebration of Loving Service to Yamuna" to add his support to the ongoing struggle to reeducate people about the importance of clean rivers. He kicked off the ceremony by administering a solemn vow (*sankalpa*) to all those who had gathered. The following is my translation of the Hindi vow distributed on paper and administered by Paliwal.

> We the people of the single family of India that consists of 26 states, 190 religious traditions, and 3,742 communities, on the auspicious occasion of the new millennium, today take this vow for the purpose of working to rid the Yamuna of pollution, and to protect the environment and the beauty of Indian culture: We will always cooperate in protecting the environment and

making it beautiful, in ending pollution, and in making the environment green; and we vow not to pollute the water of the Yamuna.

Glory be to Mother Yamuna!
Glory be to India!
Glory be to the Land of Braj!

After administering this oath to the entire crowd, Paliwal referred to a story now frequently mentioned in speeches regarding Yamuna pollution. He asserted that the time had come for everyone to emulate Krishna, who once long ago rid the Yamuna of the poisonous snake Kaliya. This well-known story is from the *Bhagavata Purana*, the most important religious text in Braj culture.[8]

The deadly multiheaded Kaliya moved into a deep pool in the Yamuna that happened to be the favorite swimming hole of Krishna and his cowherd companions. The snake's poison caused both the cows and cowherds to become seriously ill; trees near the bank of the pool withered, and birds flying over it fell dead. Discovering the source of the pollution, Krishna dove into the pool to battle Kaliya and began a death dance on the heads of the serpent (figure 12). Had it not been for the pleadings of the snake's wives, Krishna would have killed Kaliya. Instead Krishna merely expelled Kaliya from the Yamuna so that the river became free from pollution. Today many people in Braj say that Kaliya has returned in the form of the drains discharging domestic and industrial wastes into the river, that the various pipes are his many poisonous heads. They insist that Kaliya, the symbolic source of pollution, must again be defeated so that the Yamuna can once more be free from all pollution. Paliwal ended his comments by suggesting that the schoolchildren gathered before him on this occasion were a form of Krishna come again to do just that.

Next spoke Govinda Sharma, representative of the pilgrimage guides and priests of Vrindaban. The distinguishing features of Braj are the forest of Vrindaban, Mount Govardhan, and the Yamuna River, he said, declaring that Yamuna is absolutely essential for the divine love play that is celebrated in Braj. He stressed that Krishna loved Yamuna more than all his other lovers, choosing never to leave her. For this reason, she alone is designated as his Chief Lover (*patarani*). "If Krishna loved her that much," Sharma asked, "then how can we pollute her?" He concluded by announcing, "Yamuna-ji is in danger! We must all perform *seva* [loving service] to save her and make her free from pollution."

Sanjiv Mittal, the new District Magistrate who had recently assumed charge of the Mathura District, spoke next. He praised the people of

Figure 12. Krishna dancing on the multiple heads of the poisonous snake Kaliya. Paper stencil by Mohan Kumar Verma.

Vrindaban for working to end the pollution of the Yamuna. In a grandiose manner he declared Vrindaban to be one of the most environmental friendly towns in India and proclaimed that the entire Mathura District should follow suit. He concluded his optimistic remarks—which seemed to disregard the real remaining problems—by saying that the length and strength of the human chain that had occurred that morning showed that the Yamuna would soon be restored to its former condition. Encouraging words from politicians are fine, but the man who took the stage next knew well that more than words were needed to combat pollution and restore the Yamuna.

Gopeshwar Nath Chaturvedi approached the microphone. He needed little introduction, for his name is the one most associated with efforts in Braj to clean the Yamuna. He began by reviewing the achievements prompted by his High Court case. All industrial pipes and more than three dozen domestic drains had been tapped in Vrindaban and Mathura and, therefore, were no longer discharging their untreated effluents directly into the Yamuna. He checked the District Magistrate's optimism by reminding everyone that "Yamuna water at Vishram Ghat in Mathura and at Keshi Ghat in Vrindaban is still polluted." The crowd cheered and clapped loudly, however, when he declared, "But I promise that Yamuna will be free from pollution one day soon!" Chaturvedi ended his speech by saying that because of its religious significance and widespread influence, Vrindaban should become the first place where all pollution of the Yamuna is stopped.

Sewak Sharan, a resident of Vrindaban, spoke next. His environmental sensibility had been awakened one day when he observed a group of men cut down a large tree that was home to several peacocks. A worshipper of Krishna who identified trees with Krishna, he had tried to stop the men but was unsuccessful.[9] Although this experience caused him a great deal of despair, it also opened up a new awareness of the plight of the trees in and around Vrindaban. He had asked himself at the time, "What is the use of your chanting[,] and what is the use of your worship in the temples[,] and what is the use of your taking a bath daily in the Yamuna[,] and what is the use of your daily *parikrama* [circumambulation] round the sacred forest[,] if you can't protect these trees and animals which are part of your devotion[,] whom you consider to be your gurus? If you can't protect them[,] there is no use of any worship."[10] Sharan has since developed an understanding of his religion in ecological terms. He remarked, "When we talk of environment[,] we cannot leave humans out of the picture. If we have to re-create the environment, we will have to consider ourselves. When we start re-creating ourselves[,] we have to look within our hearts and see where we have erred and made mistakes. This means to be religious— to proceed towards God. In this way the environmental approach becomes the religious approach. Ultimately we will have to think for ourselves where we are going wrong in creating this imbalance in nature. If we are not kind to the tree, the ant[,] or some other animal or plant, we are not environmentalists. We have to see Krishna in every being. This is one of the requirements for the environmentalist."[11]

These realizations led Sharan to turn his simple home into a wildlife sanctuary and dedicate his life to exploring ways to save the environment of Braj. In 1991 he successfully persuaded the World Wide Fund for Nature to support a tree planting project in the Vrindaban area that would help regenerate the forest and provide a positive model for the role religion might play in restoring the environment. He was aided in this effort by Ranchor Prime, a British worshipper of Krishna who had come to Vrindaban for devotional purposes. Prime later founded the Friends of Vrindaban, an organization dedicated to cleaning the environment of Braj, planting trees to reforest the region, and working to stop pollution of the Yamuna River.[12]

Today, the organizational and theological leadership of the Friends of Vrindaban are in the hands of Michael Duffy and Shrivatsa Goswami, respectively. Duffy too was present for the January 1 celebration; I had an opportunity to interview him shortly before this occasion. He first came to Vrindaban with his wife, Robyn Beeche, who is a well-known photographer.[13] Both of them fell in love with the delightful display of colors present during Braj festivals, particularly Holi.[14] While Duffy was busy filming and documenting the culture of Braj, he began to experience a desire to do something more for this area and its people. To familiarize himself with rural India, he took long bicycle trips. This earned him the name "Mike on Bike" in the press.[15] After a long journey that followed much of the Narmada River in central India, he talked with a British trustee of the Friends of Vrindaban and together they came up with the idea of organizing a bicycle ride from Yamunotri to Vrindaban, a distance of more than five hundred miles. The purpose of this expedition would be to raise consciousness about the condition of the Yamuna and raise funds for environmental restoration in Braj. The bicycle ride, which took place in October 1996, did both, and it initiated Duffy's entry into Friends of Vrindaban activities. Funds raised by the forty cyclists allowed Friends of Vrindaban to establish itself in India as an independent nongovernmental organization.

Friends of Vrindaban under Duffy's direction began cleaning streets, since they are connected directly to the river. The group employed traditional sweepers and gave them a position of new respect with uniforms and a higher monthly salary. "Perhaps we can't do anything about what comes from upstream," explained Duffy, "but we can do something about our stretch of the river."[16] Over a decade's worth of garbage had accumulated at places on the bank of the river. Under Duffy's supervision, Friends of Vrindaban has worked to reduce these piles, establish a solid waste dumpsite away from the river, and prevent further pollution of the river. During my time spent researching in Vrindaban, local artisans hired by Duffy staged a well-attended folk play titled "Krishna, Your Yamuna Is Defiled" (*Syama Teri Yamuna Maili*). The lengthy play was performed outdoors in the center of Vrindaban. It began by celebrating the religious meaning of Yamuna, and went on to lament the current pollution of the river. Finally, the actors implored the audience to dedicate themselves to restoring Yamuna to her previously glorious condition.

I asked Duffy what motivates his commitment to this environmental work. "The Hindu concept of *seva* motivates my whole life," he told me at his home in a Vrindaban ashram. "It also gives me a sense of purpose in life." Duffy defines his *seva* as "giving loving service to Braj, and thus to the community, for a healthy environment." Under the influence of Shrivatsa Goswami, Duffy has embraced a view of Krishna as the ultimate environmentalist. "I began a relationship with Krishna as the ultimate environmentalist, and came to understand his message as having compassion for all life on Earth. And everything is living, including the trees, rocks, and rivers. I have found my role model and have finally surrendered to that Krishna. By surrendering my life to this *seva*, I feel like I am plugged in directly to grace. To do *seva* to the land is doing *seva* to Krishna. Love is what makes the world go round, and Krishna is the foundation of everything. By 'Krishna' I mean the divine couple. Very importantly this includes the female, Mother. Mother Nature is manifested fully in Braj. Love and pain for Yamuna have become very intense for me, but I can think only optimistically about environmental work, because once you are plugged directly into grace, then you know that things will develop in the right way."

Duffy's ideas have been greatly influenced by his spiritual adviser, Shrivatsa Goswami, who is actively involved in rethinking and articulating Braj Vaishnavism in face of the environmental crisis. I talked with Goswami about this issue on a number of occasions; our last conversation about it took place in his Vrindaban ashram. He was in a grave mood after the death of his aunt and about the fact that, because of the pollution, he was unable to participate in a ritual funeral bath in the Yamuna as his family had done for centuries.[17] "We religious people are hypocrites in our relationship to Yamuna. We say she is pure, but we use Bisleri [a brand of bottled water] in our temples. If Yamuna is pure, let us use Yamuna water; or else let us admit that there is a problem and get on with fixing it. The onus for change is on the religious leaders. It is we who have to do something." As one of the most active and influential eco-theologians in Braj, Goswami has on many occasions articulated an understanding of his religious tradition in environmental terms. His talks and writings are a rich resource for a contemporary Krishna-based eco-spirituality. He has said, "When theology and ecology go together, the players in the theatre of the environment will be able to restore a balanced relationship."[18]

Goswami understands that the greatest challenges we face today are related to environmental problems, and he interprets traditional Vaishnava scripture with this in mind. I asked him how he had come to an ecological way of thinking about theology. He informed me that he looks at current issues through the lens of the *Bhagavata Purana,* the primary foundational text of Braj Vaishnavism.[19] "The way the *Bhagavata* is viewed depends upon who is looking at it. My own time makes me read the *Bhagavata* in an ecological way, but the *Bhagavata* defines my predicament." Goswami claims that our problems today are so great that we need a superhuman model to show us the way out of our current crisis: "We need a historical, tangible person who has made attempts to restore the environment." Looking to his own religious roots, he identifies Krishna as such a person. In his writings, presentations, and sermons, Goswami asserts that Krishna is a model environmentalist, calling him the "ecological guru." "Krishna's whole life in Braj is an environmental story for me. Krishna came in human form to set a human model for ecological restoration." Goswami maintains that, in his incarnation as a cowherd boy, "Krishna's primary responsibility was to restore the ecological balance and conserve the environment. His life gives us a theological model, a script by which a proper play of ecology can be staged."[20]

According to Goswami, there are two dimensions to Krishna's exemplary environmentalism: repairing environmental damage and worshipping nature, "for it is in the greenery of the land of Mother Earth, that true divinity lies and where it must be protected and celebrated by her children, her devotees."[21] Regarding the first, he turns to the *Bhagavata Purana* for fruitful lessons. He points out that the Braj Krishna inhabited was not without serious problems; rather, it was in need of serious environmental restoration. "The waters of the Yamuna were poisonous,

the forest groves were on fire, the winds were in violent turmoil, and no
one paid any attention to the hills."[22] Vaishnava traditions agree that
Krishna came to Braj to give and experience joyful bliss, but Goswami
explains that, according to the *Bhagavata Purana,* this happened only
after Krishna rid the environment of its problems. "Only after Krishna
has set the environment to rights, then, does he achieve the moment of
total enjoyment and bliss."[23] Specifically, this means that he had to
restore the health of the five major elements: "The five elements make
bodily life possible. If our relationship with the five elements is not
proper, then we cannot survive."[24] Krishna restored the water by con-
quering the polluting serpent Kaliya, he restored the air by subduing the
tornadoes, he restored the forests by swallowing the destructive fires, he
restored space by filling it with beautiful melodies, and he restored the
earth by putting some in his mouth. "He said, alright, I have to play in
these grounds, I will make these grounds so pure that anybody can pick
up a little piece of earth and taste it."[25]

In a similar manner, Goswami maintains, only after the environment
has been restored can humans enjoy the divine love that occurs on the
divine playground that is the world. He asserts that the way out of the
current environmental crisis is to intentionally follow a human model of
sanity and compassion, and not to look for help from some transcendent god. "Krishna says you are responsible for your own actions, so
don't look to some transcendent god to get you out of your mess. The
environment is your concern; your duty is to be responsible for it."[26]
Krishna's life in Braj provides a model for environmental restoration,
but it is the responsibility of humans to follow it.

Goswami contends that Krishna is also a model for the worship of
nature, the other key to the ultimate experience of joy. "This path of
green devotion is demonstrated by Krishna. Among all his lilas, only
twice does he get involved in religious rituals. Interestingly, both are
confined to nature worship. He worships only Mount Govardhan, the
home of the trees, cows, animals, and birds."[27] Elsewhere Goswami
writes, "After he had purified all the five elements, Shri Krishna found
that his elders in Vraja were still worried—how to raise the money for
the annual water-tax to the great god Indra? But Krishna, in childish
simplicity[,] pointed out that they should not look to Indra to provide
water—'It is the mountains and the forests that provide the water,' he
said[;] 'Come, let us pay our tax to the forests and mountains—not in
the form of money alone, but with loving concern and care for their
well-being.' So Krishna established the environmental ritual—the worship

of the mountain, the river, the trees, and the animals."[28] According to Goswami, this represents a move away from an overly transcendent view of divinity to a more immanent view. The world itself in Braj Vaishnavism is considered divine; it is the resulting manifestation of the love affair between Krishna and his lover Radha, as well as the play-ground for further love play between the amorous god and goddess. "The cloud-blue boy passionately sought the company of the golden-yellow gopi Radha, and in the union of blue and yellow, to create a green in the spiritual as well as physical world."[29] Moreover, Krishna's worshipful acts suggest that true enjoyment of the world depends upon an appreciative or reverent attitude. For this reason, what Krishna exemplifies most significantly is love. "The ultimate aim of Krishna is to establish the human value of love. Love is the key to all sustainable living."[30]

Goswami sharply distinguishes true love from exploitation. "My story is a very short and very repetitive story, that ecological disasters come if we exploit."[31] As an alternative, "[Krishna's] love is not to sub-jugate or exploit nature, but to celebrate it."[32] Exploitation involves acts performed to satisfy one's egoistic self, whereas love involves acts performed for the satisfaction of others. "With what technique can we protect our environment?" he asks. "This technology is relation-ship through love, through devotion, through giving and serving."[33] Relationship (sambandha) comes from that feeling of being vitally inter-related with someone or something, that sense of being intimately con-nected to someone or something outside of the egoistic self. "It is the total flowing into each other, total flow of identity into each other[,] and that is what the process of love calls the religion."[34] In this way, a person does not protect some natural form primarily out of a morally imposed sense of duty, but rather out of a sense of appreciation that flows naturally from deep connection. The highest form of living, according to Goswami, does not aim for self-gain, but to please the other, to express apprecia-tive love. Thus, he remarks, "this Sambandha [loving relationship] is the key to ecology."[35] When this deep relationship flavors one's percep-tion of the world of nature, then one enters into a loving interaction with the natural world that is marked with appreciation, protection, and celebration. One's reward for this is the experience of limitless joy. "This relationship is one of love. Krishna says very clearly that the model relationship is love and love is a relationship of mutual enjoy-ment, with no other transaction than itself. Enjoyment replaces exploita-tion, it resolves differences of all kinds—social, economic, cultural, or any other. It brings us to mutuality, because the characteristic of love is enjoyment of the others' pleasure. Nature enjoys being enjoyed, as anyone who has spent time in nature understands, but reacts furiously to exploitation."[36]

Therefore, everything depends on falling in love, even with a polluted world. A world seen through the eyes of love is a very different world. Love is both a means to environmental restoration and the end result of environmental enjoyment. Krishna is once again the model: "So Krishna took this project by leading. He first fell in love with the horrible Vrindavana. He did not fall in love with a beautiful Vrindavana, I tell you. He fell in love with a Vrindavana when it was on fire, the river was totally poisonous, where the winds were hurricanes, everything was upside down. He fell in love, and love as you know is to serve and give."[37] Here again, we encounter the important idea of *seva*, loving service, that is exemplified in Krishna's own attitude toward Yamuna. "To water He gives a status of a girlfriend, not less respect than that, the highest love relationship ever possible."[38] Vrindaban is an important pilgrimage center, drawing to its sacred sites and temples thousands of people every day from all over India and other parts of the world.[39] Because of this, Goswami is working to nurture his vision of environmental health in Vrindaban, so that "it can serve to nourish a vision of nature worldwide. Efforts are underway; studies are being made so as to reawaken consciousness of Vrindavana, so that devotion to the natural world again becomes a vital part of human life."[40] He is the chief patron and theologian today behind the environmental nongovernmental organization Friends of Vrindaban, which is now housed in a temple belonging to his family, and he speaks out for protection and restoration of the Yamuna whenever he gets the chance.[41]

Sewak Sharan, representing the founders of the Friends of Vrindaban, remains deeply concerned with what is happening to the Yamuna. Thus, he too was present onstage at the "Celebration of Loving Service to Yamuna," which took place in Vrindaban on the first day of the new millennium. He concluded his remarks by saying that original Yamuna water should be allowed to flow from the source all the way to the ocean. This is a major issue for the residents of Braj, who are all too aware of what becomes of the Yamuna as it passes through Delhi.[42] Sharan's wish is to let Yamuna move as a free river from her beginning to her end. He proclaimed that "the ocean of people who have gathered here today for Yamuna *seva* can help reawaken faith and restore Yamuna to her former condition." He then shouted, "Jaya Shri Yamuna Maiya," which was echoed enthusiastically by the audience, and returned to his seat.

Lakshminarayan Pathank, then chairman of the Vrindaban municipality, approached the microphone next. "On this first day of a new millennium, we all need to recognize that Yamuna is the Mother of us all! She gives us water to drink and to grow our food. She is the Chief Lover [patarani] of Shri Krishna and should be honored by all people. Yamuna is particularly special for us in Vrindaban. It is the responsibility of all of us to make sure that we do not throw garbage from our homes into the Yamuna." He promised that the municipality would make a great effort to see that, from then on, all drains that had been tapped would be kept in good working condition so no sewage from Vrindaban would flow into the Yamuna.

The last speaker to take the stage was Swami Maheshananda, another local religious leader concerned about the environmental problems in his region. He began by identifying the essential features of the sacred land of Braj as the Vrindaban forest, Mount Govardhan, and the Yamuna River. Regarding these, he insisted that Yamuna first had to be made free from pollution, otherwise the sacred site of Vrindaban would be defiled. He too evoked the story of Krishna removing the pollution from the Yamuna in a former age by defeating the poisonous snake Kaliya, and he urged the audience to do seva for Yamuna, showing her the respect she deserved by ridding her of all pollutants.

Shouts of "Jaya Shri Yamuna Maiya!" rent the air as the speeches ended and the audience filed into a nearby exhibition showcasing the government's efforts to control pollution in the river. The exhibit was opened by O. P. Singhal, project manager for the Yamuna Action Plan in Mathura and Vrindaban. When I interviewed Singhal in his office in Mathura later in the year, he sat under a sign in Hindi that read, "Holy Yamuna is the beloved of all people. Yamuna's water is pure and cool."[43] Singhal had worked as a civil engineer for the Uttar Pradesh Jal Nigam (Water Department) since 1977 and had served as the project manager for the Yamuna Pollution Control Unit in Mathura since 1983. When the Yamuna Action Plan was inaugurated, he was put in charge of implementing the plan in the Mathura District.

The Yamuna Action Plan, or YAP, as it is commonly called, was initiated in Delhi on June 5, 1993, by Kamal Nath, then minister for the environment and forests. The plan aims to intercept, divert, and treat the municipal wastewater from six cities in the state of Haryana, eight cities in the state of Uttar Pradesh (including Mathura and Vrindaban), and Delhi.[44] The project is also to include the construction of community toilets and improved crematoria, afforestation along the river, and efforts to increase environmental awareness through public education. The estimated cost of the project is well over one hundred million U.S. dollars; it is financed by a large loan from the government of Japan. YAP was initiated as part of the second phase of the Ganga Action Plan.

The Ganga Action Plan, commonly known as GAP, was launched dramatically in the holy city of Banaras (Varanasi) on June 14, 1985, by Prime Minister Rajiv Gandhi, who promised, "We shall see that the waters of the Ganga become clean once again."[45] The stated task was "to improve water quality, permit safe bathing all along the 2,525 kilometers from the Ganga's origin in the Himalayas to the Bay of Bengal, and make the water potable at important pilgrim and urban centres on its banks."[46] The project was designed to tackle pollution from twenty-five cities and towns along its banks in Uttar Pradesh, Bihar, and West Bengal by intercepting, diverting, and treating their effluents. With the GAP's Phase II, three important tributaries—the Damodar, Gomati, and Yamuna—were added to the plan. Although some improvements have been made to the quality of the Ganges's water, many people claim that GAP has been a major failure. The environmental lawyer M. C. Mehta, for example, filed public interest litigation against the project, claiming, "GAP has collapsed."[47]

Singhal was put in charge of overseeing YAP projects in Mathura and Vrindaban, with orders to install two sewage treatment plants in each town. At the time of my first interview with him in April 2000, he told me that approximately 90 percent of the YAP projects in Vrindaban had been finished and close to 85 percent had been finished in Mathura.[48] Specifically, he said this meant that most of the drains flowing into the Yamuna from Vrindaban and Mathura had been stopped, and that the two sewage treatment plants planned for Vrindaban had already been completed and the two for Mathura were near completion. He explained that the main job remaining to be done in Mathura was the installation of a pipeline under a railway bridge that would carry treated sewage water across the river to be used for irrigation. Singhal seemed very proud of his system. I asked him if he had encountered any failures in the project. He replied confidently, "None!" and proceeded to assign the report grade of "A" for the project.

When I informed him that just the day before our talk I had seen drains in Vrindaban blocked with plastic bags and other refuse, causing untreated wastewater to spill directly into the Yamuna, he placed the blame on the municipal government. "The Vrindaban municipal government is responsible for keeping the drains clean, and they have been doing a better job than in the past. But I tell you that only 5 percent of the sewage is going into the Yamuna in Vrindaban." Singhal admitted that the greatest challenge to the sewage treatment system was ongoing maintenance. "We need to make the people maintain the system. Once a car is built, it needs a good driver. Socially vigilant people need to put pressure on the local authorities to maintain the system and to stop people from polluting the river." This, he claimed, all depends on education.

Singhal, who told me that he personally viewed the Yamuna as a "holy river," believes that environmental education in this region must be linked with religion in order to be successful. As part of the effort to raise public awareness about river pollution, his office posted many signs along the Yamuna in Mathura and Vrindaban. These give expression to a confluence of religious and environmental ideas and are perhaps significant signs of hope that environmental restoration will occur in the region. Some of them simply instruct the public to take care of the river: "Keeping Yamuna pure is your duty." "Spreading pollution in Yamuna is a punishable offense."[49] "Keep Yamuna clean." "Keep Yamuna flowing uninterrupted."[50]

A much lengthier sign has been posted at Keshi Ghat in Vrindaban as part of the YAP educational program. These, in effect, outline the *yamas* (don'ts) and *niyamas* (dos) of river care:

YOU SHOULD NOT DO THESE THINGS:

1. Don't defecate or urinate at river's edge.
2. Don't use soap when you bathe in the river.
3. Don't put dead bodies in the river.
4. Don't let animals, such as buffaloes and cows, wander unrestrained in the river.
5. Don't throw household garbage in empty places along the river.
6. Throw no leaf plates or plastic bags in the drains outside your house.
7. Don't make the river steps dirty.
8. Don't make the town dirty.
9. Don't cut trees.

YOU SHOULD DO THESE THINGS:

1. Defecate and urinate in the public toilets.
2. Bathe in the river without soap.
3. Cremate bodies in the crematorium.

4. Keep animals under control.
5. Collect household garbage and put it in a trash bin.
6. Put leaf plates and plastic bags in a trash bin.
7. Keep the river steps clean.
8. Keep the town clean.
9. Adopt a healthy, beneficial attitude toward all life and protect the greenery.

One sign even tries to unify different religious communities in a joint effort to stop pollution of the river: "Hindus and Muslims should come together and drive the pollution far from the Yamuna."[51] Others take on a much more personalized or even devout tone: "Pure Yamuna is the beloved of the people. Yamuna's water is clean and cool."[52] "Water is a priceless inheritance of nature. You should give it your love and protection."[53]

The theological shift suggested by this last sign is noteworthy: Yamuna is represented not as an all-powerful divinity but rather as a possibly vulnerable one in need of loving protection. This perspective is also evident in the most popular of the signs posted in Vrindaban and Mathura, which urges people to engage in restorative actions on behalf of Yamuna: "Mother Yamuna has given so much. Now Yamuna asks for loving service [seva]."[54] In the context of the religious culture associated with the Yamuna a few decades ago, the word seva would have referred almost exclusively to ritual acts of worship, such as offering flowers, milk, hymns, and incense to the river goddess. Now this term is increasingly being used to designate acts that would in the West be labeled environmental activism. YAP officials such as Singhal and local religious leaders alike are engaged in educational efforts that both cultivate and make use of the emerging religious view that the river Mother who cared for her human children now needs them to care for her.

The last time I saw Singhal was in November 2001, while he was in Vrindaban helping to enlist the Vrindaban boatmen in preventing future pollution of the river. He told me very hopefully on this occasion, "Now things are changing rapidly. Look [pointing toward the river]! For a long time people washed their clothes, dumped their refuse, and bathed their buffaloes in the Yamuna. Now all of that has almost completely stopped. All of the drains in Vrindaban have now been tapped, and all but three small ones in Mathura have been tapped. And all STPs [sewage treatment plants] in Mathura and Vrindaban are now functioning."[55] Regardless of whether Singhal's hopefulness about what is happening in Braj is warranted or not, one still wonders what is coming downstream from Delhi.

Most of the people I spoke with in Vrindaban and Mathura are aware that the greatest threat to the Yamuna comes from Delhi. Although Delhi is neither a great religious center, nor a site of conscious development of ongoing Yamuna theology, some of the environmental concerns and signs of hope that manifest in Braj are being expressed there too. One organization working to improve the condition of the Yamuna in Delhi is the Paani Morcha, a nongovernmental organization founded by Sureshwar Sinha.[56] I interviewed Sinha in Vrindaban, where he had come to organize a classical musical performance in celebration of a recent Supreme Court ruling ordering the government to maintain a certain minimum flow of freshwater in the Yamuna.

Sinha is the former naval officer mentioned in chapter 3 who had been stationed in Delhi since the late 1940s. Over the course of several decades, he had watched with anguish as the water quality of the Yamuna deteriorated. The day he witnessed a boy become violently ill from falling into the Yamuna, his distress moved him to take action. Realizing that children were dying because of polluted water, Sinha felt compelled to act. Aided by a naval chief, he filed a complaint with the government of Delhi in the late 1980s, but his complaint went unanswered. In 1992 he filed a PIL in the Supreme Court that aimed to stop untreated sewage from entering the Yamuna and to maintain a minimum flow of 356 cusecs of freshwater throughout the river. The government argued that nothing could be done about these problems because of the large increase in population, and the Court accepted their position. Sinha, however, would not give up.

He founded the Paani Morcha (meaning "Water Front": the group considers itself to be the "front line" of a political battle to restore the Yamuna) in 1994 in order to stop the release of untreated sewage and industrial waste into the Yamuna in Delhi and to press for regulations to maintain a minimum flow of freshwater in the river. Members of the Paani Morcha began their efforts by first conducting extensive research on water quality at points along the entire Yamuna. The organization focused on solutions in the megacity of Delhi, but it also maintained ties with the religious communities in Vrindaban and, especially, with Shrivatsa Goswami. Sinha acknowledged that his work is motivated in part by religious concerns. He explained, "I belong to a family of Shaivites, so I am a devotee of Ganga. But since Yamuna is the sister of Ganga,

I am a devotee of her too."[57] In 1995, under Sinha's guidance, Paani Morcha filed a report with the government of Delhi that expressed concern about ritual bathing in the river and offered a biological solution to the sewage problem. The report proposed the *eco-baag* (eco-garden) system, which uses a series of ponds planted with vegetation that naturally filters out sewage before the water is returned to the river. Understanding that the river needs a minimum flow in order to clean itself, Paani Morcha also promoted the PIL that Sinha had previously filed to bring this about. The Supreme Court ruled in May 1999 that a minimum flow of 356 cusecs, or about 10 cubic meters per second, must be maintained throughout the Yamuna. This order was to be executed within two weeks. Since this was not done, Sinha filed a contempt petition to put pressure on the government to enforce the Court's ruling. This effort continues.

Sinha admitted that he and his work were initially received with great hostility; but as the problems became more and more severe, people began listening to him. This included not only governmental officials but also religious people, though not all. "Pollution," he speculated, "may not yet be bad enough to affect the religious behavior of all people. The value of bathing in a river is still greater than the risk of pollution for many people. But the time may soon come when all that changes."

The institution that has allowed Sinha and other activists to pressure the government to change its river policies is the Supreme Court. The founders of the Indian nation gave the judiciary the right to stop any law or executive action that went against the Constitution. But with environmental problems growing by alarming leaps, and with the executive branch demonstrating little ability to cope with them, the Court found itself in a position to take a more proactive role in environmental protection. In the late 1980s, Supreme Court Justice P. N. Bhagwati ruled that the right to life guaranteed in the Indian Constitution included the right to a healthy environment.[58] This opened the way for a powerful public interest litigation movement that allowed concerned citizens to petition judges to rule against propagators of environmental damage. The PIL has permitted judges to close down polluting industries; protect forests and other natural features of the environment, including rivers; and raise environmental consciousness in the country. The application of the PIL to environmental problems is another sign of hope on the bleak landscape of ecological destruction. Rajeev Dhavan, a senior advocate of the Supreme Court, argues, "What PIL did was that it created a new institution of governance. In effect, the judiciary said, you just bring your problems to us and we will devise solutions for them."[59] Environmentalists' use of the PIL has been defended along constitutional lines, since the Constitution states, "It shall be the duty of every citizen to protect and improve the environment, including forests, lakes, rivers and wildlife and to have compassion for living creatures."[60]

While many would agree that the regulation of environmental protection should be located within the administrative system, the persistent failure of the executive branch of the government created a need for the courts to assume this role. And doubts remain as to whether the executive branch will resume its responsibilities as watchdog of the environment. Dhavan says, "An inactive and inept government regulatory system invited judicial activism. If judicial activism reverts to its previous less-activist discipline, will the system suddenly find an activist environmental courage which has so shamelessly deserted it in the past?"[61] India has some of the best environmental legislation in the world, but the executive branch has failed repeatedly to enforce the laws. This has left an enforcement void that the courts have attempted to fill. In 1988, for example, Justice E. S. Venkataramiah enforced the Water Pollution Control Act of 1974 by closing down tanneries polluting the Ganges.[62] The Supreme Court advocate M. C. Mehta insists, "The judiciary is the only organ in our democracy which is working. The Supreme Court of India is doing a tremendous job. It is not the ministry of environment or pollution control boards which are controlling pollution, it is the Supreme Court."[63] Thus, many continue to look to the courts for help in protecting the environment, and their numbers are increasing.

The trickle of environmental PILs that began in the 1980s had surged by the mid-1990s. One result of this torrent of activity is what has been called the "green bench." Environmental cases have become so numerous that the Supreme Court has set Fridays aside to deal with environmental matters. The question remains, however, whether the courts can actually be effective in the area of enforcement. "'Orders passed by the Supreme Court do not get translated into reality,' says Chatrapati Singh, director of the Centre for Environmental Law of the World Wide Fund for Nature (WWF)."[64] Veer Bhadra Mishra of Banaras, frustrated with the failure to enforce environmental laws, said, "The Supreme Court can even order the Yamuna to flow backwards, but they still can't make it do so."[65] The need for better executive implementation of existing laws is clearly evident.

One place the Supreme Court's proactive policies have been noticed is
Delhi. There the Court has put a great deal of pressure on industries polluting the Yamuna to clean up their act. Much of this has been the result
of a PIL filed by the environmental lawyer M. C. Mehta. The *Hindustan
Times* reported, for example, on April 9, 1998, "The Supreme Court
today directed all the water polluting industries in Delhi to either contribute their share of Rs 40 crore for setting up 28 common effluent
treatment plants (CETPs) or face closure of their units."[66] Unfortunately, such announcements are so common that one might indeed
wonder how effective judicial enforcement really is. Nonetheless, the
Supreme Court has done a good job of keeping the polluted condition
of the Yamuna on everyone's mind and maintaining pressure on the
Delhi government. The *Times of India* reported on September 20, 1999,
"Once again, the Supreme Court has intervened decisively to prevent
further degradation of the Yamuna by asking industries discharging
effluents into the river to install treatment plants by November 1 or face
closure."[67] Hundreds of polluting units had been shut down by the end
of 1999, and hundreds more had been served notice at the beginning of
the new millennium.[68] The *Hindustan Times* published a similar report
but added that the Delhi government has sought extensions while claiming that "the industries would need more time to set up effluent treatment plants and [that] their sudden closure would lead to a lot of
unemployment."[69] On January 24, 2000, the *Hindustan Times* reported,
"Taking serious note of the pollution level of the Yamuna river, the
Supreme Court today banned discharge of untreated industrial effluent
into the river or any drain leading into it in the Capital and Haryana."[70]
According to this article, the Supreme Court chided the Delhi government for failing to comply with its earlier order that fixed November 1,
1999, as the deadline to stop all discharge of untreated effluent into the
river. The bench ruled that "public health should be given top most
priority even at the cost of a few jobs."

The government of Delhi, however, keeps dragging its feet. On
May 12, 2000, a front-page article in the *Hindustan Times* read,
"Incensed over the Delhi Government's inaction to improve the quality
of the Yamuna's water, the Supreme Court today slapped a fine of
RS10,000 on the Government saying 'mere promises to improve the
quality of the water is not enough.'"[71] Justice B. N. Kirpal and Justice
Ruma Pal ruled, "The Government must govern, implement and
enforce its own rules and regulations to ensure that the river is clean. . . .
We will hold the Government responsible [for not implementing the

Court's orders]. You [the Government] have ample powers to set things right. . . . Excuses are all we got." The *Times of India* also covered this case, reporting that the Supreme Court justified the fine because "the Yamuna today is worse than a drain with no dissolved oxygen in it."[72] This article also reported that two days after the fine was given, it had already been suspended upon the government's assurance that it was doing its best. One wonders what went on behind the scenes.

The Supreme Court has also pressured the Delhi government to more effectively treat domestic sewage and has been frustrated in this area as well. On July 10, 2000, *The Hindu* reported, "Exasperated with the Delhi government's inept steps to clean the Yamuna, the Supreme Court on Tuesday warned the administration of stringent penalty if the quality of the river water was not improved within three months."[73] The Court threatened fines and "further action," remarking, "Yamuna is only a drain which resembles a river in the monsoons and remains a drain for the rest of the year." This same article reported that the Court noted that the permissible level of coliform—an indicator of human sewage—was 5,000 per 100 ml, whereas levels of over 1 million per 100 ml had been recorded in the Yamuna in Delhi. The Court has also locked horns with the National River Conservation Authority in Delhi. In May 2001 it identified the main source of pollution as untreated sewage and questioned a 2005 deadline set by the National River Conservation Authority for Delhi to stop releasing untreated sewage into the river. "A bench headed by Justice B. N. Kirpal had asked the Centre on August 4 'to explain why, despite orders having been passed regarding the cleaning up of the Yamuna, the river regarded as holy by many, will continue to be polluted at least until 2005.'"[74] On April 10, 2001, the Supreme Court set a firm deadline, ordering the Delhi government to clean up the river by March 31, 2003.[75] The *Indian Express* recorded the judgment: "The Supreme Court today set March 31, 2003, as the deadline for cleaning up the Yamuna after it grew tired of telling agencies the importance of keeping the 'life-line of Delhi free from pollution.'"[76] With increasing frustration, the Court asked the Delhi government to file an affidavit laying out "what steps would be taken to improve the quality of water, so that the river can no longer be called '*mailee* [dirty] Yamuna' after March 31, 2003."[77]

Efforts to clean the Yamuna in Delhi have been spearheaded publicly by Delhi's chief minister, Shiela Dixit. In June 2000 she traveled to London to investigate whether the successful effort to revive the Thames River could be applied to the Yamuna. Upon her return she announced,

"Yamuna river can be cleaned and given a new look following the methodology adopted at river Thames. . . . Even river Thames was as dirty as river Yamuna not long ago. But British experts took timely measures and brought down the pollution level."[78] Under Dixit's guidance, Delhi's Department of Environment published notices in the city's newspapers. One shows a picture of a flock of pigeons perched on a log floating in the Yamuna. The caption above the picture reads, "Yamuna river does not belong to Man alone."[79] Below the picture are the words "Nature has given Delhi a very precious gift of the river Yamuna. But we, the people of Delhi, have turned this gift into a garbage dump— now polluted by dirt, dead animals, harmful toxins and effluents. This once beautiful river is now a sewer of slime and poison. But all is not lost. If we, the citizens of Delhi, believe in the goodness of Nature, let us start by not polluting our river. Because we must always remember that the Yamuna does not belong to Delhi. Delhi belongs to the Yamuna." Large bold letters at the bottom of the notice drive home this last point: "YAMUNA PRESERVATION. We belong to the river." In another newspaper ad, Dixit's picture is positioned beside a bold caption that reads, "Clean water is everyone's right. Let's conserve our natural resources. Generations to come will pay the price. *Stop Polluting Yamuna.*"[80] Delhi's government plans to clean the Yamuna are listed in this public notice. These include raising the sewage treatment plants' capacity significantly over the next several years, building fifteen common effluent treatment plants for industrial waste, monitoring and closing polluting industries, and repairing the major drain systems in the city. Under pressure from the Supreme Court, Delhi's government also organized a drive to clean up the riverbanks, collecting plastic bags and other accumulated refuse. Thirty-six truckloads of waste were hauled away after five days of work by volunteers in June 2001. Chief Minister Dixit was pictured in the newspapers participating in the cleanup drive and pressing for greater public awareness about river pollution.

Critics of the government's efforts allege, however, that they simply disguise the government's failure to take the steps necessary to stop the pollution and clean the river. Manoj Nadkarni of the Centre for Science and Environment insists, "Efforts to clean Yamuna have ended up as photo opportunities, while the actual problems are still unaddressed."[81] An article titled "The Great Sham" that appeared in the Centre for Science and Environment's fortnightly magazine, *Down to Earth,* alleges that the Delhi government's efforts are "more to create drama than to serve any real purpose."[82] Many featured in the article argued that Dixit's program serves only to camouflage serious problems. For example, Anupam Mishra, an environmentalist who is current head of the Gandhi Peace Foundation, says regarding the government's campaign to clean the Yamuna, "The government is fooling the people. The campaign is a sham." R. C. Trivedi, a senior scientist with the Central Pollution Control Board asks, "How can the government generate public awareness about the Yamuna when it doesn't even know how to clean it? . . . Cleaning the river in just a few days is impossible." He repeated his well-known position that the quality of the water in the Yamuna will improve only after a minimum flow of water is maintained by the government; despite court orders, the government has not done so. Sureshwar Sinha, chairperson of Paani Morcha, remarks, "This drive may just clean the banks, but will make little difference to the river." Picking up refuse scattered on the banks of the Yamuna will have a positive aesthetic effect, but does not tackle the more serious problems. The article's authors claim, "Not a single sewage treatment plant is functioning, thus making Yamuna a colossal drain for Delhi." Concerned citizens of India look to see whether the government's efforts will produce concrete changes to cope with the more egregious problems of domestic and industrial waste. But many people simply wonder whether the government will continue to simply "YAP YAP YAP."[83]

At the close of 2002, the *Hindustan Times* ran an article summing up the efforts to date: "Despite the government pouring in lakhs of rupees into the second phase of the Ganga Action Plan, which envisaged restoring the Yamuna to its old pristine self, the pollution levels in the river remain very high. The ambitious plan to clean the river has clearly flopped."[84] Delhi's government produced many words but undertook little action to stop the release of untreated sewage into the Yamuna by the March 31, 2003, deadline set by the Supreme Court. Another article published in the *Hindustan Times* at the end of 2002, titled "Deadline Near, but Yamuna Dirty," read, "With just three months to the Apex Court deadline on cleaning Yamuna and the river as dirty as ever, the Delhi state government is clearly in trouble. Most of the Yamuna Action Plan, drawn after the Supreme Court fixed a deadline of March 31, 2003, to make the river water potable, is still on paper."[85] Messages from my contacts in Delhi communicated very clearly that the deadline came and went without any significant change,[86] and I concluded my own tracking of this issue on this date. A full year after the Supreme Court's deadline, Subijoy Dutta, who established the Yamuna Foundation for Blue Water to address social justice issues related to Yamuna's pollution in the Agra region, wrote to me, "Yamuna Devi is really getting hurt, and I am afraid that one day she may just give up the life support she is providing to the millions of poor people living on her bank in the Delhi-Agra stretch."[87] Governmental words and actions seem to represent well the hope and hopelessness of the situation for rivers in northern India today.

As noted earlier, after the confluence of the Yamuna and Ganges at Allahabad, the combined rivers are called the Ganges, despite the fact that more water enters the joint channel from the Yamuna than from the Ganges. Nonetheless, many devotees of the Yamuna continue to regard the combined rivers as the Yamuna.[88] Regardless of perspective, the Yamuna and Ganges are intimately related and are often referred to as "sisters." Religio-environmental events happening along the Yamuna have their parallel on the Ganges and are centered on the most significant religious site located on the bank of the combined rivers: Banaras. The person most connected with religiously motivated environmental efforts in this holy city is Veer Bhadra Mishra, internationally the best known of those working on river pollution in India. He is also known simply as Mahant-ji, a title indicating his position as head priest of Sankat Mochan, the famous temple of the sixteenth-century saint Tulsidas.

Mahant-ji has a fascinating dual identity: in addition to being head priest of one of Banaras's most important temples, he is also a professor of hydraulic engineering in the Civil Engineering Department at Banaras Hindu University, one of the best academic institutions in India. The latter identity gives him access to scientific perspectives on river pollution (he even supervises a lab designed to monitor pollution levels in the Ganges), while the former locates him within a traditional Hindu world. Noting with increasing concern the worsening pollution of the Ganges, in 1982 Mahant-ji founded the Sankat Mochan Foundation, a nongovernmental organization dedicated to cleaning this sacred river. Since then, he has campaigned tirelessly for environmental causes connected with cleaning and protecting the Ganges; he has been a watchdog against pollution of the Ganges and has been directly involved in designing sewage technology appropriate for Banaras. Mahant-ji represents this work in deeply religious terms; he is a fervent devotee of the Ganges who organizes and participates in both private and public worship of the river goddess. He knows much about the dangerous pollution in the river, and yet continues to honor her by immersing himself in her daily.

"I know all about the pollution, but I cannot leave my Mother," Mahant-ji told me during an interview at his home on the bank of the

Ganges in Banaras.[89] He spoke about the polluted condition of the river with much anguish but also expressed a deep love for her. The combination of this knowledge and love "created a great turmoil in my life that has manifest itself in this work." He explained his lifework this way: "God has given me a heart and a mind. There is a road for the heart and a road for the mind. The heart must respond to the goddess, while the mind must tend to the pollution. Religion and science must work together like two banks of a river." Following this twofold track, Mahant-ji has employed his dual vocation as religious priest and university professor to bring both spheres to bear on the problem of river pollution.

Mahant-ji's concerns are not only for Mother Ganges but also for the religious sentiments of her devotees. An increase in river pollution signals a decrease in river worship. "Human beings have carried faith in rivers for thousands of years, but now people who worship rivers are an endangered species. For their sake too the rivers should not be polluted." According to Mahant-ji, not only do humans have a right to worship rivers but also river worship is the key to environmental protection of rivers. "If religion is not there, people will not work to clean Ganges. Religion is the main motivation for environmental work." In fact, Mahant-ji maintains that talk of pollution alone diminishes people's faith and will only deter them from joining in efforts to clean the river, whereas talk of the need to do *seva* for Mother Ganges will encourage them.

Mahant-ji is well aware of the efforts and challenges to restore the Yamuna in the region of Braj. He told me to take the following message back to people working to clean the Yamuna in Braj, "Why are you cleaning a nonexistent river? Minimum flow is a necessary condition of any river. Court actions are not enough to correct the situation. Citizen actions are desperately needed. Someone in Vrindaban or Mathura must lead a citizens' action to force them to maintain minimum flow. Being nice is fine, but there comes a point when you have to fight. After all, even Rama had to fight one day!"

Mahant-ji was hopeful that efforts to clean the Ganges and Yamuna will ultimately be successful. "I am optimistic through and through. Some day it will happen, I tell you. Even if this is an irrational statement, it doesn't matter. This is my faith. Pessimism will only defeat us. Ganges and Yamuna are in the hearts of millions. People support this work; thus we will be successful—though it may take many years."

The degree of success that Mahant-ji and others in Banaras achieve will largely depend upon what happens upstream. Just as the health of the Yamuna in Braj is linked to what happens upstream in Delhi, so too the health of the Ganges in Banaras is linked to what happens in the large industrial city of Kanpur, the major source of pollution for the Ganges.[90] In addition to the domestic sewage of the city, which has a population of more than three million, Kanpur has a huge tanning industry, which consists of more than four hundred tanneries. Several of these date back to when Kanpur was the major center for supplying the British colonial army with leather saddles and other leather products. Particularly worrisome is the large amount of chromium used in the modern tanning process and then released into the Ganges with industrial effluents. But Kanpur too has its spiritual eco-warrior in the figure of Rakesh Jaiswal, founder of Eco-Friends, a nongovernmental organization established in Kanpur to fight the pollution of the Ganges.

One day in 1993, Jaiswal opened the tap in his house and black, foul-smelling water came out. He investigated and found out that his water came from the Ganges. He took a closer look at the condition of the river and was horrified by what he found. Urgent action was called for. He stopped work on his doctorate in political science and founded Eco-Friends, an organization that has done much to raise awareness about pollution in the Ganges. Recognizing that environmental action is limited without environmental education, he visited many schools, colleges, and universities in his area to awaken students to the deteriorating condition of the Ganges and inspired them to demonstrate their concerns in political rallies. In June 1994 he organized an expedition from Kanpur to Gomukh, the glacial source of the river; and in 1997 he organized a boat journey from Kanpur to the oceanic end of the river, near Calcutta. The boat was equipped with a temple dedicated to the goddess Ganges. Jaiswal held seventy meetings, drawing large crowds along the course of the journey to educate people about the condition of the river, to worship the river, and to rally support to save Mother Ganges.

Following these journeys, Jaiswal resolved to initiate legal action. Like Gopeshwar Nath Chaturvedi in Mathura, he filed public interest litigation in the High Court of Allahabad. The aim of his litigation was to stop the discharge of untreated domestic sewage and industrial effluents into the Ganges in the entire state of Uttar Pradesh. The case is still pending, but in May 1998 the court ordered the closure of all industries without primary effluent-treatment plants. As a result of Jaiswal's PIL, 117 tanneries were closed in Kanpur, 40 sari-printing factories were closed in Banaras, and 10 carpet-dyeing units were closed in Mirzapur. The court also ordered the Uttar Pradesh Pollution Control Board to set up river police and monitor the river quality in the state. Jaiswal also works to keep pressure on the municipality of Kanpur to limit the amount of untreated sewage it releases into the Ganges. There is a large gap, however, between court orders and implementation in India today. Although Jaiswal accomplished much, he was determined to demonstrate that more needed to be done. What did he have in mind and what motivated him?

I met Jaiswal in Kanpur in early March 2000, the day before Shiva Ratri, the most important festival day for the god Shiva in the Hindu calendar. Jaiswal described himself as a deeply religious man, a devotee of Shiva, and told me that his work is inspired by Shiva. He represented his environmental work as a way of honoring Shiva and rendering loving service, or *seva,* to the goddess Ganges. Jaiswal emphasized the close relationship between Shiva and Ganges, who is often viewed as Shiva's consort. Jaiswal's first name, Rakesh, a name of Shiva that means "Lord of the Moon," comes from images of Shiva with the moon and the Ganges intertwined in his hair. Jaiswal said this means that, as a devotee of Shiva, he is intimately connected to the Ganges. Thus, Jaiswal chose the day of Shiva Ratri to organize a direct action that would block one of the biggest of the drains that still flowed from many of the tanneries of Kanpur straight into the Ganges.

"There is no better day to block this drain than on Shiva Ratri," Jaiswal explained, "because working to stop the pollution of the Ganges on that auspicious day will be the greatest form of devotion to Lord Shiva. For the river flows from his matted locks, and polluting the river is equivalent to insulting Lord Shiva by dumping all the sewage on his head."[91] (Water from the Ganges is ritually poured over Shiva lingams as an expression of worship.) The direct action he organized was successful. The police, who were present throughout the well-organized event, did not dare to arrest Jaiswal but instead begged him to stop the action for fear of a riot. Soon after the drain was blocked, a troupe of Eco-Friends left in triumph, shouting, "Ganga Maiya ki Jaya! [All Glory to Mother Ganges!]" This is another example of direct action motivated by strong religious conviction; Jaiswal explicitly articulated his environmental work as *seva* to Shiva and the goddess Ganges.

Environmental education and action motivated by religious sentiment is also happening further upstream at the sacred places of Haridwar and Rishikesh. For example, Swami Chidanand Saraswati, often called simply "Muni-ji," of the Parmarth Niketan Ashram has established a program called the Parmarth Ganga Seva Nidhi, which is dedicated to cleaning the Ganges in both Banaras and Rishikesh. Muni-ji organized a camp at the January-February 2001 Kumbha Mela in Allahabad. His program there included a five-day conference, "Ecology and the Ganges," and a nightly waving of the *arati* flames at the confluence of the Yamuna and Ganges. The conference included discussion of the environmental condition of the sacred rivers in India, with a special emphasis on cleaning and protecting the Ganges. In a pamphlet produced by the Parmarth Niketan for this occasion, Muni-ji wrote, "India is the only land where rivers, mountains, trees and animals are not only respected, but also worshipped. In today's age of environmental awareness and ecological conservation, everyone knows that mountains, rivers, and trees are great natural resources which must be preserved, conserved and used wisely. We have seen the devastating consequences of deforestation, over-industrialization and the pollution of our water sources. Yet, Indian culture has preached reverence for nature since its inception so many thousands of years ago. The nectar that Kumbha Mela must disseminate today is a renewed respect for our Earth and her animals, a re-dedication to the laws of our scriptures, and a re-kindled fire of spiritual yearning in our souls."[92]

The Parmarth Niketan Ashram is helping spread a new consciousness about environmental awareness on a continuous basis. One of the stated objectives of the ashram in Rishikesh is: "To protect the sacred natural resources, and cultivate wide-spread consciousness of environmental sanctity."[93] The ashram sponsors nightly worship ceremonies of the Ganges in both Banaras and Rishikesh that culminate with the waving of large, flaming brass *arati* lamps before the river. This is usually accompanied with celebratory music and dramatic ritual performances.

I met with Muni-ji in his Rishikesh ashram shortly after the last Kumbha Mela and asked him whether he saw any connection between the beautiful worship service I saw performed on the banks of the Ganges in his ashram and efforts to restore the Ganges. "Definitely!" he replied. "Religion is the key to environmental work in India. I am trying to spread awareness of the need to keep the river clean. People come to the *arati* at Parmarth and get the message that worship of the river and care for the river are linked. The key is generating awareness, and religion can do this better than anything."[94] As examples of concrete action, he told me, many people staying in his ashram patrol the banks of the Ganges to pick up plastic bags and other garbage, and he was considering making all who stay in his ashram clean the Ganges for a short time as part of their daily spiritual practice (*sadhana*). He described plans to organize a campaign along the Ganges from its source at Gangotri to its oceanic end at Gangasagar to convince people to care for the section of the river on which they live. He explained that, although the connection between ecology and religion is new in Hinduism, it is definitely a rapidly growing movement. "The connection between ecology and religion is essential these days. If you just talk about ecology, no one will come; but if you tie it into religion, then many people will come and listen." Most important, Muni-ji believes, a worshipful attitude reinforced by the performance of rituals is an important element in all this. "Worshipping Ganga is the key to developing ecological consciousness about Ganga."

Muni-ji, then, provides another example of the growing connection between religion and ecology in India: his environmental activism is intimately connected with his religious view of the river.[95] In him and the many others introduced in this chapter, we clearly witness the emergence of eco-religious activism in India today in a particularly Hindu mode. But will such developments be sufficient to stem the tide of the environmental destruction of India's sacred rivers?

CHAPTER 6

A Matter of Balance

There's nothing like seeing a river through the eyes of
somebody who really cares about it.

Bill Painter

If we could get people to see the goddess in the river, they
would worship her and stop polluting her.

Deepu Pandit

This book examines environmental and cultural transformations that
are still in motion and, therefore, not yet complete, so it is difficult to say
at this point what the outcome will be. There are roughly three possibilities for what might happen to Yamuna. We may be witnessing a "death
of a goddess" movement. If the environmental conditions of the Yamuna
continue to worsen, people may abandon their religious connection with
the physical river. Many people who now say that Yamuna is sick or
even dying tend to assume a strong connection between the river and the
goddess. Krishna Gopal Shukla of Vrindaban, who believes Yamuna
might be dying, said, "If the physical river goes, then the goddess goes
too."[1] A priest who tends a small Krishna shrine in Vrindaban represented the final consequence of this development: "The river is dead
because of pollution. I used to bathe in the river with faith when she was
alive, but now she is dead. . . . I don't worship her anymore."[2]
    If conditions deteriorate further, this trend may spread, as is happen-
ing among worshippers of the Ganges. Rakesh Jaiswal, founder of
Kanpur's Eco-Friends, told me that he thinks the Ganges is dying. When
I pressed him to clarify his theological perspective, asking him if this
included the goddess, he said, "Yes, Ganga Devi too will die."[3] When the
gates of the Tehri Dam on the Ganges were closed on December 2, 2001,
damming the river and flooding Sunderlal Bahuguna out of his home,

he performed the Hindu *shraddha* death ritual for his Mother Ganges. The *Indian Express* reported that Bahuguna performed the death rite for Mother Ganges by shaving his head. "I have shaven off my beard and [shaven my] head as I have lost my mother," Bahuguna said.[4] This striking death ritual may have been the first ever performed to mourn the demise of a river goddess.

Another possibility is that, as circumstances deteriorate further for Yamuna, the transcendent strands of the theological traditions that disassociate the power of the goddess from the conditions of the physical river will gain in strength and become dominant. Many whom I talked with, particularly the pilgrimage priests of Vishram Ghat, who have much to gain economically by this position, acknowledged that there was pollution in the river but denied that it had any effect on Yamuna as an all-powerful goddess. These priests, who make their living performing *puja* worship services for the pilgrims, insisted, "Yamuna-ji is not polluted in any way. She can never be polluted."[5] The claim that Yamuna is not polluted is usually concomitant with a theological position that maintains a significant distinction between the physical river and the goddess. Those who hold this view are relatively unconcerned about the pollution. Lina Gupta made a similar point about the Ganges after discussing what she views as problematic notions of the river's purity: "When these presumptions about Ganga's purity are linked, one can see why Hindus do not appear to be motivated enough in salvaging Ganga from her polluted condition. When seen as pure in this way, Ganga herself too often becomes other-worldly and disengaged from the Earth, even disassociated with the river that bears her name."[6] This position is in line with that of the pilgrim priests whom Kelly Alley studied at Dasashvamedha Ghat on the Ganges in Banaras. She contends that, for them, "Ganga's purity has lapsed into a fixed transcendent state."[7] And she argues that this viewpoint undermines efforts to clean the river. The most extreme development of this possibility would be a complete disassociation of the goddess from the physical river.

Recent research suggests that there may be historical precedent for such disassociation, although the determining factors would have been quite different. Modern satellite technology has confirmed that thousands of years ago a mighty river flowed out of the Himalayas, but as a result of tectonic movement, it disappeared into other river systems.[8] Scholars in India have identified this river as the Sarasvati, a river often referred to in the Rig Veda, but which now survives solely as a goddess of aesthetic culture. If this is true, the transformation of Sarasvati from an association with an actual physical river to today's goddess, completely divorced from any physical river, demonstrates how a river goddess might survive the demise of a physical river by becoming thoroughly transcendent. A significant difference, however, is that the Sarasvati disappeared because of geological events, whereas the destruction of the Yamuna is due to human activities. Moreover, it is important to note that such a transformation to radical transcendence would be perceived as an utter failure by many devotees of Yamuna, who would see this as the death of a vital aspect of the river goddess as a result of environmental destruction, as well as a signal of the end of a healthy human world. As Chamanlal Bhatta of Mathura said about the river, "Yamuna-ji is the Mother of life. We cannot live without her."[9]

A third possibility is that the social, political, and environmental changes necessary to reverse the degradation of the Yamuna and restore her to a healthy condition will take place before it is too late. The signs of hope showcased in chapter 5 point in this direction. This is certainly the outcome most desired by environmental activists striving to restore the Yamuna. Both religious leaders and governmental officials working toward this end insist that, if this is to happen, the confluence of religion and ecology will have to grow into a more effective popular and widespread movement. Many scholars support this contention. Vasudha Narayanan remarks, "We know that the environmental problems facing India are tremendous, but there is also no doubt that religion is a potential resource for raising peoples' consciousness about these problems."[10] Bruce Sullivan concurs: "Emphasizing the religious significance of nature in India seems an especially effective approach to encourage ecological activity."[11] Public administrators such as the Additional District Magistrate R. D. Paliwal, hydraulic engineers such as O. P. Singhal, religious leaders such as Shrivatsa Goswami and Veer Bhadra Mishra, and environmental activists such as Gopeshwar Nath Chaturvedi and Rakesh Jaiswal all agree that "religion is the key" to an effective environmental movement in India that will work to save her sacred rivers. The religious leader Muni-ji of Rishikesh is optimistic about this development. When I asked him if the connection between religion and ecology is important in the work being done to restore the Ganges to health, he said, "Oh yes! It is essential. This is a growing movement; it is definitely happening."[12]

When I began this study of the Yamuna, I was worried that as a student of religion I would read too much religion into the environmental work being done on the Yamuna and other sacred rivers of northern India. I discovered in the course of my research, however, that this concern often kept me from seeing the prominent and ubiquitous role religion does indeed play in the environmental effort. Christopher Chapple affirms the religious nature of Indian environmentalism: "Whereas in the American context the early rallying cry for environmental action came from scientists and social activists with theologians only taking interest in this issue of late, in India, from the outset there has been an appeal to traditional religious sensibilities in support of environmental issues."[13] The aspects of Hinduism most invested in the worship of natural forms as divine beings seem to provide the greatest resource for environmental care.

While they recognize the negative consequences of certain kinds of religious views and practices, all the major players involved in promoting the protection and restoration of the Yamuna spoke of the vital place that religion does and must assume in motivating people to take the action necessary for saving the river. Echoing Lynn White (see chapter 1), these leaders acknowledged that, although certain aspects of religion may be part of the problem, religion must also be part of the solution. Paliwal maintained that the revival of a religious consciousness that worships natural forms is key to achieving a new environmental awareness and more positive behavior toward the river. Veer Bhadra Mishra, cofounder of the Sankat Mochan Foundation, insisted that "the main motivation for environmental work in India is religion."[14] He said, "Those in the know feel the best way to remedy the situation is to revert to that which has been distorted: religion. If we care for the environment, we have to go back to our roots."[15] In this book, I have tracked the beginning of such a return—or perhaps more accurately, a reformation of aspects of the Hindu tradition under the environmental pressures caused by recent developments. As Muni-ji insisted, "If you just talk about ecology, no one will come; but if you tie it into religion, then many people will come and listen."[16] He explained that people who come to the celebrations of the Ganges that he has arranged at his ashrams in Rishikesh and Banaras come away with a clear message: the worship of the river and care for the river are linked. Religion is central in the efforts to restore sacred rivers in India.

The specific nature of the role religion plays centers on the concept of *seva*. A few decades ago, *seva* would have referred specifically to "loving service" that took the form of standard acts of worship, such as making offerings of hymns, flowers, fruit, milk, and incense. These days, however, a significant cultural transformation is under way: although the word still retains the older meaning, increasingly it includes actions that we in the West would label "environmental activism." Gopeshwar Nath Chaturvedi, for example, used the term "Yamuna *seva*" to refer to his organizational efforts to clean the Yamuna and to his legal work within the courts to stop untreated sewage and industrial effluents from being released into the river. He said that *seva* now means both worshipping (*puja karna*) and environmental protection (*paryavaran surakshan*). The word *seva* as used in the most popular sign posted along the Yamuna in Braj, and as featured as an epigraph at the beginning of chapter 5, means environmental restoration, not offering milk and so forth. *Seva* in this context is environmental action understood and expressed as a form of religious devotion. It is usually performed out of strong sentiment or love (*bhava*, to use the religious word) for a particular form of divinity, in this case Yamuna. Many people told me that it was their *bhava* that both allowed them to perceive the true form of Yamuna—called the *svarupa*—and motivated their activism. Religious love is a strong motivation for environmental activism in India, which fairly well distinguishes it from the dominant form of environmental activism typically found in the United States.

A major motivation behind much American environmentalism stems from the belief that we are now living on the brink of, and rushing rapidly toward, an environmental catastrophe. Fear of this motivates many to work to avoid it. A book by former vice president Al Gore, *Earth in the Balance,* is a good example of this.[17] This book was written to argue that we are on the threshold of a massive and systemic environmental catastrophe, and that unless we deal with it in an effective manner soon, the life of all future generations is endangered. Gore claims, therefore, that there is no greater political challenge than addressing the environmental crisis. The scientific community too has announced time and again, in many varied and increasingly louder voices, that we are heading toward a disaster that threatens the very future of humanity. On November 18, 1992, the Union of Concerned Scientists, based in Cambridge, Massachusetts, issued a statement, *The World Scientists' Warning to Humanity.*[18] The statement was initially signed by more than seventeen hundred of the world's leading scientists, and has now been signed by more than three thousand, including more than one hundred Nobel laureates. Among them is the prominent Harvard biologist Edward O. Wilson, who has asked publicly and persistently, "Is humanity suicidal?"[19]

The scientists' statement opens with a warning: "Human beings and the natural world are on a collision course. Human activities inflict harsh and often irreversible damage on the environment and on critical resources. If not checked, many of our current practices put at serious risk the future that we wish for human society and . . . may so alter the living world that it will be unable to sustain life in the manner that we know. Fundamental changes are urgent if we are to avoid the collision our present course will bring about." The statement concludes, "Warning: We the undersigned, senior members of the world's scientific community, hereby warn all humanity of what lies ahead. A great change in our stewardship of the earth and the life on it is required if vast human misery is to be avoided and our global home on this planet is not to be irretrievably mutilated."[20]

Similarly, the Worldwatch Institute has warned repeatedly that there is little time left to turn things around in order to avoid an irreversible environmental meltdown that would most certainly bring into question the very future of humanity. Indeed, such alerts are commonplace in the American environmental movement. Those who can pierce through the currently socially sanctioned denial are well aware of these statements and their implications for future human life on this planet. Desire to stave off imminent disaster provides incentive for much environmentalism in the United States.

Another feature of mainstream environmentalism in the United States is its primary concern for human beings. This anthropocentric viewpoint focuses on human well-being, often at the expense of any concern for nonhuman beings. Anthropocentrism is currently being challenged in more radical environmental circles,[21] but all parties recognize that it still dominates Western environmentalism.

I do not mean to portray American environmentalism in terms that are too simple and reductionistic. To be sure, there are eco-centric schools of thought as opposed to anthropocentric schools of thought operative in the American environmental movement—perhaps most notably those associated with the name *deep ecology*. As noted in chapter 1, the first of the eight basic principles articulated by deep ecologists Arne Naess and George Sessions reads, "The well-being and flourishing of human and nonhuman Life on Earth have value in themselves (synonyms: intrinsic value, inherent value). These values are independent of the usefulness of the nonhuman world for human purposes." More important for our concerns, they go on to elaborate this principle: "The term 'life' is used here in a more comprehensive nontechnical way to refer also to what biologists classify as 'nonliving': *rivers,* landscapes, ecosystems. For supporters of deep ecology, slogans such as 'Let the river live' illustrate this broader usage so common in most cultures."[22] Common in most cultures, but not in modern Western culture, the authors point out. The dominant forms of environmentalism in the United States aim to save the environment for human use, advancement, and pleasure.

An illustration of this point is the case of the Hudson River in New York State. One could argue that the Hudson River was the first real battleground of the American environmental movement that took shape in the 1960s. The environmental lawyer Robert Kennedy Jr. and fisherman John Cronin write, "While the Hudson is cursed with more than its share, it was blessed since the early 1960s with an activist community that engaged polluters with an intensity and ingenuity that made the Hudson the most critical legal battleground of the modern environmental era."[23] The organization most responsible for these achievements was the Riverkeepers, an admirable association of commercial and recreational fishermen that came together in the 1960s to track down Hudson River polluters and bring them to justice. From the outset, the group's aim was to restore the river to public control, so that powerful corporations would stop polluting the river and a healthy fish population could return to the river for the benefit of fishermen. Riverkeepers remains an effective movement, now protecting rivers nationwide. The writings of David James Duncan might also be mentioned in this context. His work showcases how river environmentalism in the northwestern United States has been led by fishermen concerned with the health of the salmon and trout populations in the rivers of this region.[24]

River environmentalism in the United States was spearheaded first by fishermen, and second by river adventurers. A quick glance at *The River Reader,* an anthology of river writings, supports this assertion.[25] Herein rivers are celebrated almost exclusively for their human recreational value. In sum, American environmentalism is fundamentally motivated by fear of an impending catastrophe and is primarily anthropocentric in that it aims to defend human ends. River environmentalism, in particular, exemplifies these trends and has been dominated by fishermen.

In contrast, we observe something quite different in the river environmentalism represented by Gopeshwar Nath Chaturvedi and others working to save rivers in northern India. Here we encounter a river-centered approach rather than a human-centered approach. I never once heard Chaturvedi say, for example, that the river should be saved for current or future generations of humans (though his work may contribute to such an outcome). Instead, he said, "We do this for our Mother." Moreover, we find a motivational attitude of love over fear: Chaturvedi and others like him report that they engage in environmental actions as *seva* for Yamuna because of their *bhava* (love) for her. We also encounter the involvement of river worshippers rather than that of fishermen. River environmentalists in India are much more likely to be seen waving *arati* lamps, rather than fishing poles, over rivers. It is evident that environmental activism is part of the religious life of those working to save rivers in northern India.

Veer Bhadra Mishra, or Mahant-ji, is aware that much Western environmentalism is based on fear, but he told me that, "in our country, fear of environmental disaster is not there."[26] Instead, he explained, the main motivation behind the environmental work that he and others are doing for the Ganges and Yamuna is "religious." "People worship Ganga as a goddess, or simply as 'Ma.' We work *for her*." Mahant-ji went on to characterize this environmental work as *seva*, acts of "loving service." Mahant-ji and his group are not trying to restore the Ganges in order to save human beings (although their efforts may result in this), but from love for the river herself, conceived in their culture as a magnificent goddess and loving mother. In an article that appeared in the *New Yorker*, Alexander Stille stresses this point: "The mahant is also convinced that science and religion have to mesh if the Ganges is to be saved. The Western approach, based on fear of a possible ecological disaster, will not work, he says. 'If you go to the people who have a living relationship with Ganga and you say 'Ganga is polluted, the water is dirty,' they will say, 'Stop saying that. Ganga is not polluted. You are abusing the river.' But if you say 'Ganga is our mother. Come and see what is being thrown on the body of your mother—sewage and filth. Should we tolerate sewage being smeared on the body of our Mother?' you will get a very different reaction, and you can harness that energy."[27] It is clear that Mahant-ji is a fervent devotee of Ganges. He organizes and participates in both private and public worship of Ganges. He knows more than most about the dangerous pollution in the river and yet immerses himself in her daily as a way of honoring her. His ongoing struggles to save this river are motivated by devotional love. There may be a lesson in this for all who have ecological concerns and hope to take effective environmental action. What it suggests is that love builds and goes somewhere—perhaps like a river—whereas fear might foster greater denial and serve to dam up effective action. The Yamuna devotee Vasishthagiri told me, "The way to tap into the infinity of love is to give it infinitely. It flows like a river but becomes stagnant when it is stopped, dammed, or held onto out of fear or selfishness."[28]

A common religious aim within Hindu culture is to cut through the limited consciousness of egoistic ignorance and selfishness to see (sakshat darshan) the true and vast nature of reality and establish a beneficial relationship (sambandha) with some form of it. Those who are unaware of this larger perspective are not inclined to act lovingly in the world, as love involves healthy connections. A selfish outlook produces fearful obsession with the egoistic self and obscures the true nature of reality, causing one to make a mess of the world. The resulting mess only makes it more difficult to see the true nature of the world. Within the religious culture associated with the Yamuna, this means it is necessary to become aware of her svarupa, her "own true form" or "essential nature," and develop a loving relationship with Yamuna as an exquisite goddess, or risk remaining blind to her true nature. A boatman in Vrindaban told me, "The power [shakti] of the river does not become less with pollution, but because of the pollution our access to it has become less. We can't see clearly because the filth gets in our eyes."[29] This is comparable to the difficulty of seeing stars at night because of light pollution. The stars are always shining with bright and majestic intensity, but urban light pollution—which does not affect the power of the stars—keeps us from seeing them. Yamuna's devotees tell us that her wondrous power is always there in all its majesty, but the pollution keeps us from seeing it. Gopeshwar Nath Chaturvedi put it this way: "The river is just like a murti [embodied form of divinity worshipped in a temple]. You can throw dirt on it, but you cannot kill God. You can, however, destroy your ability to see God."[30] The physical river is a vital link to divinity. This all raises the question: How might one come to see more clearly?

As a powerful goddess of love, Yamuna possesses the ability to transform her devotees' nature, to initiate and nurture them into a world of divine love. It is a function of Yamuna herself, therefore, to take her devotees' minds out of the limited ego consciousness of samsara and reveal the true nature of reality as the Beloved. Rupa Gosvamin celebrates in his "Yamunashtakam" Yamuna's ability to burn up the selfish arrogance of those who worship her.[31] In his commentary on the ninth verse of Vallabhacharya's "Yamunashtakam," Hariray explains that the phrase "[Yamuna] conquers one's nature [svabhava vijaya]" means that "one's desire is changed from being directed toward the self to being directed toward everything—to see the self in all beings." He relates this transformation to the idea of self-realization expressed in Upanishadic texts: shifting one's identity from the ego self to the Self that is interconnected with everything.[32] From this perspective, then, spiritual clarity is understood to be a matter of grace, and those who engage in environmental activism as *seva* are really responding to the call of the highest divinity. Yet even within traditions that recognize the important role of grace, strategies and techniques for realization have been developed by practitioners eager for advancement, and Yamuna's devotees are no different.

On a warm spring morning during one of my many visits to Vishram Ghat in Mathura, I sat quietly observing a colorful array of people as they came to worship Yamuna. One man in particular impressed me with the gracefulness of his actions and the seeming sincerity of his demeanor. After politely removing his sandals at the top of the ghat, he approached the river with peaceful concentration. He cleaned a spot on a large stone step just inches above the surface of the water, unrolled a grass mat and sat down, meditating on the river for about thirty minutes. He then took water from the river in his right hand and sipped it three times. Next, as he offered red rose petals into the river, he sang with a melodious voice Vallabhacharya's "Yamunashtakam," the Sanskrit devotional hymn known by almost all serious devotees of Yamuna. For a while after this, he sat calmly gazing into the river with a slight smile on his face. He then filled a small copper pot with water, stood, and started up the stone steps. As he was putting on his sandals, I joined him to ask some questions about the conditions of the Yamuna and his relationship with her.

His name was Dinesh Chaturvedi. He said that the real source of pollution today lies within: "Pollution comes out of polluted hearts."[33] Because of this, people don't see the true nature of Yamuna. He told me about the transformation in his own life that led him to become a daily worshipper of Yamuna: "I used to see Yamuna-ji as an ordinary polluted river. I used to wear my sandals down to her bank." (He now views this as a grave insult. In fact, his concerns about showing disrespect with his feet are so strong that he never steps into Yamuna, and therefore does not bathe in her, but only sips her water respectfully from the bank.) "But then I met my guru, and he told me to start worshipping Yamuna-ji. At first I was a little resistant, but I did what he said. Soon, I began to see her *svarupa* [true form] and realized how wonderful [*adbhut*] she really is. So now I worship her everyday with love. The main benefit of worshipping Yamuna-ji is an ever-expanding love. I want to live in her world of love."

Dinesh Chaturvedi's words suggest that his guru understood something important. The act of worship leads to a perspectival awakening: through a reverent act of worship, one comes to see the true nature of something and experiences a new attitude toward it. Once that true nature is revealed and one has an experience of its marvelousness, one enters spontaneously into an appreciative and worshipful attitude and engages naturally in acts of loving service aimed to care for it. Or perhaps more simply, love is both a means (a physical practice) and an end (a wonderful state). According to a saying in Braj, "The beloved is found through love itself" (Pritama prita hi te peyi). Something reveals its true nature only in the face of love. Chaibihari Sardar of Gokul put it this way: "Just as butter slowly comes from milk, the *svarupa* gradually came to me by meditating on Yamuna-ji with love."[34] Muni-ji of Rishikesh said something similar while stressing a more environmental message aimed at protecting the Ganges: "Worshipping Ganga is key to developing ecological consciousness about Ganga."[35] Vasishthagiri told me that people pollute rivers because they don't recognize their supernatural side. When I asked him why this was so, he replied, "Because our vessels are not clean enough."[36] How are we to clean our vessels? "By doing *seva* to others, to the rivers and other forms of Mother Nature. There is no other way." *Seva*, then, is both an intentional act of physical worship or loving service and a natural expression of love. There is something wonderfully circular about all this.[37] Awareness of the true nature (*svarupa*) of Yamuna generates love for her, and love enables one to see her *svarupa* more fully. How does one break into this circle? The emphasis here is on action over ideas. Loving acts toward a being generate loving feelings toward that being, which further motivate more loving acts. By doing acts of Yamuna *seva* intentionally, one develops the love that leads to realization of Yamuna's *svarupa*, which in turn further enhances love for her, leading to more acts of *seva*—and on and on, the circle grows into an "ever-expanding love," as Dinesh Chaturvedi put it. Worshipful acts, then, are the very doorway into an inner world of realization; they are concrete levers for opening up new perspectives. As Vasudha Narayan remarks, "Devotional [*bhakti*] exercises seem to be the greatest potential resources for ecological activists in India."[38]

While pollution, I was told again and again, is the result of people having a limited perspective on the world, many I spoke with stressed that a positive and ecologically healthy relationship with the Yamuna depends on a loving awareness of her true nature, or *svarupa*. Giriraj of Gokul,

one of the Pushti Margiya priests who tend the Yamuna temple at
Thakurani Ghat, explained, "Yamuna is polluted because people see her
as something ordinary and are not aware of her as Yamuna-ji. They are
not aware of her *svarupa*."[39] I heard this notion expressed repeatedly:
a specific and primary recommendation articulated by those working to
save the Yamuna is for people to learn to perceive her essential nature.
Harekrishna of Gokul contended that such an awareness is crucial to a
beneficial relationship with Yamuna. "The people who do not see the
svarupa are polluting her. The *svarupa* is not polluted, but there is pollution in the water. The water is also part of her *svarupa*, but the people
who are not aware of the *svarupa* are polluting her."[40] A Nimbarki priest
in Vrindaban agreed: "People pollute Yamuna because they see her as a
simple river. If they saw her as the lover [*patarani*] of Krishna, they
would never pollute her."[41] Deepu Pandit of Gokul expressed this in an
even more prescriptive manner: "If we could get people to see the goddess in the river, they would worship her and stop polluting her."[42]
He went on to say, "Pushti Margiyas don't pollute Yamuna, because
they see the river in this way. I have never seen a Pushti Margiya polluting the river. They only worship her. People who don't understand the
svarupa of Yamuna-ji are polluting her. We must make them understand
the real nature of Yamuna-ji, and then they will stop polluting." The
widow Anantadasi of Vrindaban spoke of the true inner (*antar*) nature
of Yamuna and claimed that unlike devotees, polluters are ignorant of
her inner nature. She went so far as to suggest that polluting is the mark
of a sinner: "If a person pollutes a river, he or she is not a devotee but is
a sinner [*papi*]. This is the true test whether one is a devotee or a sinner."[43]
These and many other Yamuna devotees agreed, then, that pollution
comes from people who are unaware of the real nature of Yamuna.
Anyone who has this awareness not only refrains from polluting the
river but also enters into a worshipful relationship with Yamuna. An
awareness of the true nature of reality leads one into a world of divine
love wherein pollution becomes unthinkable.

Yamuna's *svarupa*, many devotees insist, is unaffected by the pollution. As Giriraj of Gokul declared, "The *svarupa* is not affected by the
pollution. It never changes."[44] While Giriraj himself expressed great
concern that the river be cleansed of all pollution, is there not a possible
danger in this perspective? What if an awareness of Yamuna's *svarupa*
were divorced from any concern with conditions of the concrete physical world? This attitude is expressed by some river worshippers. Alley
shows how the theological perspective of certain pilgrim priests in

Banaras regarding Ganges has become locked into radical transcendence. There is an economic benefit to this move for those whose livelihood depends on maintaining the idea of Ganges's eternal purity even as the river becomes more and more polluted. Some pilgrim priests in Mathura have expressed a similar view about the Yamuna. By and large, however, I found this position to be a minority one. Almost everyone I spoke with linked the goddess and the physical river; many identified them as the same (*sama*). This position is promoted by the Yamuna theological traditions of Braj in general, and by that of the Pushti Marga in particular.

There is perhaps no religious figure more influential in the development of Yamuna theology in Braj than the sixteenth-century saint and founder of the Pushti Marga, Vallabhacharya. We have seen that his "Yamunashtakam" is the foundation stone of much of the theological thinking about Yamuna in Braj, and that almost every Yamuna devotee knows it by heart. In one of his other texts, the *Siddhantamuktavali*, Vallabhacharya compares three different forms of the Ganges to the different dimensions of the ultimate reality of Krishna. He explains that the water that is the Ganges is like the physical world, the spiritual power that is the Ganges is like the unchanging and unmanifest *brahman*, and the goddess that is the Ganges is like the supreme personality, Krishna. Vallabhacharya points out that all three dimensions of reality are interconnected and fully divine. The third dimension of divinity, in fact, encompasses the other two dimensions. This was conveyed to me in the context of the Yamuna during a conversation with the head priest of the main Vallabhacharya shrine near the Yamuna temple in Gokul: "The water is the physical form [*adhibhautika-rupa*]. For inner cleansing we look to the spiritual form [*adhyatmika-rupa*]. And the divine form [*adhidaivika-svarupa*] is the goddess, the lover of Krishna. But they are all Yamuna-ji."[45] Pushti Marga theology distinguishes itself from the world-denying ascetic philosophies, such as Shankara's Advaita Vedanta, by insisting that the physical world is fully divine, and that the highest divinity is not divorced from the world.[46]

A Pushti Marga teacher I met stressed that embodied beings can reach the highest dimension of divinity only through the physical world. He compared the physical world to the material of a television set, spiritual power to the electricity that runs the television, and vision of the highest divinity, or supreme personality, to the picture that appears by means of the other two. His point was that, if you destroy the physical dimension of reality, you have destroyed access to the highest divinity. When this is applied to the Yamuna, it implies that one cannot have a relationship with Yamuna as the highest divinity that is radically separated from the physical river. This was exactly the point emphasized by many Yamuna devotees during my conversations with them. Most simply, in the words of Anantadasi of Vrindaban: "The river and the goddess are one!"[47] The key to a beneficial relationship with Yamuna and the key to her environmental restoration, then, turn out to be the same: a loving awareness of her *svarupa*. Those who are aware of her *svarupa* fall deeply in love with her and would never consider polluting her. Seeing the *svarupa* properly, however, means seeing it as encompassing the physical realm of the world, not somehow opposing or radically transcending it.

The commentaries on Vallabhacharya's *Siddhantamuktavali* make it clear that this is a matter of perception. The whole world is divine, but not all humans can see it as such. The perceptual example Vallabhacharya uses in this text is again the Ganges. Some people look at the river and see only "water," in a completely objective sense. In the terminology of the commentaries on the *Siddhantamuktavali,* this means they can see only the physical form, the *adhibhuta* dimension of reality. Others are more perceptive and see the specialness of the Ganges, that dimension that draws pilgrims to her to cleanse themselves of sins and prepare for a good death. In the terminology of the commentaries, these have the ability to perceive the spiritual form, the *adhyatma* dimension of reality. Finally, others see more than this; they perceive the river as a magnificent presence, as a divine being worthy of reverent worship and appreciative devotion. They see the river as a goddess. In the terminology of the commentaries, this is the divine form, the *adhidaiva-svarupa* dimension of reality with which one can have a loving relationship. And most important for ecological considerations, those who reflect on the environmental crisis from this perspective say that this complete and all-inclusive perspective is the one most needed to restore a healthy relationship with the world. For the devotees of Yamuna immersed in this perspective, this means opening oneself to the river to the point where one can perceive the *adhidaiva-svarupa* of Yamuna. Once this occurs, polluting the river becomes as impossible as dumping garbage on the face of one's lover.

Yamuna theology makes it clear that there is a dimension of her that is beyond the physical world. Her *adhidaiva-svarupa* is unaffected by the pollution and yet is very much present in the world. Many I spoke with insisted that the water itself is somehow part of Yamuna's *svarupa*. Ghanashyam Sharma of Gokul said, "The water [*jal*] is part of the original *svarupa* of Yamuna-ji."[48] Paramananda Sharma of Gokul asserted, "The water [*jal*] is the direct form of Yamuna's *svarupa* [*sakshat svarupa*]."[49] Although dirt and pollution can be added to the river, the water itself remains fully divine and beyond pollution. Water can have pollution *in* it, but the H_2O is still distinct from the pollution. The British travel writer Bill Aitken narrates how he came to a similar realization at the confluence of the Yamuna and Ganges in Allahabad. An Indian acquaintance he was traveling with went into the river for a bath and beckoned Aitken to join him. Aitken writes, "He resurfaced in exaltation and wearing a smile of original bliss shouted, 'Jump in. It's the best tonic in the world.' I didn't know what disgusted me more, the cold or the filth. It seemed a bad bargain if in washing away your sins the river should give you a communicable disease. 'It's too dirty,' I hollered back. My friend's reply hit like a moment of Zen insight: 'It isn't the water that's dirty. It's the rubbish in it.'"[50] In a sense the polluted river is its troublous *samsarik* form; it is the form created by those heavily enmeshed in the egoistic perspective of *samsarik* alienation. For those living in the troublous world of *samsara,* however, dealing with the pollution is absolutely necessary; many maintained that it is our duty (dharma) to take care of it.

All this suggests that the right perspective for a healthy relationship with Yamuna is a matter of balance. The general consensus of Yamuna devotees is that people pollute the river because they don't see her true form, her *svarupa;* they see her merely as some inert object. For these people, the prescribed remedy is the acquisition of a loving awareness of Yamuna's living *svarupa*. A focus on the *svarupa* divorced from any concern for the physical river, however, also results in a problem: extreme transcendence fosters an unbalanced worldview that undermines concern for environmental health. What is called for is an awareness of Yamuna's *svarupa* that includes the realization that it is intimately connected to the physical river. The river is the physical body of the goddess and must be cared for as such. Wonder at the marvelous nature of Yamuna's *svarupa* must be linked significantly to a responsible concern for the river itself. Without this, some Yamuna devotees are beginning to speculate, a limit to Yamuna's motherly love will soon be reached, and she will begin to punish human polluters with diseases caused by the pollution itself.

Yamuna today is both a river of delights and a river of troubles; Yamuna devotees insist that to ignore either side will only invite further problems.[51] She is concurrently a goddess and a (now polluted) river.

She has an infinite side and a finite side, what one devotee called her "supernatural side" and her "natural side," and another her "inner face" and her "outer face." Thus, she is simultaneously unmanifest and manifest, powerful and vulnerable, big and small. I am reminded of a story found in the writings of the Chinese Taoist master Chuang Tzu.[52] He tells of a frog who lives in a well, thinking he is master of an immense realm. One day a huge turtle from the vast ocean comes to visit the frog and reveals to him just how small his well really is. Chuang Tzu informs us that the frog—who occupies the position of the human in the story—lives in a false consciousness and needs to become aware of the bigger picture. In a certain sense, the well is no big deal. And yet, if the well becomes polluted the frog will suffer and die. What seems to be required is both a wisdom that apprehends the immensity of reality and the limitations of human efforts, and a compassion that is deeply concerned with the particular tangible and fragile reality immediately before us. Yamuna will survive with or without human beings—rivers flowed on this planet before any biological life was established and will most likely continue to flow even if all biological life becomes extinct—but her songs say she came to nurture life; and if she is going to do this, mutual care is necessary.

One day Gopeshwar Nath Chaturvedi suggested to me that the true environmental activist must be a karma yogi. He made this remark during a conversation about the importance of maintaining an awareness of Yamuna's *svarupa* while engaging in the concrete work of environmental protection. I have since thought much about this. The karma yogi is a central figure in the Bhagavad-gita. Herein the karma yogi is characterized as one who is neither too attached to the outcome of personal actions nor too detached from them.[53] The ordinary human condition is marked by an egoistic sense of self and an ignorance that obscures the ultimate nature of the world, making it appear to consist of autonomous objects under one's control. Being too attached to the outcome of one's own actions, assuming one is "in control," can lead to "burn out" in fighting environmental problems, whereas environmental action as *seva* is surrendered action: it involves fighting the battle lovingly each moment while surrendering to the bigger picture. The karma yogi is one who cuts through egoistic ignorance and unhealthy attachment with a sword of knowledge (*jnana*) that reveals the ultimate nature (*brahman*) of everything, showing it to be interconnected and infinite. The Bhagavad-gita rejects the renunciation of engagement in the world; the karma yogi is a warrior who is deeply involved, for the manifest world of finite and changing forms is a precious reality declared to be fully real.[54] The karma yogi must eschew both extremes of ordinary attachment and ascetic indifference for a middle path that simultaneously values the finite and the infinite, though in different ways.[55]

The environmental activist as karma yogi must in effect learn to see everything in the world concurrently with two very different eyes: one trained on the finite and one trained on the infinite. The eye trained on the finite is the eye of compassion. It focuses on the small, the fragile, the ever-changing tangible and precious world that is right before our eyes.[56] This is the realm in which life occurs. It is the immanent dimension of divinity. The compassionate eye leads one to care for each and every particular being that appears in front of it. It is the eye that enables one to develop personal relationships and accept personal responsibility. From the perspective of this eye, the Yamuna is in trouble; she is polluted and unhealthy and is pleading for our help. The response she deserves is a tender one. Here *seva* means loving acts of kindness that aim to alleviate her pain. In this perspective, time is of the essence; we need to act now.

The eye trained on the infinite is also the eye of knowledge. It focuses on the big, the indestructible, the eternal world beyond immediate manifestations. This is the transcendent dimension of divinity that is beyond the contingency of everyday life. It involves a humble recognition of the majestic power of the goddess as the very source of all life. Here *seva* is an expression of amazement and appreciation. In a sense the knowledgeable eye is somewhat indifferent to the transitory world, understanding that everything is beyond personal control and human agency. Every being that is born dies; death is an ingredient of life. In the cosmic scheme of things, human beings are short-lived and powerless. Within the perspective of this eye, time is vast. Yamuna cannot be polluted indefinitely and will flow on into the future with or without a human presence on the planet.

Again, this is a matter of balance. The woman pictured in figure 13 carries a water pot on her head (filled with Yamuna water?). Modeling an elegant balancing act, she is an exemplary karma yogi or eco-warrior showing the way into a healthy future. She must balance the water pot carefully, or it will spill. To insure safe delivery of the water, she must be mindful not to veer too far to one side of the path or the other, and she must be attentive. If she is not, the pot will spill. On the other hand, if she becomes too fixated on the pot and loses sight of where she is going, she will spill it. Safe handling requires attention that is neither too loose

Figure 13. Woman carrying a pot of water. Paper stencil by Mohan Kumar Verma.

nor too tight, and both eyes must be wide open. If the eye of compassion is closed, indifference to this world becomes extreme; nothing matters. Within the range of religious possibilities, there exists a life-negating temptation to devalue this world for some other: we become mere sojourners passing through this world on our way to a heavenly home elsewhere, rather than inhabitants of Earth or children of Yamuna. If the eye of knowledge is closed, one can become crushed in the face of the inevitable losses encountered in this world. One loses sight of the "bigger picture," that all this is part of an immensity. The rain forest activist John Seed reported that he experienced a breakdown upon observing forest after forest destroyed by bulldozers and chainsaws. He was restored to mental health and an ability to continue his fight to save rain forests by reading accounts of Earth's long history of previous extinctions. This assured him of the resilience of biological life on this planet and enabled him to contextualize his struggles in a larger and more hopeful frame-work.[57] The deep ecologist Freya Mathews remarks, "I think that it is vital for our own spiritual health, and for the health of the environ-mental movement, that we assure ourselves that we cannot bring about a death of nature."[58] The trick is to be radically life-affirming while at the same time accepting human limitations. To fight the battle for envi-ronmental protection enthusiastically each moment while surrendering the outcome to the bigger picture beyond human control is to engage in the battle as a karma yogi.

One final question remains: How to live in an age of pollution? Yamuna's devotees suggest that we need to respond with love to the now-damaged world in which we live, specifically a love accompanied by an ongoing awareness and appreciation of the wondrous divinity of the world as we sustain a well-grounded and life-affirming commitment to stop human-caused environmental destruction. One seductive lure away from loving action is to deny the existence of the pollution or to discount it in some cheap gesture toward transcendence. The other danger is to get too stuck in the pollution, not seeing the wonder and power beyond current problems. The strongest love is one that can take the pollution into itself, neither denying it nor succumbing to disem-powering depression. Yamuna's devotees tell us that the key to true and marvelous love is an awareness of the *adhidaiva-svarupa*—that amazing divine reality of the world. The infinite breaks open the claustrophobia of the finite; yet, as eco-feminists remind us, a sense of wonder must involve care. Regarding the earthly bodies of God, Sallie McFague writes, "We cannot in good conscience marvel with aesthetic delight at the one and not identify with the *pain* of the other: bodies are beautiful and vulnerable. If God is physical, then, the aesthetic and the ethic unite: praising God in and through the beauty of bodies entails caring for the most basic needs of all bodies on the planet."[59] Any temptation to drift off into a disconnected realm of transcendence must be resisted; true love is well-grounded. Thus, any extreme fixation on the infinite must be remedied with a good dose of the needy finite.

No one really knows what will become of the Yamuna or, for that matter, the rest of the life-support systems of the natural world; only time will tell. In the meantime the message for action according to Yamuna devotees is clear: regardless of the outcome, human life finds its highest aim in loving service. A possible link between religion and ecology is clearly evident among those who dedicate their lives to saving sacred rivers in northern India. They call for a renewed recognition of the sacrality of the world—the reenchantment mentioned in the opening chapter—identified specifically among Yamuna devotees as the goddess's *svarupa*. And they stress that what is needed is a wise, all-inclusive, and engaged love that expresses itself in a direct and caring relationship with the physical river or with other natural embodied forms of divinity that make up this world.[60] A Yamuna devotee from Vrindaban proclaimed, "Love is the key to all sustainable living."[61] This suggests that what is most needed in this age of pollution is a vast outpouring of love, a mighty river of love that will nourish and sustain us while washing away the pollution that is threatening the very fount of all life.

Translations

"YAMUNASHTAKAM" OF RUPA GOSVAMIN

Rupa Gosvamin, one of the most important theologians of the developing movement of Gaudiya Vaishnavism, came from Bengal to Vrindaban in the sixteenth century to help establish the major tenets and practices of this religious tradition. This is an *ashtakam,* an eight-versed hymn; a ninth verse has been added in this case to specify the benefit of singing the hymn.[1] Themes of the purification of sins and protection from the torments of Yama, Lord of Death, are present, but more important is the expression of Yamuna's charming beauty and ability to increase devotional love.

[1]

She frees one from being taken away to the land of her
    brother, Lord of Death;
She carries even the worst of sinners across the ocean of sins
    by her sight;
She attracts all people's hearts with the sweetness of her water;
May the Daughter of the Sun always purify me.

[2]

She beautifies the spacious forests with her flow of alluring
    water;

She dances with the birds and bees flying about her lotus
    fields;
She completely destroys all disease, sickness, and sin for
    those who desire to bathe in her;
May the Daughter of the Sun always purify me.

[3]

She eradicates the evil consequences of former births for
    the person who touches but a few drops of her water;
She increases the stream of loving devotion for Krishna,
    Son of Nanda;
She fulfills the wishes of those who gather on her banks;
May the Daughter of the Sun always purify me.

[4]

She demarcated the seven oceans and inhabits many
    continents;
She knows the supreme divine love play performed by
    Shri Krishna;
She outshines a heap of Indra's blue sapphires with her
    brilliant sparkles;
May the Daughter of the Sun always purify me.

[5]

She adorns the entire region of Braj with her charming
    beauty;
She widens the path for devotees of Krishna who have found
    supreme love;
She worships the feet of Krishna with the play of her armlike
    waves;
May the Daughter of the Sun always purify me.

[6]

She is embellished with herds of cows lowing on her pleasing
    banks;
She is covered with flowers from divinely perfumed *kadamba*
    trees;
She is delighted by the union of Krishna and her devotees;
May the Daughter of the Sun always purify me.

[7]

She is accompanied by the songs of thousands of swans and
    feathery geese;
She is worshipped by the gods, saints, and celestial musicians
    all filled with devotion;
She annihilates the obstacles of birth with sweet fragrances
    flowing along her banks;
May the Daughter of the Sun always purify me.

[8]

She pervades the Earth, atmosphere, and heavens with her
    playful stream of consciousness;
She burns up the very root of great sins and selfish arrogance
    for those who praise her;
She is fragrant with the waves of passion coming from the
    body of Krishna;
May the Daughter of the Sun always purify me.

[9]

O Lotus-Eyed Goddess, Daughter of the Sun, Destroyer of
    All Sins,
May you who move with pure waves and who are attended
    by all gods
Increase the torrent of devotion streaming toward Krishna
    for that intelligent and content person who sings this
    hymn to you.

"YAMUNASHTAKAM" OF SHANKARACHARYA

This eight-versed hymn to Yamuna is attributed to the famous eighth-century expounder of Advaita Vedanta, Shankaracharya (also simply called Shankara).[2] Although many devotional hymns are attributed to Shankara, there is much uncertainty regarding their authorship. This hymn was most likely composed long after the time of Shankara, as it features the devotional qualities of Radha. It shows signs of being influenced by the religious culture of Braj. Nonetheless, this is a fairly well-known Yamuna hymn and expresses themes of purification and beauty.

[1]

She flows with water beautified by the darkness of Krishna's
    body.
She destroys the sorrows of the three worlds and makes
    Indra's heaven seem like straw.
Her rapturous flow animates the many love bowers on her
    enchanting banks.
May Yamuna, Daughter of Kalinda, always remove the
    impurities of our minds.

[2]

She is endowed with powerful enchanting water that
    completely destroys all impurities.
She is capable of destroying the sins of those who surrender
    to her with limitless joy.
Her heart is always colored with passion for the beautiful
    body of Krishna.
May Yamuna, Daughter of Kalinda, always remove the
    impurities of our minds.

[3]

Gentle breezes on her banks relieve the exhaustion of those
    engaged in divine love play.
The charm of her water is beyond anything that can be
    expressed with words.
All rivers on Earth are purified when they mix with the
    current of her water.
May Yamuna, Daughter of Kalinda, always remove the
    impurities of our minds.

[4]

She destroys the sins of all beings who come in contact with
    her shining waves.
Her fresh sweetness sustains the *chataka* birds born from
    devotion.
She fulfills the desires of those perfected devotees who have
    taken refuge with her and dwell on her banks.
May Yamuna, Daughter of Kalinda, always remove the
    impurities of our minds.

[5]

Passionate fragrances flowing into her water from Krishna's
    body attract swarms of bees.
She wears a garland of *champaka* flowers that have fallen
    from Radha's wavy hair.
Devotees serving the Lord always come to bathe in
    her waters.
May Yamuna, Daughter of Kalinda, always remove the
    impurities of our minds.

[6]

She is passionately colored with the beautiful body of
    Radha, who sported in her water.
She shares the essence of graciousness that even the most
    excellent devotees find difficult to obtain.
She is skilled at dividing the seven oceans produced by
    the gods.
May Yamuna, Daughter of Kalinda, always remove the
    impurities of our minds.

[7]

She is full of passion from her waves being in contact with
    the love play occurring on her sandy shores.
She is adorned with sweet blossoms and rays of the
    autumn moon.
She is skilled at extinguishing the fierce fire of worldly
    trouble with her cool waters.
May Yamuna, Daughter of Kalinda, always remove the
    impurities of our minds.

[8]

She is lined with lovely bowers always used for Krishna's
    love play.
She glistens with pollen from the blossoms of *kadamba* trees
    growing on her banks.
She carries those who always bathe in her water across the
    ocean of worldly trouble.
May Yamuna, Daughter of Kalinda, always remove the
    impurities of our minds.

FORTY-ONE YAMUNA POEMS

This collection of forty-one poems is famous in the region of Braj and
beyond, especially among Pushti Margiya Vaishnavas, many of whom
recite these poems every day. Eight very well-known sixteenth-century poet-
saints, known collectively as the Ashta Chap, each wrote four of the poems.
These eight poets are Govindaswami, Chitaswami, Chaturbhujadas,
Nandadas, Surdas, Kumbhandas, Krishnadas, and Paramanandadas.
All eight wrote many other poems and were connected with the Shri
Natha-ji temple that once stood atop Mount Govardhan in Braj. Two
additional poets each wrote four poems in this collection: the influential
figure Hariray, who signs his poems Rasika Pritama, and Ganga Bai, a
celebrated female poet associated with the Shri Natha-ji temple, who
signs her poems Shri Vitthal. The collection is usually capped with a
longer poem by the Ashta Chap poet Krishnadas, bringing the number
to forty-one. These poems, composed in the Braj Bhasha language, are
second only to Vallabhacharya's Sanskrit "Yamunashtakam" as a source
of Yamuna theology for Pushti Margiya Vaishnavas.[3]

[1]
Full of love, she plays with her beloved.
She signals her beloved to give her bliss to everyone.
Her heart is overjoyed when he says he will do this.[4]
She is greatly celebrated, for everything is in her hands.
She showers incalculable grace on those who invoke her name.
Look at her, touch her, and meditate in your heart on her
Who always wanders with Krishna, Lord of Braj.
She grants supreme bliss and destroys all sorrows.
The bliss she gives surpasses that promised by all others.
Understanding Yamuna in this way, sing about her great
    qualities,
And obtain the priceless jewel of Rasika Pritama.[5]

[2]
Krishna's abode of bliss is wherever her name is uttered.
Night and day the Lord of Life comes and resides in the
    heart of those fortunate ones who sing of her glory.
Again and again she is declared to be the very essence of this
    world.
She is the foundation of all, and the treasure of the needy.

One attains the gift of fearlessness by invoking the name
    Shri Yamuna.
The Beloved of Rasika Pritama is under her control.[6]

[3]

She has been verified as the very essence of scripture.
What can anyone accomplish without her, Friend?
She destroys worldly and otherworldly sorrows,
And showers one with complete bliss.
Her left arm quivers when a soul is initiated into the divine
    relationship.[7]
She runs noisily while going to her beloved.
She becomes delighted as her heart is filled with great bliss.
Her name is a priceless jewel that cannot be stolen by anyone.
A devotee should make a necklace of it and wear it on the
    heart.
The person upon whom the Beloved of Rasika Pritama
    showers his grace can understand the true form of
    Shri Yamuna-ji.

[4]

Now fill your eyes with the Daughter of the Sun.
When she plays with her beloved, bumblebees swarm around
    them.
She flows with divine sweat produced from blissful
    lovemaking.
Her course is twisted and she enchants her beloved.
He cannot live without her for a single second.
The Beloved of Rasika Pritama performs the love dance on
    Shri Yamuna's banks.
She is the fortune of those who have nothing else.

[5]

Being united with Dark Krishna, Shri Yamuna herself is dark.
Her flow of drops of love sweat rushes toward her beloved
    ocean.
She is like a young lover who is so restless that she cannot
    remain in her own home.
Look at her beautiful form; she surpasses millions of cupids.

She makes love with Krishna, the young holder of Mount
    Giriraj.
Lord Govinda becomes exceedingly happy while looking
    at her.[8]
She comes to him like a new bride.

[6]

There is no greater giver than Shri Yamuna.
She instantly gives union with Lord Krishna to the person
    who takes refuge with her.
How can one tongue possibly describe her qualities,
    which are a treasure of nectar?
Why didn't the Creator give me a thousand tongues to
    do this?
Govinda offers his body, mind, and wealth to her completely.
She holds all souls in her hand.

[7]

The person who sings the glories of Shri Yamuna in this
    world has Krishna, the very Lord of Life, under control.
That person's eyes and voice become filled with divine
    nectar.
This is not available in the Vedas and Puranas since
No one is able to grasp the subject of love.
Govinda says: The person upon whom Shri Yamuna showers
    her grace enters the refuge of Shri Vallabha's lineage.

[8]

Shri Yamuna, you grant the dust from the Lord's lotus
    feet.
You save souls in this decadent age.
You cut through all sins with your powerful stream
    of water.
Shri Natha-ji, Vallabha, and Vitthalnatha all came for the
    benefit of the devotees.
And you are the ladder to reach all bliss.
Govinda says: She cannot live for a single second without
    her Lord.
Her eyes quiver with great impatience.

[9]

Rush to the bank of Shri Yamuna!
Now, how can anyone begin to describe her greatness?
Go and touch her body, liquid love.
Night and day, Krishna, the Enchanter of Hearts,
Plays with his Lover in a crowd of devotees.
Chitaswami's Lord, Shri Vitthal, Holder of the Mountain,[9]
Cannot tolerate a single second without her.

[10]

Shri Vallabha blesses the person who sings the name
     Shri Yamuna.
That person is able to understand Shri Yamuna.
When you offer everything—body, mind, and wealth—to
     youthful Krishna,
Your mind will become fastened to his feet.
Chitaswami says: Then Shri Vitthal, Holder of the Mountain,
Manifests the divine love play for your eyes.

[11]

Blessed Shri Yamuna gives the divine treasure.
Ignorance and sins are removed by singing about her qualities.
And one achieves a meeting with the Lover and Beloved.
If any doubt about this arises, hold this in mind:
She causes great happiness for those following the Path of
     Grace.
She causes them to enter into that mass of love in the love
     bower,
While filling them with the nectar of love.
Shri Yamuna, the beloved Shri Natha-ji,
Vallabha, and Vitthalnatha all shower kindness upon the
     soul.
Chitaswami says: She came here with Shri Vitthal, Holder of
     the Mountain, for the purpose of enhancing love.

[12]

How can one mouth possibly describe her limitless qualities?
Abandon all religious practices and worship the name of Shri
     Yamuna-ji.

By this means alone, you will obtain Krishna, the youthful
    Holder of the Mountain.
She knows everything about the way of pure divine love.
Therefore, firmly grab onto her lotus feet.
Chitaswami asks: Now where is there to go if one
    leaves the great treasure Shri Vitthal,
    Holder of the Mountain?

[13]

Hold Shri Yamuna in your mind night and day.
Under the influence of her devotees, she showers her
    grace.
Always, this is the nature of Shri Yamuna-ji.
The person who utters the name Shri Yamuna
Is connected to her and goes to her without delay.
Chaturbhujadas now says to everyone: Call out the name
Shri Yamuna! Shri Yamuna!

[14]

Krishna, Lord of Life, wanders playfully on the bank of
    Shri Yamuna.[10]
Bumblebees dwell there, attracted by the sweet aroma of
    Krishna,
Who is like a lotus that has opened fully upon seeing the
    rising sun.
When Krishna makes music with his flute,
The women of Braj hear it and lose consciousness of their
    bodies.
Chaturbhujadas says: But Krishna, the youthful Holder of
    the Mountain, sways with bliss in the ocean of
    Shri Yamuna's love.

[15]

Again and again one should sing the qualities of Shri
    Yamuna.
That person whose tongue drinks the divine nectar of her
    name is very fortunate.
The Daughter of the Sun is exceedingly kind and
    compassionate.

One should live continuously hoping for her.
Chaturbhujadas says: One who is soaked with the divine
    nectar of Shri Yamuna-ji resides near the Beloved.

[16]

Shri Yamuna favors her devotees and grants entrance into
    the love bower.
There Krishna, the Supreme Connoisseur of Love, makes
    love night and day.
To what extent can one describe that gathering of love?
Hearing Krishna's flute, the river stopped flowing
    and the women of Braj became enraptured.
No one can resist its sound.
Chaturbhujadas says: Yamuna is like a lotus,
My mind buzzes around her like a bumblebee.

[17]

Shri Yamuna showers amazing grace upon her devotees.
She leaves her own abode and comes to Earth
To reveal to her devotees the divine love play.
She fulfills the highest aim of all her devotees,
Giving them a very wonderful body.[11]
Nandadas says: Understanding this, grab onto her feet
    firmly!
How can one tongue possibly describe her special nature?

[18]

Out of great affection Shri Yamuna came here first.
Knowing completely the state of the devotees' hearts, she ran
    here quickly.
She fulfills whatever wish exists in the devotees' hearts.
Coming like that, she is worshiped by the virtuous.
Nandadas says: The Lord is very pleased with those who
    sing about the fame of Shri Yamuna-ji.

[19]

Sing Shri Yamuna! Shri Yamuna!
Shesha sings with his thousand mouths night and day[12] but
    cannot achieve the highest aim.

Yet through her, it can be achieved.
She gives all bliss, so utter her name.
Say it again and again so as not to forget it.
Nandadas says: Shri Yamuna fulfills all hopes.
So keep her in your mind constantly.

[20]

Shri Yamuna gives fortune and supreme blessedness.
Abandon ordinary things and worship Yamuna in her
    nurturing form.
Then you will meet Krishna, the youthful Holder of the
    Mountain.
Talk to her great devotees and take their teachings,
And you will always be in the presence of the Playful
    Lord.
Nandadas says: That person upon whom Shri Vallabha
    showers his grace is continually under
    Shri Yamuna's power.

[21]

Know the greatness of her name.
By saying her name, those following the lawful path obtain
    ordinary satisfaction,
And those following the graceful path of love obtain
    supreme love.
A drop of *svati* rainwater becomes different things
    depending upon the nature of the vessel into which it falls.
Know Shri Yamuna to be a vast ocean of grace while *svati*
    rainwater is variable.[13]
Sur asks: How can anyone fully describe her qualities?

[22]

Shri Yamuna makes the inaccessible accessible for her
    devotees.
All sins are washed away for the person who bathes in her in
    the morning;
And Yama, Lord of Death, joins his hands in honor of that
    person.
What does the experiencer know without experience?
The one whose heart has not been stolen by the Beloved

Cannot understand the secret essence of the ocean of love.
Sur asks: What then would be the use of bathing this
body?[14]

[23]

One knows the form of a reward when that reward is achieved.
How can you believe anyone if you have not seen it or heard
about it?
A priceless jewel is placed only in the hand of one who is
capable of recognizing it as such.
Sur says: Always remain far from cruel people.
Strain out the waste and drink the name Shri Yamuna.

[24]

The devotees of the Lord of Shri Yamuna have a special
characteristic.
They live among accomplished devotees,
And Krishna, Lord of Life, remains in their hearts.
Those who are able to understand Shri Yamuna's deep and
secret nature, have their eyes fixed on Krishna,
Enchanter of the Heart.
Sur says: This is the essence of happiness,
Obtained only by the grace of Shri Vallabha.

[25]

Bow your head to Shri Yamuna, the treasure house of divine
love.
She gives all bliss to those devotees who know her greatness.
They receive whatever they ask for.
By taking her name, the fallen soul is made pure and is able
to cross over.
Grab onto her feet firmly, and don't go anywhere else.
Kumbhandas says: I wish to look at the face of Krishna,
Holder of the Mountain, without the interruption
of a single blink.

[26]

It is not possible to count the countless qualities of Shri Yamuna.
One can acquire a new body from the sands on Yamuna's
bank.[15]

How can one even speak of the greatness of the bliss
    she gives?
Whatever the devotee asks for, she gives in a second.
Acting in this way, she carries out her vow.[16]
Kumbhandas asks: How can the heart ever get enough of
    looking at the face of Krishna,
    Holder of the Mountain?

[27]

Offer your body, mind, wealth, and life to
    Shri Yamuna.
Who can describe her pure glory?
Fasten your eyes on her without a moment's break.
Keep her lotus feet in your mind,
And let your mouth recite her name night and day.
Kumbhandas says: With her grace one is able to behold
    the face of Krishna, the youthful Holder of the
    Mountain.

[28]

Shri Yamuna-ji fulfills the devotee's wish.
She gives what is best without even being asked.
How can one begin to describe her beneficial nature?
She is just like anyone's mother.[17]
Krishna makes love with the women of Braj on the bank
    of Shri Yamuna.
With a gentle smile he steals their hearts.
Kumbhandas says: I desire to look upon the face of
    Krishna, the youthful Holder of the Mountain.
Shri Yamuna fulfills my wish.

[29]

Know Shri Yamuna-ji to be an ocean of the nectar of divine
    lovemaking.
Her body is a mighty river in an ever-changing form.
She keeps the Lord in the middle of her heart.
She assumes the burdens of her devotees,
And gives them her own dear Lord,
While speaking sweet, sweet words.

Shri Vitthal says: She has Krishna,[18]
Holder of the Mountain, under her control.
Who then is able to describe her greatness?

[30]

She frees her devotees from worldly snares and protects
   them.
She always keeps those who utter the name Shri Yamuna
   with her in her nectar of love.
How can anyone begin to describe her grace?
She cares for her people just like a mother cares for her son.
Shri Vitthal says: She plays with Krishna, Holder of the
   Mountain, but does not forget her devotees
   even for a second.

[31]

That person who invokes the name of Shri Yamuna is very
   fortunate.
The person who always reflects on her true nature is
   not affected by this decadent age and remains attached
   to love.
The essence of the Path of Grace is difficult to attain through
   ritual actions.
So leave them all and become saturated with supreme love.
Shri Vitthal says: Without them even asking,
Yamuna gives to the devotees the treasure of Krishna,
Holder of the Mountain.

[32]

Who is able to describe Shri Yamuna-ji?
Krishna, the beloved Enchanter, enchants the mind of
   everyone, but she steals his mind.
Krishna, the Wealth of the Soul, cannot remain without her
   for a single second.
She is so blessed that she provides bliss for the heart of
   Krishna, the Moon of Braj.
Shri Vitthal says: She came with Krishna, Holder of the
   Mountain, having assumed incarnation for the
   good of the devotees.

[33]

Shri Yamuna-ji, you are the one for me.
Be kind and give me sight of yourself night and day.
Inspire me to sing your praises.
By obtaining you, a person obtains all treasures.
My bumblebee mind hovers about your lotus feet.
Krishnadas says: Whoever resides near you, including trees
    and creepers, must have performed successful
    religious austerities.

[34]

She showers such grace that we may take her name.
Shri Yamuna is worshiped by the whole world.
Who can count the qualities of her whose consort is
    Krishna,
The Beautiful Dark Lord?
Beloved Krishna is so greatly under her control that
    he gives the blissful nectar of union to her devotees.
Just hearing about her great fame,
A person's desires are all fulfilled.
Krishnadas says: Shri Yamuna does not remain for a single
    second without doing good for her devotees.

[35]

All sins are destroyed through Shri Yamuna-ji's name.
Krishna, the youthful Holder of the Mountain, has such love
    for hearing about her qualities that he comes and appears
    before one singing about them.
All the devotees' efforts are accomplished in a second, and
    they join with their group of Braj women.
Krishnadas asks: Now who is there to fear when
    Shri Yamuna is pleased with you?

[36]

One who invokes the name Shri Yamuna-ji becomes
    attached to Krishna, the Son of Nanda.
That person offers everything and lives in divine
    proximity.

The person who really understands this is able to accept it
   fully in his heart.
For without recognition how can one attain it?
Krishnadas says: Shri Yamuna's name is a boat for the
   devotee to use to cross over the ocean of
   worldly suffering.

[37]

A devotional servant wishes for Shri Yamuna.
With folded hands, I ask with mind, voice, and actions to
   remain in your presence night and day where
   Radha and Krishna, the pair of divine connoisseurs,
   meet to make love.
Paramanandadas says: I have now found Krishna, the Moon
   of Braj.
I see his gentle smile and cool eyes.

[38]

The Lord now wanders with Shri Yamuna.
She fulfills all desires in the devotee's heart.
Who can describe her song?
She is adorned with various garments and ornamentations.
The beauty of her body cannot be expressed.
Paramanandadas says: I have now found Krishna, the Moon
   of Braj.
Keep me in your shelter as you flow.

[39]

Shri Yamuna, you have the beloved Krishna under your
   control.
You captured him with the snare of love and keep him close
   to you.
You have managed to purchase this priceless jewel.
He always runs wherever you send him.
He is soaked in the nectar of your love.
Paramanandadas says: I have now found Krishna, the Moon
   of Braj.
Shri Yamuna is so generous that she gave him to me as
   a gift.

[40]

Shri Yamuna makes her dear Lord Krishna very happy.
She makes him remember those loving souls he had
    forgotten.
How can anyone describe her goodness?
When she sings with her beloved Krishna, she is flooded with
    the rapture of loving joy and keeps the beat by clapping
    her hands.
Paramanandadas says: I have now found Krishna, the Moon
    of Braj, because she knows all the ways of love.

[41]

She safeguards refuge and increases love for Gopala.
She makes you a lover and gives you the abode of the Lord.
She who is filled with unlimited compassion and is the other
    half of Krishna's body places you in front of him.
Humble people know her as an abundance of love, the
    goddess of the love bower who plays the love dance with
    Beloved Krishna night and day.
She grants devotion, carries you across the ocean of all
    worldly troubles, and destroys all the sins of ruined people.
Krishna, Son of Nanda, remains near her banks night
    and day,
And there the cowherd men and women always play in the
    middle of the very source of love.
Yamuna's body is the color of Krishna,
She has the qualities and character of Shri Krishna,
She is filled with Krishna's love play,
And she is a source of Krishna's pleasure.
Ganges obtained Krishna from merging with Yamuna,
And she became filled with the power to grant all spiritual
    powers, and capable of removing all sins.
Shri Yamuna is full of the nectar of grace,
She is a stairway to heaven,
She is famous throughout the world,
And she adorns the head of Shiva.[19]
Establish yourself at her lotus feet,
Leave everything else and behold her eyes.
She is kind and her smile is gentle and sweet.

With both hands joined together, Krishnadas prays:
Bless me now, O Daughter of Kalinda Mountain.

SURDAS'S FAMOUS POEM TO YAMUNA

I have included the following poem because it is one of the most widely
known of the Yamuna poems composed in Braj. Although it is not
included in the "Forty-One Poems," many Vaishnavas, especially Pushti
Margiyas, know it well and sing it in their daily worship. It is typically
sung in the early morning in *raga* Bhairava.[20]

Shri Yamuna-ji, sight of you gives me much delight.
You flow past the town of Gokul, bringing the beauty of
    your waves.
You remove all sorrows and grant all joys, Shri Yamuna-ji,
For those who rise early in the morning and bathe in
    your waters.
You are the Lover of Krishna, the Enchanter of Love,
And are called his Chief Lover [Patarani].
You make love happen in the forest of Vrindaban,
While enchanting Krishna plays the flute.
Surdas's Lord Krishna unites with you,
Whose pure splendor is sung about in the holy scriptures.

"SHRI YAMUNA CHALISA"

*Chalisa*s constitute a genre of short sacred texts that consist of forty
verses of praise. (Two additional verses proclaim the benefits of reciting
this text.) It is likely that all *chalisa*s are modeled on the "Hanuman
Chalisa," a text attributed to the famous sixteenth-century saint Tulsidas.
This particular *chalisa* is addressed to Yamuna and was written in
Gokul in the Braj Bhasha language by Pannalal Purushottam Shastri.[21]

1. One who sings "Shri Yamuna! Yamuna!" is flooded with love
   for the feet of Hari [Krishna].

2. You alone, O Yamuna, give all spiritual powers and establish
   one's relationship with Hari.

3. There is no greater means than you for one seeking refuge from
   the terror of Death.

4. The sages Narada, Sanaka, and Vyasa meditate eternally on your banks, driving away all misfortunes.

5. The divine couple Shyama [Radha] and Shyam [Krishna] sit there on an extremely beautiful seat situated in the middle of a love bower.

6. One who bathes in your water will never experience Death's noose.

7. Uttering your name eliminates all troubles just as a lion's roar drives away an animal.

8. You are the true love of Madan Mohan [Krishna] and completely control Murari [Krishna] in many powerful ways.

9. Saras cranes, swans, parrots, peacocks, and partridges sing with delight on your banks.

10. The village Gokul adorns your banks and great happiness abounds where Nanda's house stands.

11. All glory to Queen Yamuna, Krishna's Lady, Daughter of the Sun!

12. When the young women of Braj sing your praise, they attain Nandalal [Krishna] as their lover.

13. Ganges was purified by uniting with you and thereby became situated permanently on the head of Shiva.

14. O Chief Lover of the Aesthetic Jewel of Supreme Love [Krishna], scripture proclaims your greatness.

15. Your milk flows with great charm. Seeing you brings joy to my heart.

16. O Kalindi, you are a brilliant young woman. Those who drink your milk are most fortunate.

17. The holy city of Mathura is located on your bank, delighting all with its splendor.

18. We know that you save the wretched. You are the Queen of Braj, upon whom even the Lord of Braj depends.

19. Mother, there is no one equal to you. You give all eight spiritual powers and all nine spiritual treasures.

20. Your stream split into the seven seas and you manifest to uplift the world.

21. You keep one's body free from all disease and suffering during all parts of the day.

22. Whoever performs loving service [*seva*] to you, O Yamuna, is united with the young King of Braj [Krishna].

23. By presenting you with elegant clothing, offering you food, and serving you cool, sweet milk . . .

24. Your devotees become especially dear to Gopal [Krishna], the best of lovers, who wears yellow cloth and a peacock feather crown.

25. Your body is adorned with infinite qualities that astonish Shiva, Indra, and the holy sages.

26. As an ocean of compassion, your body is a supreme refuge; you destroy all problems.

27. You are the wishing stone of the devotees; you help them to cross over the ocean of worldly troubles.

28. You are the lover of the Lord of Gokul [Krishna]; you are the darling of the mighty sun king.

29. You are the tool that destroys all sins; you are the stairway by which one arrives at heavenly Goloka.

30. You are the light of the whole world, a most fortunate mother, and daughter of the sun.

31. You transform bad situations and cause one to be fastened to the feet of Hari.

32. One who sings about Hari's qualities on your bank is immediately released from all other connections.

33. Ah Mother, we residents of Gokul delight in the dust from the feet of the Lord of Gokul.

34. Love for the Lord increases from sight of you; you cause one to remember one's own true form.

35. You came from Mount Kalinda to Gokul to manifest the graceful divine play [*pushti lila*] here.

36. O Mother, you protect the devotees and punish the wicked.

37. You destroy the faults of this decadent age and accomplish incomparable devotional love.

38. You play many roles in the Lord's divine drama and unite the devotees with Hari.

39. Your brother is Judge of Righteousness [Yama, Lord of Death]; by your kindness he releases us.

40. All glory to the Sister of Yama! All glory to the Savior of the World! You are the Supreme Queen of the highest bliss.

41. One who recites this "Shri Yamuna Chalisa" will witness all the spiritual powers of the Goddess of Braj.

42. All desires of the heart are fulfilled for the one who recites this *chalisa*.

"SHRI YAMUNA YASHA PACHASA"

A *pachasa* is a fifty-verse hymn in praise of a deity. (Two additional verses are added to proclaim the benefit of reciting the hymn.) This one addressed to Yamuna is very recent; it was written in Vrindaban by Vrindaban Bihari Mishra on the occasion of the new millennium. It demonstrates the continuity of literature composed to celebrate Yamuna that stretches back over three thousand years to the early Vedic period. The title may be translated as "Fifty Verses in Praise of Yamuna's Grandeur."[22]

All glory to Yamuna!
All glory to Krishna's lover!
All glory to the blissful splendorous abode!
Radha and Krishna play eternally on your blessed banks.

1. All glory to Yamuna! All glory to the Daughter of the Sun! All glory to the Lover of Krishna-Chandra!

2. All glory to Krishnaa, the Mother who saves the world![23] Your father is the Sun and your brother is Yama, Lord of Death.

3. You flow as a river from the heavenly abode of Shri Goloka; your essential form consists of an abundance of purity.

4. You know how the sun manifested the world; for this reason you are considered to be the Daughter of the Sun.

5. Mount Kalinda performed great asceticism and so you appeared there on Earth.

6. You flow as a powerful and swift stream from your source of Brahmakunda at Yamunotri, uttering sounds as you go.[24]

7. You reduce mighty boulders to grains of sand that move along with your pure waters.

8. When one utters your name, "Kalindi," and understands your essential form as Shyam [Krishna], the world becomes blissful.

9. You give bliss as a river as dark in color as Krishna, and your strong current is like a sharp chisel that cuts through all sins.

10. You came to Earth with Krishna's kindness; you give bliss to the holy men, saints, and devotees.

11. Your clothing is dark and your stream is dark; you support the love play of Radha and Krishna.

12. You enhance the beauty of the land of Braj as you pass through the middle of the circle of Braj.

13. All sins are destroyed by bathing in Yamuna; all afflictions are destroyed by sipping her water.

14. All sorrows vanish immediately upon having sight of her. Thus people shout, "Shri Yamuna! Yamuna!"

15. The messengers of Death [Yama] do not come near the person who sings about the magnificence of Yamuna.

16. She holds a lotus garland in her hand for Krishna, offering it to this Son of Nanda.

17. She has lotuslike feet and lotuslike eyes on her face. The nectarlike water from her feet confers complete bliss.

18. She is Krishna's primary queen in the city of Dwarka, where her mind is immersed in the loving service of the Lord.

19. Murari [Krishna] met her in Indraprastha when he went there with mighty Arjuna.[25]

20. Abandoning Indra, she took Vishnu [Krishna] for her beloved; immersed in his loving service, she delights Krishna.

21. Anyone who bathes in Yamuna achieves the highest place; anyone who sips her water attains the glory of supreme love.

22. She immediately destroys the sorrows of one who honors her, and causes the eternal auspiciousness of Krishna's kindness to shower upon that one.

23. Yamuna carries a mass of dust that was certainly obtained from the feet of Krishna-Chandra.

24. She adorns Krishna with elaborate ornaments and plays gentle music with the ankle bells on her lotus feet.

25. On Bhai Duj, sister Yamuna adorns her brother Yama Raja [Lord of Death] with all decorations.

26. After applying an honorific mark [*tilak*] on his forehead, Yamuna feeds her brother Yama. He rewards his sister with presents and kind words.

27. Brothers and sisters who come together on the second day of the bright half of the lunar month of Kartik . . .

28. And bathe in Yamuna's water have the sins of lifetime after lifetime destroyed.

29. Those who bathe in Yamuna on Bhai Duj never approach the door of Yama.

30. One who says "Shri Yamuna! Yamuna-ji!" is always united with Krishna.

31. The Sister of Yama saves one from the realm of Death and carries that one to the heavenly abode of Shri Goloka.

32. Yamuna destroys the troubles of this decadent age; the gods, sages, and people praise and worship her.

33. Having left Mount Kalinda, she descended onto the plains and revealed herself at Indraprastha.

34. Balarama dragged her with his plow so that her face looked eastward from this offensive hold.

35. She then came to blessed Vrindaban and, encircling it like a bracelet, she made it blissful.[26]

36. The divine couple play on the banks of Yamuna. The waves of Yamuna are her arms.

37. The Dark Lord [Krishna] delights Radha by himself steering her through the forest in a boat.

38. Yamuna makes a beautiful necklace around Vrindaban that shines just like blue sapphires.

39. Making an offering to her beloved Krishna, she begins to circumambulate his sacred land.

40. She flows on all sides of Vrindaban uttering "Hari, Hari" with her waves.

41. She then flows by Mathura forming the shape of a half moon.

42. Flowing past the many ghats there she gives great bliss. She destroys all sins and is a stairway to Hari's abode.

43. Then moving on south to Gokul, she spreads divine bliss over Gokul.

44. Further downstream Yamuna embraces Ganges and merges with the heart of Sarasvati.

45. Yamuna unites with Ganges at Prayag and there turns her dark.

46. From here on, the river is Yamuna in form but Ganges in name, and they flow on together to Gangasagar.[27]

47. Upon reaching the ocean, she travels to Dvaraka and there becomes the chief queen of Krishna.

48. She steals the heart and mind of Krishna and his lovers and performs all beneficial work for her own devotees.

49. Bathing in Yamuna, offering her milk, worshipping her, offering her food, . . .

50. Bowing to her, and feeling love for her, one attains all spiritual powers through Yamuna's kindness.

51. She gives the energy and bliss of all spiritual powers. All glory be to Shri Yamuna, the mother of the world!

52. Recite this twelve times with an engaged mind and you will achieve the state of supreme love through Yamuna's kindness.

All glory to Yamuna, who consists of drops of supreme love!
All glory to Yamuna's water, whose essential form is consciousness!
A human life becomes blessed by bathing in her and always worshipping her.

YAMUNA ARATIS

Dozens of *aratis,* hymns of praise, are sung by various worshippers of Yamuna. I have included these two to exemplify this genre of Yamuna hymns. The first is posted near the Yamuna temple at Keshi Ghat in Vrindaban. It is sung early every morning and every evening by those who gather together to worship Yamuna at this temple. The second is commonly known in Braj.[28] I translated these hymns for their meaning only; their rhyming and rhythmic quality does not survive translation. Both were composed in the Braj Bhasha language.

"Yamuna Arati"

All glory to you Mother Yamuna!
Balaram's brother, Krishna, dances on your banks.
One who drinks your water does not go to the abode
     of Death.
One who sings about you does not suffer the torments
     of Death.
You are a river of liquid Brahman and in you reside all
     worthy pilgrimage sites.
All sins are destroyed for the one who bathes in you on
     Yama Dvitiya.
You appear in the eternal love play as a river equal to the
     lover Radha.
Your different ways of moving appear as variations in your
     pure current.
Sickness, poverty, and death never come near your water,
     which shines like a blue sapphire.
Day and night you destroy all impurities for those who
     worship you with fruit, milk, and words.
Krishna is charmed by each and every one of your drops
     of water.
Mother Yamuna, you are associated with the happiness of
     Krishna's form.
Singing these verses with love, you remain with me.

"Shri Yamuna-ji ki Arati"

All glory to you, Mother Yamuna!
Om, all glory to you, Mother Yamuna!
You break the noose of Death
     and are a boat to the other shore.
Om, all glory to you, Mother Yamuna!
You are the Daughter of the Sun
     and Sister of Death.
O Dark Goddess, Shyama Kalindini,
You fulfill the desires of all those who worship you.
Om, all glory to you, Mother Yamuna!
You are the lover of Krishna, Son of Nanda.
You both have the same complexion.

You remove all misfortune and disease
   for those who are mindful of you.
Om, all glory to you, Mother Yamuna!
You are a stream of loving devotion.
One who is immersed in you passes beyond all troubles.
Your water turns a wild jungle into Vrindaban, the forest
   of love.
Om, all glory to you, Mother Yamuna!

Organizations Working on River Issues in Northern India

ORGANIZATIONS THAT WORK ON THE YAMUNA

Friends of Vrindaban　A Vrindaban-based environmental organization that works on environmental issues in the Braj region. This work includes cleaning the banks of the Yamuna and stopping the flow of refuse into the river. Web site address: www.fov.uk.org.

Paani Morcha　A New Delhi-based organization that works to stop the pollution of the Yamuna in the capital region and to increase the minimum flow of freshwater in the river. Web site address: www.paanimorcha.com.

We for Yamuna　A Delhi-based youth initiative committed to cleaning the Yamuna. Web site address: www.weforyamuna.8m.com.

Yamuna Foundation for Blue Water　An organization that addresses social issues and works to clean the Yamuna in the area around Agra. Web site address: http://yamuna.sdutta.tripod.com/yamuna.htm.

ORGANIZATIONS THAT WORK ON THE GANGES

Eco-Friends　A Kanpur-based environmental organization whose efforts include cleaning the Ganges in Kanpur and educating the public about environmental issues in the area. Web site address: www.ecofriends.org.

Sankat Mochan Foundation   A Banaras- (Varanasi-) based organization dedicated to stopping the pollution of the Ganges in this holy city. Web site address: www.friendsofganges.org. Information can also be found under "International Projects" on the Oz Green Web site: www.ozgreen.org.au.

RESEARCH INSTITUTIONS

Centre for Science and Environment   A New Delhi-based research organization dedicated to studying the environmental challenges of India and informing the public about them. This organization has done much work on the Yamuna. Web site address: www.cseindia.org.

GOVERNMENTAL ORGANIZATIONS

Central Pollution Control Board   An Indian governmental branch that monitors environmental conditions of India, including those of the Yamuna. Information on the Yamuna can be found in the "Water Quality" section of this Web site: www.cpcb.nic.in.

Yamuna Action Plan   This governmental project, which began in 1993, aims to build sewage treatment plants and stop the flow of pollution into the Yamuna. The home page for this project can be found at: http://yap.nic.in.

Notes

INTRODUCTION

1. "The growing pollution of our rivers constitutes the biggest threat to public health," reports India's Centre for Science and Environment. The organization names the Yamuna as one of India's most polluted rivers. Anil Agarwal, Sunita Narain, and Srabani Sen, eds., *The Citizens' Fifth Report: State of India's Environment* (New Delhi: Centre for Science and Environment, 1999), 58.

2. See the conclusion of *Purifying the Earthly Body of God: Religion and Ecology in Hindu India,* ed. Lance E. Nelson (Albany: State University of New York Press, 1998), 332.

3. Central Pollution Control Board, *Water Quality Status of Yamuna River* (Delhi: Central Pollution Control Board, 2000), 7.

4. The state of Himachal Pradesh holds 1.2 percent of the Yamuna's catchment area; Haryana, 8.6 percent; Rajasthan, 31 percent; Madhya Pradesh, 38.3 percent; Uttar Pradesh, 20.5 percent; and the Union Territory of Delhi, 0.4 percent. Government of India, Central Water Commission, *Water Quality Studies: Yamuna System, Status Report, 1978–1990* (New Delhi: Government of India, Central Water Commission, 1991), 1.

5. This bicycle expedition, which was sponsored by the Friends of Vrindaban, took place October 5–26, 1996.

6. See Heinrich von Stietencron, *Ganga und Yamuna Zur symbolischen Bedeutung der Flussgottinnen an indischen Tempeln* (Wiesbaden: Otto Harrassowitz, 1972). This volume includes many photographs and an introduction in English.

7. Several residents of Dakpathar told me in conversation that they believed Yamuna was a goddess only upstream from the Dakpathar dam, and at Dakpathar,

the Yamuna as goddess ended. Although this viewpoint could be said to account for the seriously degraded state of the Yamuna downstream from Dakpathar, it is denied completely by the residents of Braj, who claim that the Yamuna is most sacred when she arrives in Braj and unites with Krishna, her Beloved, who is often identified with the land of Braj.

8. Cited in Arundhati Roy, *The Greater Common Good* (Bombay: India Book Distributors, 1999), 7. From C. V. J. Sharma, ed., *Modern Temples of India: Selected Speeches of Jawaharlal Nehru at Irrigation and Power Projects* (New Delhi: Central Board of Irrigation and Power, 1989).

9. Much of the following information is based on Bhajan Singh Giani, *Gurdwara Sri Paonta Sahib: A Short History* (Paonta Sahib, Himachal Pradesh: Parbandhak Committee, 1997).

10. See Abha Singh, "Irrigating Haryana: The Pre-Modern History of the Western Yamuna Canal," in *Medieval India: Researches in the History of India, 1200–1750*, ed. Irfan Habib (Delhi: Oxford University Press, 1999), 50–52.

11. Ibid., 53.

12. Ibid., 57–58.

13. See Central Pollution Control Board, *Water Quality Status of Yamuna River.* This fact was also related to me personally by Dr. R. C. Trivedi, a senior scientist working for the Central Pollution Control Board.

14. H. K. Kaul, *Historic Delhi* (Delhi: Oxford University Press, 1996), xviii.

15. Muhammad Ghuri defeated the Rajputs under the leadership of Prithviraj in the second battle of Tarain in 1192. For more on this, see Romila Thapar, *A History of India*, vol. 1 (Middlesex, U.K.: Penguin Books, 1966), 236–38 and 266–68.

16. This occurred in the year 1857, the year of the so-called Indian Mutiny. For more on the history of these times, see Stanley Wolpert, *A New History of India* (New York: Oxford University Press, 1982), 201–38; or Percival Spear, *A History of India*, vol. 2 (London: Penguin Books, 1978), especially chapter 11.

17. I confess that I have not counted these temples and suspect that this number is exaggerated. The number 108 is a sacred number, and if there are not actually 108, the point is that there are in spirit.

18. B. K. Chaturvedi, *Yamuna*, Gods and Goddesses of India, no. 12 (Delhi: Books for All, 1998), 62.

19. Pandit Mishra, *Shri Bateshwar Nath va Shauripur* (Shikohabad: Jaya Ma Enterprises, 1983), 20–21.

20. Central Pollution Control Board, *Water Quality Status of Yamuna River,* 6.

21. *Narada Purana* 1.6.5. See *Narada Purana*, trans. G. V. Tagare (Delhi: Motilal Publishers, 1980), 126.

22. The pilgrimage literature available at this site still refers to it by this name.

23. See K. S. Valdiya, *Saraswati: The River That Disappeared* (Hyderabad: Universities Press, 2002).

24. Within yogic culture, the Yamuna, Ganges, and Sarasvati are identified with the three inner channels of the subtle body, respectively the right *pingala*, left *ida*, and central *sushumna*. See, for example, Jean Varenne, *Yoga and the Hindu Tradition* (Chicago: University of Chicago Press, 1976), 161–62.

25. *Prayag Mahatmya* (Allahabad: Shri Durga Pustak Bhandar, n.d.), 3.

26. *Padma Purana* 6.24.1–15. See *Padma Purana,* pt. 7, trans. N. A. Deshpande (Delhi: Motilal Banarsidass, 1991), 2407.

27. *Padma Purana* 6.127.42–45. *Padma Purana,* pt. 8, p. 2771.

28. *Prayag Mahatmya,* 6.

29. Expressed commonly in Hindi as "Ganga nam, lekin Yamuna rup." Also, for example, as "Yamuna rup, Ganga nam" or "Rup ki Jamuna, Nam ki Ganga," in Vrindaban Bihari Mishra, *Shri Yamuna Yasha Pachasa* (Vrindaban: Shivahari Press, 1999), 6 and 13. I translate this text in appendix 1.

1. A RIVER OF DELIGHTS, A RIVER OF TROUBLES

Epigraph: Henry David Thoreau, reflecting on the Concord River in Massachusetts; see *The River: Selections from the Journal of H. D. Thoreau* (New York: Bramhall House, 1963), 52.

1. Lester Brown and Ed Ayres, eds., *The World Watch Reader on Global Environmental Issues* (New York: W. W. Norton, 1998), 174.

2. Ibid., 294.

3. See Ed Ayres, *God's Last Offer* (New York: Four Walls Eight Windows, 1999), 9–25.

4. The American Museum of Natural History, in New York City, conducted a national survey of biologists in 1998 and found that the great majority of them believe we are in the midst of a very serious mass extinction that poses a threat to all life on the planet. Furthermore, they believe: "This mass extinction is the fastest in Earth's 4.5-billion-year history and, unlike prior extinctions, is mainly the result of human activity and not of natural phenomena." See www.amnh.org/museum/press/feature/biofact.html. See also Edward O. Wilson, *The Diversity of Life* (New York: W. W. Norton, 1999).

5. See, for example, the *World Scientists' Warning to Humanity* released by the Union of Concerned Scientists in 1992. The statement, signed by more than seventeen hundred of the world's leading scientists—including the majority of Nobel laureates in the sciences—reads: "Human beings and the natural world are on a collision course. Human activities inflict harsh and often irreversible damage on the environment and on critical resources. If not checked, many of our current practices put at serious risk the future that we wish for human society and the plant and animal kingdoms, and may so alter the living world that it will be unable to sustain life in the manner that we know." The statement is available on many Web sites, including that of the Union of Concerned Scientists: www.ucsusa.org.

6. See Al Gore, *Earth in Balance: Ecology and the Human Spirit* (New York: Houghton Mifflin, 1992).

7. "Human similarities to other life-forms are more striking than the differences. Our deep connections, over vast geological periods, should inspire awe, not repulsion." Lynn Margulis, *Symbiotic Planet: A New Look at Evolution* (New York: Basic Books, 1998), 4.

8. Personal communication with Dr. Indu Tikekar, Gandhi Ashram, Delhi, October 17, 1996.

9. Lina Gupta, "Ganga: Purity, Pollution, and Hinduism," in *Ecofeminism and the Sacred,* ed. Carol Adams (New York: Continuum, 1993), 101.

10. Lynn White Jr., "The Historical Roots of Our Ecologic Crisis," *Science* 155, no. 3767 (March 1967): 1203–7; Lynn White Jr., "Continuing the Conversation," in *Western Man and Environmental Ethics,* ed. Ian G. Barbour (Reading, MA: Addison-Wesley, 1973), 55–64.

11. White, "Historical Roots of Our Ecologic Crisis," 1205.

12. Poul Pedersen cautions us to avoid "explanations which assume that values and norms directly determine behaviour" ("Nature, Religion, and Cultural Identity: The Religious Environmental Paradigm," in *Asian Perceptions of Nature,* ed. Ole Bruun and Arne Kalland [Richmond, U.K.: Curzon Press, 1995], 264). It is important to remember that many factors come into play to determine human behavior. Nonetheless, religious values do have a significant effect on shaping human attitudes toward the natural world. Pedersen himself embraces a middle path: "I do not say that values are unimportant for the way people relate to their environment" (265).

13. White, "Historical Roots of Our Ecologic Crisis," 1206–7.

14. Ibid., 1206–7, and "Continuing the Conversation," 61. White ends his first article by suggesting that Saint Francis should become the patron saint for ecologists. In 1960 the University of Michigan zoologist Marston Bates proposed that Saint Francis should be the patron saint of those who loved nature. The combined voices of Bates, White, and others led the Vatican in 1980 to officially dub Saint Francis the patron saint of ecologists. Francis's "Canticle of Brother Sun, Sister Moon" has now found its way into much eco-spiritual liturgy. See, for example, George Sessions and Bill Devall, *Deep Ecology: Living as If Nature Mattered* (Salt Lake City: Gibbs Smith, 1985), 92.

15. White, "Continuing the Conversation," 57.

16. Ibid.

17. Perhaps the strongest evidence of this is a remarkable series of ten conferences—organized by Mary Evelyn Tucker and John Grim—on the major religions of the world and ecology that took place at Harvard University's Center for the Study of World Religions from 1996 through 1998. These conferences brought together more than eight hundred scholars representing a variety of disciplines from numerous countries to explore the important roles religions play in environmental issues. Harvard University Press has published ten volumes resulting from these conferences in a series titled Religions of the World and Ecology. The conferences also led to the formation of an ongoing academic organization known as the Forum on Religion and Ecology, now based at the Center for the Environment at Harvard University. The Forum maintains a Web site at http://environment.harvard.edu/religion. Moreover, courses are being offered in the area of religion and ecology in increasing numbers in religious studies and anthropology departments in colleges and universities around the country, and there is growing recognition in environmental studies programs and research centers that religion is a significant factor in thinking about the environmental crisis. This is documented in the 2002 edition of *The World Watch Reader,* which contains a section on religion that was expanded into a Worldwatch Paper: Gary Gardner, *Invoking the Spirit: Religion and Spirituality in the Quest for a Sustainable World,* Worldwatch Paper 164 (Washington, DC: Worldwatch Institute, 2002).

18. See "The Greening of Religion," chapter 4 of Roderick Nash's *The Rights of Nature* (Madison: University of Wisconsin Press, 1989), for a good summary discussion of this development.

19. Lynn White, for example, argued, "Especially in its Western form, Christianity is the most anthropocentric religion the world has seen" ("Historical Roots of Our Ecologic Crisis," 1205).

20. White places this in the historical context of Christianity's destruction of European animism. "In Antiquity every tree, every spring, every stream, every hill had its own *genius loci*, its guardian spirit. . . . By destroying pagan animism, Christianity made it possible to exploit nature in a mood of indifference to the feelings of natural objects. . . . The spirits *in* natural objects, which formerly had protected nature from man, evaporated. Man's effective monopoly on spirit in this world was confirmed, and the old inhibitions to the exploitation of nature crumbled. . . . For nearly 2 millennia Christian missionaries have been chopping down sacred groves, which are idolatrous because they assumed spirit in nature" (ibid., 1205–6).

21. A good example of this was an antienvironmental statement by Ronald Reagan's secretary of interior, James Watt, who said that we should not be so concerned with preserving this world, as our real concern should be with a heavenly world beyond this one. Considering Watt's influential position, this incident stands as testimony to the powerful hold that religious worldviews have on human attitudes and behavior toward the world.

22. See, for example, Thomas Berry, *The Dream of the Earth* (San Francisco: Sierra Club Books, 1990). Berry has articulated a religious vision that shows great concern for the health of the Earth and views all living beings as a community of subjects rather than a collection of objects. Berry has inspired a whole generation of Catholic nuns, many of whom have turned their communities into experimental living and learning centers for sustainability and eco-spirituality. Prime examples of this are Genesis Farm in New Jersey and Saint Mary of the Woods in Indiana, especially their White Violet Center for Ecojustice. See also Rosemary Radford Ruether, *Gaia and God: An Ecofeminist Theology of Earth Healing* (San Francisco: Harper, 1992); Sallie McFague, *The Body of God: An Ecological Theology* (Minneapolis: Fortress Press, 1993); Matthew Fox, *Original Blessing* (Santa Fe: Bear and Company, 1983); Charles Cummings, *Eco-Spirituality* (New York: Paulist Press, 1991); and Mark Wallace, *Finding God in the Singing River: Christianity in an Ecological Age* (Minneapolis: Fortress Press, 2005).

23. Ruether, *Gaia and God*, 48.

24. Parallel developments are also taking place in Judaism, as is evident from the establishment of the Coalition on Environment and Jewish Life. See also Hava Tirosh-Samuelson, "Nature in the Sources of Judaism," *Daedalus* 130, no. 4 (Fall 2001): 99–124.

25. A large number of journals (e.g., *Environmental Ethics*), books, and courses germane to environmental philosophy began to appear in the academy during this time.

26. Arne Naess, "The Shallow and the Deep, Long-Range Ecology Movement: A Summary," *Inquiry* 16 (1973): 95–100. Reprinted in *The Deep Ecology Movement: An Introductory Anthology*, ed. Alan Drengson and Yuichi Inoue (Berkeley: North Atlantic Books, 1995), 3–9.

27. In his introduction to his own commentary on the Bhagavad-gita, Gandhi wrote, "This self-realization is the subject of the Gita, as it is of all scriptures." Mohandas K. Gandhi, *The Bhagavad Gita, According to Gandhi,* ed. John Strohmeier (Berkeley: Berkeley Hills Books, 2000), 17.

28. Mohandas K. Gandhi, *All Men Are Brothers* (Lausanne: United Nations Educational, Scientific, and Cultural Organization, 1958), 118.

29. Arne Naess, "Self-Realization: An Ecological Approach to Being in the World," in *The Deep Ecology Movement: An Introductory Anthology,* ed. Alan Drengson and Yuichi Inoue (Berkeley: North Atlantic Books, 1995), 13.

30. Bill Devall, "The Ecological Self," in *The Deep Ecology Movement: An Introductory Anthology,* ed. Alan Drengson and Yuichi Inoue (Berkeley: North Atlantic Books, 1995), 104.

31. While camping in the desert of Death Valley, California, on the occasion of John Muir's birthday in April 1984, Arne Naess and George Sessions articulated eight principles that they thought best summarized fifteen years of thinking about deep ecology. These have been reprinted in Drengson and Inoue, *The Deep Ecology Movement,* 49–53.

32. Ibid., 50. Emphasis added.

33. Ibid.

34. Although many see philosophical roots of deep ecology in the thought of such figures as Henry David Thoreau, Ralph Waldo Emerson, John Muir, Robinson Jeffers, Rachel Carson, Dave Bowers, and other prominent environmentalists, deep ecology as articulated by Naess was introduced to Americans largely by Bill Devall and George Sessions, authors of *Deep Ecology: Living as If Nature Mattered.* These two also acknowledge the contributions of Asian religious traditions, such as Taoism and Zen Buddhism, particularly as represented to Americans by Alan Watts and Gary Snyder, the latter of whom is recognized as being nearly equal to Naess in terms of his importance to the development of deep ecology. The peace activist Joanna Macy and ritual specialist Delores LaChapelle have identified themselves with the deep ecology movement in the United States. Moreover, deep ecology has gained public awareness in the United States through the publicity arising from the environmental activist group Earth First! and through the writings of the group's founders, such as Dave Foreman, who applied deep ecological ideas to liberating nature: "Free shackled rivers! . . . The finest fantasy of eco-warriors in the West is the destruction of [Glen Canyon] Dam and the liberation of the Colorado [River]" (Nash, *The Rights of Nature,* 161). Alan Drengson has identified himself with deep ecology in Canada, as has Yuichi Inoue in Japan, and Pat Fleming in England. Deep ecology has found an advocate in Australia in the rain forest activist John Seed and more recently in Freya Mathews and Warwick Fox. Shifting to India, Sunderlal Bahuguna, the recognized "father of Indian environmentalism," identifies with and professes many deep ecological principles.

Indeed, many radical environmental groups have identified themselves with the deep ecological movement. See Christopher Manes, *Green Rage: Radical Environmentalism and the Unmaking of Civilization* (Boston: Little, Brown, and Company, 1990).

35. Significantly, they all also acknowledge Lynn White's 1967 article as a major contributing factor in their respective thinking.

36. See Kazimuddin Ahmed, Suverchala Kashyap, and Samir Kumar Sinha, "Pollution of Hinduism," *Down to Earth* (Centre for Science and Environment, New Delhi) (February 15, 2000): 27–37.

37. Ole Bruun and Arne Kalland, "Images in Nature: An Introduction to the Study of Man-Environment Relations in Asia," in *Asian Perceptions of Nature,* ed. Ole Bruun and Arne Kalland (Richmond, U.K.: Curzon Press, 1995), 2–3.

38. Gupta, "Ganga," 101.

39. Rita Dasgupta Sherma, "Sacred Immanence: Reflections of Ecofeminism in Hindu Tantra," in *Purifying the Earthly Body of God: Religion and Ecology in Hindu India,* ed. Lance E. Nelson (Albany: State University of New York Press, 1998), 89–90.

40. Pedersen, "Nature, Religion, and Cultural Identity," 266.

41. Exceptions to this tendency might include Ranchor Prime, *Hinduism and Ecology* (Delhi: Motilal Banarsidass, 1994); and Christopher Chapple, "Hinduism and Deep Ecology," in *Deep Ecology and World Religions,* ed. David Barnhill and Roger Gottlieb (Albany: State University of New York, 2001). Peter Marshall goes so far as to declare, "Unlike the Judeao-Christian [*sic*] tradition, mainstream Hinduism is deep ecological" (*Nature's Web: Rethinking Our Place on Earth* [London: Simon and Shuster, 1992], 24).

42. Many Western representations of Hinduism expressed by those with environmental concerns also assume that the ascetic dimensions of religion have nothing to contribute to ecological health. Christopher Chapple, however, has shown that this is not the case. See his "Hinduism and Deep Ecology."

43. Tom Hayden, *The Lost Gospel of the Earth* (San Francisco: Sierra Club Books, 1996), 49.

44. Warwick Fox, *Toward a Transpersonal Ecology: Developing New Foundations for Environmentalism* (Albany: State University of New York Press, 1995), 110. Note the reduction of "Indian thought" to a single position.

45. Ibid., 111.

46. Ibid. Fox's association of Gandhi with the Bodhisattva ideal of Mahayana Buddhism denies the strong presence of otherworldly, ascetic-monastic ideals within Mahayana Buddhism. The Buddhist scholar Jan Nattier argues that early Mahayana Buddhism is—far from being this-worldly—more like a monastic "marine corp." See her *A Few Good Men: The Bodhisattva Path According to* The Inquiry of Ugra (Honolulu: University of Hawai'i Press, 2003).

47. Fox, *Toward a Transpersonal Ecology,* 109, 259.

48. Ibid., 109.

49. See David Kopf, *British Orientalism and the Bengal Renaissance* (Berkeley: University of California Press, 1969), 41.

50. H. T. Colebrooke, "On the Vedas, or Sacred Writings of the Hindus," *Asiatic Researches* 8 (1808): 494.

51. Ibid., 496.

52. See Andrew Tuck, *Comparative Philosophy and the Philosophy of Scholarship* (New York: Oxford University Press, 1990), chapter 1.

53. Paul Deussen, *Outline of the Vedanta* (London: Luzac and Company, 1907), vii. Emphasis added.

54. Tuck, *Comparative Philosophy,* 27. Emphasis added.

55. For more on this, see my *Journey through the Twelve Forests: An Encounter with Krishna* (New York: Oxford University of Press, 1994), especially 24–29.

56. Ronald Inden, *Imagining India* (Oxford: Blackwell Publishers, 1990), 105.

57. Mulk Raj Anand, *Untouchable* (London: Penguin Books, 1940), 152–53.

58. Inden, *Imagining India,* 128. Emphasis added.

59. David L. Haberman, "On Trial: The Love of the Sixteen Thousand Gopees," *History of Religions* 33, no. 1 (August 1993): 44–70.

60. Ramachandra Guha maintains that "it is probably fair to say that the life and practice of Gandhi have been the single most important influence on the Indian environmental movement" ("Mahatma Gandhi and the Environmental Movement in India," in *Environmental Movements in Asia,* ed. Arne Kalland and Gerard Persoon [Richmond, U.K.: Curzon Press, 1998], 65–66). The quote is from Mohandas K. Gandhi, *An Autobiography: The Story of My Experiments with Truth* (Boston: Beacon Press, 1957), 67. Gandhi remarked in his autobiography that "to me the Gita became an infallible guide of conduct" (65).

61. Naess wrote several books and articles on Gandhi, including *Gandhi and Group Conflict: An Exploration of Satyagraha* (Oslo: University of Oslo, 1974), and *Gandhi and the Nuclear Age* (Totowa, NJ: Bedminister Press, 1965). See also Fox, *Toward a Transpersonal Ecology,* 107.

62. David Kinsley, *Ecology and Religion: Ecological Spirituality in Cross-Cultural Perspective* (Englewood Cliffs, NJ: Prentice Hall, 1995), 187.

63. Arne Naess, *Ecology, Community, and Lifestyle: Outline of an Ecosophy,* trans. David Rothenberg (Cambridge: Cambridge University Press, 1989), 195.

64. See his introduction to *The Bhagavad Gita, According to Gandhi,* ed. John Strohmeier (Berkeley: Berkeley Hills Books, 2000), 17.

65. See Ramachandra Guha, *The Unquiet Woods: Ecological Change and Peasant Resistance in the Himalaya* (New Delhi: Oxford University Press, 1999), 162. The environmental activist and Chipko spokesperson Sunderlal Bahuguna frequently quotes from the Gita to support his own ecological theology. See chapter 2 of the present volume.

66. Ahmed, Kashyap, and Sinha, "Pollution of Hinduism," 28, 37.

67. Knut A. Jacobsen, *"Bhagavadgita,* Ecosophy T, and Deep Ecology," *Inquiry* 39 (June 1996): 219–38; and Lance E. Nelson, "Reading the Bhagavadgita from an Ecological Perspective," in *Hinduism and Ecology,* ed. Christopher Key Chapple and Mary Evelyn Tucker (Cambridge: Harvard University Press, 2000), 127–64.

68. Jacobsen, *"Bhagavadgita,"* 219.

69. Naess classifies both Buddhism and Taoism as eco-friendly Asian traditions, but, perhaps because Hinduism is assumed to be a strange and eco-hostile tradition, Naess does not identify it as the source of his own ideas about self-realization, but instead refers to the source as "certain Eastern traditions." See Naess, "The Deep Ecological Movement: Some Philosophical Aspects," in *Deep*

Ecology for the 21st Century, ed. George Sessions (Boston: Shambala, 1995), 79–80.

70. Jacobsen, *"Bhagavadgita,"* 220.

71. Ibid., 222.

72. Ibid., 223.

73. Ibid., 227.

74. Ibid., 233.

75. Ibid., 228

76. Gandhi, *An Autobiography,* 330.

77. Jacobsen, *"Bhagavadgita,"* 220.

78. Ibid., 233.

79. The world (*jagat*) has been identified with another important term that appears throughout the Gita: *kshara* (transitory forms). Verse 15.16 makes it clear that the *kshara* dimension of reality, though recognized to be changeable, is still fully real and divine.

80. See Shyam Das, trans., *Ocean of Jewels: Prameyaratnarnava of Lallu Bhatta* (Baroda: Shri Vallabha Publications, 1986), 16.

81. Verse 2.47 situates the path of *karma-yoga* in a creative middle ground between ordinary action (*karma*) and ascetic withdrawal from action (*akarma*).

82. Richard H. Davis, *Ritual in an Oscillating Universe: Worshiping Siva in Medieval India* (Princeton: Princeton University Press, 1991), 7.

83. See Bhagavad-gita 8.1–4 and 15.16–19.

84. This is expressed throughout the text, but see especially Bhagavad-gita, chapter 7, wherein Krishna is identified with everything that is (*Vasudeva sarvam*) (7.19).

85. Gandhi, *The Bhagavad Gita,* 17. In his essay "My Hinduism," Gandhi identifies his background as being Vaishnava. He writes, "I am a born Vaishnavite" (143). Evidence suggests that, growing up where he did in Gujarat, he had significant exposure to the Vaishnava tradition of Vallabhacharya known as the Pushti Marga.

86. Quoted in Naess, "Self-Realization," 22.

87. Gandhi, *An Autobiography,* 504.

88. Quoted in Naess, "Self-Realization," 23.

89. Gandhi, *All Men Are Brothers,* 119.

90. Nelson, "Reading the Bhagavadgita from an Ecological Perspective," 135.

91. Ibid., 136.

92. Ibid., 137 and 140.

93. Ibid., 142. But as Lee Siegel points out, within Vaishnavism "matter matters." See *Sacred and Profane Dimensions of Love in Indian Traditions as Exemplified in the Gitagovinda of Jayadeva* (Delhi: Oxford University Press, 1978), 12.

94. Ibid., 151–52.

95. The historian of Indian philosophy Surendranath Dasgupta writes, based on statements made in the *Mahabharata:* "For the Gita was in all probability the earliest work of the *ekantin* school of the Bhagavatas." Dasgupta dates the composition of the Gita to pre-Buddhist times, and states, "It is not improbable that

the Gita, which summarized the older teachings of the Bhagavata school, was incorporated into the Maha-bharata, during one of its revisions, by reason of the sacredness that it had attained at the time" (*A History of Indian Philosophy*, vol. 2 [Delhi: Motilal Banarsidass, 1975], 548 and 552). Whether they agree with Dasgupta's dating or specific identification of the Gita with the Ekantins, many scholars endorse his argument that the Gita is the product of the Bhagavata school. Mitsunori Matsubara, for example, identifies the Gita as "the earliest and most important Bhagavata text" (*Pancaratra Samhitas and Early Vaisnava Theology* [Delhi: Motilal Banarsidass, 1994], 135).

96. The term *Bhagavata* can often be used interchangeably with the terms Pancaratra, Satvata, Ekantika, or even Vaishnava, since it is usually defined as a cult of devotion to Vishnu (See Romila Thapar, *A History of India*, vol. 1 [Middlesex, U.K.: Penguin Books, 1966], 186). Since, however, the term *Vaishnava* is often used to refer to a broad range of contemporary Hindu traditions, I use the term *Bhagavata* to refer to the cult that has very old historical roots, and that is the origin of all contemporary Vaishnava traditions. For a brief history of the Bhagavata cult, see Ramkrishna Gopal Bhandarkar, *Vaisnavism, Saivism, and Minor Religious Systems* (New Delhi: Asian Educational Services, 1987), 1–65.

97. Dasgupta, *A History of Indian Philosophy*, vol. 3, p. 12.

98. Ibid., 105.

99. Jan Gonda, for example, says the Purusha concept of Rig Veda 10.90 is central to the development of Vaishnava theology. See his *Visnuism and Sivaism* (London: University of London, 1970), 20 and 25. Matsubara demonstrates how the *Purusha Sukta* has been used in the elaboration of Vaishnava theology. See his *Pancaratra Samhitas and Early Vaisnava Theology*, 117ff.

100. Gonda, *Visnuism and Sivaism*, 25.

101. The *Brihadaranyaka Upanishad* is the oldest and largest of the Upanishads, foundational texts for much Hindu philosophy. On the importance of the Satapatha Brahmana for early Vaishnavism, see Matsubara, *Pancaratra Samhitas and Early Vaisnava Theology*.

102. *Brihadaranyaka Upanishad* 2.3.

103. *Shvetasvatara Upanishad* 1.8. I translate from J. L. Shastri, ed., *Upanishatsamgraha* (Delhi: Motilal Banarsidass, 1980), 135.

104. See ibid., 136–37.

105. This is especially true of the Pushti Margiya Vaishnavas.

106. Bhagavad-gita 8.3–4.

107. Ibid., 15.16–18.

108. Vasudha Narayanan, "Water, Wood, and Wisdom: Ecological Perspectives from the Hindu Tradition," *Daedalus* 130, no. 4 (Fall 2001): 185.

109. Gandhi, *The Bhagavad Gita*, 17.

110. This is exactly what the sixteenth-century Vaishnava theologian Vallabhacharya does in his texts, such as the *Shastrarthaprakarana* and *Siddhantamuktavali*. We will see how he also employs this strategy to articulate a Yamuna theology.

111. Bhagavad-gita 4.6; Nelson, "Reading the Bhagavadgita from an Ecological Perspective," 137.

112. Jacobsen, "*Bhagavadgita*," 222.

113. See J. A. B. Van Buitenen, *Ramanuja on the Bhagavadgita* (Delhi: Motilal Banarsidass, 1968).

114. Gupta, "Ganga," 113.

115. *Bhagavata Purana* 2.1.23ff.

116. A similar identification is made between the goddess and these various natural features in the *Devibhagavata Purana* (7:33, 21–41). See David Kinsley, "Learning the Story of the Land," in *Purifying the Earthly Body of God*, ed. Lance E. Nelson (Albany: State University of New York Press, 1998), 230.

117. McFague presents the metaphor of the world as the body of God in her book *The Body of God*. This tendency in Asian cultures has already been noted by some scholars. Roderick Nash, for example, writes, "In the 1960s Alan Watts restated the idea as 'the world is your body.' Of course this kind of organicism had long been a staple of Eastern faiths, and many new environmentalists saw ecology as the Western equivalent" (*The Rights of Nature*, 151). For more on Vaishnava claims to the world being the body of God in a manner that moves beyond McFague, see Patricia Mumme, "Models and Images for a Vaisnava Environmental Theology: The Potential Contribution of Srivaisnavism," in *Purifying the Earthly Body of God*, ed. Lance Nelson (Albany: State University of New York Press, 1998), 133–61.

118. See also, for example, *Devi Mahatmya* 1.57, wherein the goddess is addressed as "you who consist of the world" (Thomas Coburn, *Encountering the Goddess: A Translation of the Devi Mahatmya and a Study of Its Interpretation* [Albany: State University of New York, 1991], 37).

119. In a similar vein Vasudha Narayanan remarks, "What I am urging is a shift in our perspective from the *tattva/moksha* texts to the resources that have a more direct relevance to worldly behavior. These are the popular practices embodied in the dharmic tradition and in the *bhakti*/devotional rituals" ("Water, Wood, and Wisdom," 202).

120. Diana L. Eck, "Ganga: The Goddess in Hindu Sacred Geography," in *Devi: Goddesses of India*, ed. John S. Hawley and Donna M. Wulff (Berkeley: University of California Press, 1996), 140.

121. Betty Heimann, *Facets of Indian Thought* (London: George Allen and Unwin, 1964), 107. Cited in Eck, "Ganga," 141.

122. Janet Bord and Colin Bord, *Sacred Waters* (London: Granada Publishing, 1985), 111.

123. Mircea Eliade, *Patterns in Comparative Religion* (New York: Meridian Books, 1963), 188ff.

124. Bord and Bord, *Sacred Waters*, 5.

125. Migene Gonzalez-Wippler, *Santeria: The Religion* (St. Paul, MN: Llewellyn Publications, 1994), 59.

126. Patrick McCully, *Silenced Rivers: The Ecology and Politics of Large Dams* (London: Zed Books, 2001), 10.

127. Ibid., 9–10.

128. Bill Aitken, *Seven Sacred Rivers* (New Delhi: Penguin Books, 1992), 1.

129. "Jamunajal ko naman kar,/jamunajal ko pan./Jamunajal puni dhyan dhari,/jamunajal asanan."

130. Surinder Bhardwaj maintains that the reverence for rivers has been continuous in India since Vedic times. See his *Hindu Places of Pilgrimage in India* (Berkeley: University of California Press, 1983).

131. Translated by Wendy Doniger (O'Flaherty), *The Rig Veda* (Middlesex, U.K.: Penguin Books, 1981), 231.

132. Rig Veda 10.75 is specifically addressed to the rivers. Hymn 10.30 is one of the many hymns that address rivers as "mother of the world." See Ralph T. H. Griffith, *The Hymns of the Rig Veda* (London, 1889; reprint, Delhi: Motilal Banarsidass, 1973), 552.

133. See, for example, Rig Veda 1.32. When the seven rivers are named, Yamuna typically appears in the list. See 10.75.

134. *Padma Purana,* pt. 6, trans. N. A. Deshpande (Delhi: Motilal Banarsidass, 1990), 2110.

135. *Skanda Purana,* pt. 11, trans. G. V. Tagare (Delhi: Motilal Banarsidass, 1997), verses IV.ii.92.3–6, p. 382.

136. Swami Pavitrananda identifies the Ganga, Yamuna, Sarasvati, Godavari, Narmada, Sindhu, and Kaveri as the seven sacred rivers. See his "Pilgrimage and Fairs," in *The Cultural Heritage of India,* vol. 4 (Calcutta: Ramakrishna Mission, 1956), 500.

137. See, for example, *Bhagavata Purana* 10.15.

138. See my *Journey through the Twelve Forests,* 25 and 126–27.

139. *Bhagavata Purana* 10.11.36.

140. I have in mind specifically the Vaishnava *sampradaya*s of the Gaudiyas, the Pushti Margiyas, the Radhavallabhis, the Nimbarkis, and the followers of Swami Haridas. The followers of the southern school of Shri Vaishnavism residing in Braj also often agree with this perspective.

2. THE SOURCE

1. This story was also told to me by several of the Yamunotri priests.

2. Patrick R. Dugan, *Biochemical Ecology of Water Pollution* (New York: Plenum Press, 1972), 3.

3. Robert Bowen, *Geothermal Sources* (London: Elsevier Applied Science, 1989), 36.

4. James Rattue, *The Living Stream: Holy Wells in Historical Context* (Woodbridge, U.K.: Boydell Press, 1995), especially 11 and 33.

5. I thank Arvind Prasad Uniyal, one of the Yamunotri priests, for providing me with a handwritten narration of the story of the seven sages and the origins of the Yamuna. I met Arvind in Yamunotri during the month of September 1999.

6. The Ganges once flowed as a celestial river, but she descended to Earth by the power of Bhagiratha's ascetic activities to purify the ashes of his relatives, the sixty thousand sons of King Sagara, who had been incinerated by the fiery glance of sage Kapila. The funerary waters of the Ganges freed Bhagiratha's relatives for a peaceful residence in heaven. For more on this, see Diana L. Eck, *Banaras: City of Light* (Princeton: Princeton University Press, 1983), 211ff.

7. This point was communicated to me by Chandramani Vedprakash, Yamunotri, October 28, 2001.

8. See Wendy Doniger "Saranyu/Samjna: The Sun and Shadow," in *Devi: Goddesses of India,* ed. John S. Hawley and Donna M. Wulff (Berkeley: University of California Press, 1996), 155–72.

9. Rig Veda 10.10. See *The Rig Veda,* trans. Wendy Doniger (O'Flaherty) (Middlesex, U.K.: Penguin Books, 1981), 247–50.

10. B. K. Chaturvedi writes that, "in those primordial days when the Indo-Brahma primal glacier began to melt towards its southern tilt having the Kalinda mount of darker ambience, it began attracting sun-rays quite copiously towards it and issuing a tiny stream of water" (*Yamuna, Gods and Goddesses of India,* no. 12 [Delhi: Books for All, 1998], 27).

11. Ludo Rocher, *The Puranas,* The History of Indian Literature, no. 2, ed. Jan Gonda (Wiesbaden: Otto Harrassowitz, 1986), 12–13.

12. Regarding the source of rivers in India, Anne Feldhaus writes, "Most rivers are formed by the coming together of numerous tiny streams and rivulets, some of them sometimes dry, no one of them obviously 'the' source of the river. It is thus remarkable that for all of the major, and some of the minor, rivers that originate in Maharashtra, one particular spot is, in fact, identified as 'the' source of the river, is marked as such, and becomes a site for worship and pilgrimage. The choice of this spot is an excellent example of what might be called the 'cultural construction' of the landscape: the location of 'the' source is agreed upon by everyone, is hardly ever questioned by anyone, and is yet in some respect quite arbitrary" (*Water and Womanhood: Religious Meanings of Rivers in Maharashtra* [New York: Oxford University Press, 1995], 21).

13. See, for example, Rambharosa, *Sadhana Paddhati* (Haridwar: Paliwal Press, 1998), 142. Rambharosa is a holy man who lives year-round in a Hanuman temple at Yamunotri.

14. Personal conversation with Shrivatsa Goswami, Vrindaban, November 1999. Regarding this negative aspect of pilgrimage, Lance Nelson writes, "The reverencing of a sacred space itself can, ironically, exact a heavy toll on the land in terms of pilgrimage traffic and other factors" (*Purifying the Earthly Body of God: Religion and Ecology in Hindu India* [Albany: State University of New York Press, 1998], 340).

15. This Sanskrit text is printed with a Hindi translation by Rambharosa in *Sadhana Paddhati,* 147–53.

16. Ibid., 147.

17. Personal conversation with Chandramani Vedprakash, Yamunotri, October 28, 2001.

18. Rambharosa, *Sadhana Paddhati,* 147.

19. Ibid., 147.

20. See *Agni Purana* 50:17, translated by N. Gangadharan (Delhi: Motilal Banarsidass Publishers, 1984), 133.

21. The holy man Rambharosa, also called Nepali Baba, has lived at Yamunotri for more than thirty years without leaving.

22. Rambharosa, *Sadhana Paddhati,* 150.

23. See Kusum P. Merh, *Yama: The Glorious Lord of the Other World* (New Delhi: D. K. Printworld, 1996).

24. Ralph T. H. Griffith, *The Hymns of the Rig Veda* (London, 1889; reprint, Delhi: Motilal Banarsidass, 1973), 528.

25. Merh, *Yama,* 263.

26. Nandalal Chaturvedi, *Shri Yamuna Mahima* (Mathura: Shri Govardhan Granthmala Karyalay, 2004), 9.

27. Rambharosa, *Sadhana Paddhati,* 150.

28. See Vrindaban Bihari Gosvami, *Yamuna evam Yamunashtaka* (Vrindaban: Vrindaban Research Institute, 1990), 24.

29. See *Padma Purana,* trans. N. A. Deshpande (Delhi: Motilal Banarsidass, 1990), 1443–46.

30. Ibid., 1443.

31. Ibid.

32. Ibid., 1445.

33. Ibid., 1444.

34. Ibid.

35. Personal conversation with Baba Ramananda Giri, Barkot, September 6, 1999.

36. *Padma Purana* 3.6.31.

37. C. Sivaramamurti, *Ganga* (New Delhi: Orient Longman, 1976), 49.

38. Heinrich von Stietencron demonstrates that lunar mythologies are associated with death, whereas solar mythologies are associated more with life blessings and other religious goals. He points out that Yamuna's animal mount, the turtle, "sustains the earth." *Ganga und Yamuna: Zur symbolischen Bedeutung der Flussgottinnen an indischen Tempeln* (Wiesbaden: Otto Harrassowitz, 1972), 137.

39. This difference is also expressed in Indian mythology, which states that the Ganges flows from Narayana's foot, whereas Yamuna flows from Narayana's heart.

40. Personal conversation with Vasishthagiri, Barkot, October 25, 2001.

41. Personal conversation with anonymous pilgrim, Janaki Chatti, September 7, 1999.

42. Personal conversation with Chandramani Vedprakash, Yamunotri, September 8, 1999.

43. Personal conversation on trail to Yamunotri, September 7, 1999. Note how Yamuna is approached here in search of some benefit for one's self. Compare this to the ideal expressed in Braj that one should approach Yamuna without any concern for personal gain (*niskam*), but rather only out of loving appreciation for the goddess.

44. Personal conversation with this group of pilgrims in Janaki Chatti, June 6, 2000.

45. Personal conversation with anonymous pilgrim on trail to Yamunotri, September 7, 1999.

46. Personal conversation with anonymous pilgrim on trail to Yamunotri, September 7, 1999.

47. Personal conversation with anonymous pilgrim on trail to Yamunotri, June 7, 2000.

48. Personal conversation with Arvind Prasad Uniyal, Yamunotri, September 9, 1999.

49. Personal conversation with anonymous pilgrim on trail to Yamunotri, September 7, 1999.

50. Personal conversation with anonymous pilgrim on trail to Yamunotri, September 7, 1999.

51. Personal conversation with Vasishthagiri, Barkot, October 25, 2001.

52. Personal conversation with anonymous pilgrim on trail to Yamunotri, June 6, 2000.

53. Personal conversation with anonymous pilgrim on trail to Yamunotri, September 7, 1999.

54. Personal conversation with anonymous pilgrim on trail to Yamunotri, June 6, 2000.

55. The accounts of Yamuna in Braj have it that she is rushing anxiously to meet her lover Krishna in Braj. See chapter 4.

56. Several residents of Dakpathar told me in conversation that they believed Yamuna was a goddess only upstream from the Dakpathar dam, and at Dakpathar the Yamuna as goddess ended. Although this accounts for the seriously reduced state of the Yamuna downstream from Dakpathar, this viewpoint is denied completely by the residents of Braj who claim that the Yamuna is most sacred when she arrives in Braj and unites there with her Beloved, Krishna.

57. Arundhati Roy, *The Greater Common Good* (Bombay: India Book Distributors, 1999), 7; C. V. J. Sharma, ed., *Modern Temples of India: Selected Speeches of Jawaharlal Nehru at Irrigation and Power Projects* (New Delhi: Central Board of Irrigation and Power, 1989).

58. Uttar Pradesh Irrigation Department, *Yamuna Hydro Electric Project* (Dehra Dun: Uttar Pradesh Irrigation Department, n.d.).

59. Patrick McCully, *Silenced Rivers: The Ecology and Politics of Large Dams* (London: Zed Books, 2001), 10.

60. See Roy, *The Greater Common Good*. Roy is primarily concerned with stopping construction of the massive Sardar Sarovar dam on the Narmada River, a project that has received a great deal of international attention.

61. N. Patrick Peritore, "Environmental Attitudes of Indian Elites: Challenging Western Postmodern Values," *Asian Survey* 33, no. 8 (1993): 815.

62. Madhav Gadgil and Ramachandra Guha, *Ecology and Equity* (New Delhi: Penguin Books, 1995), 84.

63. Since my visits with Bahuguna in Tehri, the dam has been completed and the town flooded into oblivion.

64. When completed, the Three Gorges Dam on the Yangtze River in China will claim this title.

65. Ramachandra Guha, "Mahatma Gandhi and the Environmental Movement in India," in *Environmental Movements in Asia,* ed. Arne Kalland and Gerard Persoon (Richmond, U.K.: Curzon Press, 1998), 65.

66. Sunderlal Bahuguna, *The Message of Aranya Culture and Tradition: A Continual Renewal* (Tehri-Garhwal: Chipko Information Centre, n.d.), 483.

67. This version of the history of the Chipko Movement is based on Sunderlal Bahuguna, *Chipko: The People's Movement with a Hope for the Survival of Humankind* (Tehri-Garhwal: Chipko Information Centre, n.d.).

68. "The first demonstration was in Yamuna valley, where 17 people had been killed in 1930 and in front of whose memorial people in 1968 had pledged to re-establish the harmonious relationship between forests and people" (ibid., 769).

69. Ramachandra Guha credits Chandi Prasad Bhatt with the idea of hugging trees to save them. See *The Unquiet Woods: Ecological Change and Peasant Resistance in the Himalaya* (New Delhi: Oxford University Press, 1999), 157.

70. Anil Agarwal, Sunita Narain, and Srabani Sen, eds., *The Citizens' Fifth Report* (New Delhi: Centre for Science and Environment, 1999), 145–49.

71. Gadgil and Guha, *Ecology and Equity,* 72.

72. Ibid., 72.

73. Bahuguna, *Chipko,* 7.

74. Bahuguna, *The Message of Aranya Culture and Tradition,* 1.

75. Personal interview with Sunderlal Bahuguna, Tehri, June 10, 2000.

76. This interview took place in Tehri on June 10, 2000.

77. When I was in India from December 2002 to January 2003, I learned that the Tehri Dam had been finished and its full operation had commenced. I learned also that Bahuguna, who considered the Ganga to be his mother, had shaved his head and performed for Ganga Devi a *shraddha,* the traditional funeral rite that a dutiful son performs on the occasion of his mother's death. This was, in effect, a "death of goddess" ritual. Importantly, however, Bahuguna has inspired many in India to work to save the environment. Even though his simple home was lost to the floodwaters of the dam, he has left behind a beautiful expression of human sanity.

78. I heard this from others also. Krishna Gopal Shukla of Vrindaban, for example, told me, "Barrages lessen the *shakti* in the water because they stop it from flowing. If we disturb nature, she will disturb our life. If we dam Yamuna-ji, our lives will be disturbed" (personal communication, Vrindaban, October 17, 2001).

3. RIVER OF DEATH

Epigraphs: Anil Agarwal, Sunita Narain, and Srabani Sen, eds., *The Citizens' Fifth Report* (New Delhi: Centre for Science and Environment, 1999), 58; personal interview with Krishna Gopal Shukla, Vrindaban, December 1, 1999.

1. *Hindustan Times* (Delhi), December 13, 1999.

2. *Times of India* (New Delhi), September 20, 1999.

3. *Hindustan Times* (Delhi), April 22, 2000.

4. Agarwal, Narain, and Sen, eds., *The Citizens' Fifth Report,* 62.

5. Samar Halarnkar, "The Rivers of Death," *India Today* (Delhi) (January 15, 1997): 102–7.

6. Ibid., 102.

7. Ibid., 103.

8. Vir Singh, *Earth Times News Service,* December 14, 1997.

9. Rajat Banerji and Max Martin, "Yamuna: The River of Death," in *Homicide by Pesticides,* ed. Anil Agarwal (New Delhi: Centre for Science and Environment, 1997), 47–98.

10. Ibid., 48.

11. We for Yamuna is an organization of college students in Delhi committed to cleaning the Yamuna. This message appeared in 2001 on their home page, www.weforyamuna.8m.com.

12. Personal interview, New Delhi, October 22, 1999.

13. See Central Pollution Control Board, *Water Quality Status of Yamuna River* (Delhi: Central Pollution Control Board, 2000).

14. Ibid., 14 and 29.

15. Personal interview, New Delhi, January 12, 2000.

16. Banerji and Martin, "Yamuna: The River of Death," 48.

17. Acknowledging this, the CPCB states that, "unless the pollution abatement action is taken at Delhi, the objectives of the Yamuna Action Plan can not be achieved" (Central Pollution Control Board, *Water Quality Status of Yamuna River*, 57).

18. Ibid., 29.

19. Ibid., 1.

20. Ibid., 9.

21. Shrivatsa Goswami, personal communication, Vrindaban, September 18, 1999.

22. Anil Chaturvedi, personal communication, November 23, 1999.

23. Government of India, Ministry of Environment and Forests, *Yamuna Action Plan* (New Delhi: Government of India, Ministry of Environment and Forests, 1993), 9.

24. Central Pollution Control Board, *Water Quality Status of Yamuna River*, 31.

25. Banerji and Martin, "Yamuna: The River of Death," 59–60.

26. Agarwal, Narain, and Sen, eds., *The Citizens' Fifth Report*, 69.

27. Vandana Shiva, *The Violence of the Green Revolution: Third World Agriculture, Ecology, and Politics* (London: Zed Books, 1991), 121.

28. Brij Gopal and Malavika Sah, "Conservation and Management of Rivers in India: Case-Study of the River Yamuna," *Environmental Conservation* 20, no. 3 (Autumn 1993): 250.

29. Shiva, *The Violence of the Green Revolution*, 128.

30. Government of India, Central Water Commission, *Water Quality Studies: Yamuna System, Status Report, 1978–1990* (New Delhi: Government of India, Central Water Commission, 1991), 3.

31. Banerji and Martin, "Yamuna: The River of Death," 63.

32. Ibid., 53.

33. Ibid., 67.

34. Central Pollution Control Board, *Water Quality Status of Yamuna River*, 35.

35. Banerji and Martin, "Yamuna: The River of Death," 66.

36. Halarnkar, "The Rivers of Death," 103.

37. Banerji and Martin, "Yamuna: The River of Death," 67.

38. Central Pollution Control Board, *Water Quality Status of Yamuna River*, 36, figure 9.

39. See the Central Pollution Control Board Web site: www.cpcb.delhi.nic.in/projresearch1.html. This Web site also reports for the same time period that,

although the maximum acceptable level for fecal coliform bacteria is 5,000 per 100 ml, readings at Okhla were 105,000,000 per 100 ml.

40. See Halarnkar, "The Rivers of Death," 103.

41. Personal interview, Delhi, November 5, 2001.

42. Personal interview, Delhi, April 8, 2000.

43. Sureshwar Sinha, personal interview, Vrindaban, November 24, 1999.

44. Personal interview, Vrindaban, November 11, 1999.

45. See H. K. Kaul, comp. and ed., *Historic Delhi: An Anthology* (Delhi: Oxford University Press, 1996).

46. Central Pollution Control Board, *Water Quality Status of Yamuna River,* 21.

47. These statistics are reported on the Municipal Corporation of Delhi's Web site, www.medline.gov.in.

48. Kazimuddin Ahmed, Suverchala Kashyap, and Samir Kumar Sinha, "Pollution of Hinduism," *Down to Earth* (Centre for Science and Environment, New Delhi) (February 15, 2000): 28 and 30. Elsewhere Shrivatsa Goswami writes, "What are we doing? We have these *kumbha melas.* You know I went to Ganga maiyya [Mother Ganges], beyond [the bridge] Laksmana jhula[,] and you know she was crying like hell. I said 'Ma, why are you crying? What is your problem?' What does she say? She says, this *kumbha mela* is coming and I will be tortured like anything. . . . By whom? By the religious people, that is my pain" ("Religion and Environment," *Jnana-Pravaha Bulletin* [Centre for Cultural Studies, Banaras] [1998–99]: 80).

49. Ahmed, Kashyap, and Sinha, "Pollution of Hinduism," 30.

50. See Central Pollution Control Board, *Water Quality Status of Yamuna River,* 2.5 in 1999 report.

51. *Hindustan Times* (Delhi), September 18, 2000.

52. A Central Pollution Control Board publication quantified Delhi's daily wastewater output at about 2,160 million liters in 1999. *Water Quality Status of Yamuna River,* 23.

53. Cited in *Hindustan Times* (Delhi), April 14, 2000.

54. Halarnkar, "The Rivers of Death," 103.

55. *Times of India* (New Delhi), February 7, 2000.

56. Central Pollution Control Board, *Water Quality Status of Yamuna River,* 43.

57. M. E. Farago, A. Mehra, and D. K. Banerjee, "A Preliminary Investigation of Pollution in the River Yamuna, Delhi, India: Metal Concentrations in River Bank Soils and Plants," *Environmental Geochemistry and Health* 11, no. 3–4 (1989): 155.

58. P. K. Jha, V. Subramanian, R. Sitasawad, and R. Van Grieken, "Heavy Metals in Sediments of the Yamuna River," *Science of the Total Environment* 95 (1990): 7.

59. "A River of Death? Scientists Detect Cancer-Causing Agent in Yamuna," *Asian Age* (September 22, 1998). See also "Poisoning the Yamuna," in *Down to Earth* (April 15, 1999): 14.

60. Farago, Mehra, and Banerjee, "A Preliminary Investigation of Pollution in the River Yamuna," 154–55.

61. Dr. R. C. Trivedi, personal interview, New Delhi, January 12, 2000.

62. Trivedi, quoted in Banerji and Martin, "Yamuna: The River of Death," 69–70.

63. Central Pollution Control Board, *Water Quality Status of Yamuna River*, 8.

64. *Times of India* (New Delhi), February 7, 2000.

65. Personal e-mail, December 9, 2001.

66. *Times of India* (New Delhi), February 7, 2000.

67. "Revive the Yamuna," *Down to Earth* 8, no. 20 (March 15, 2000): 15.

68. "Yamunanagar Power Unit Shows Decline," *Hindustan Times* (Delhi), November 24, 1999.

69. *Hindustan Times* (Delhi), September 27, 1999.

70. Central Pollution Control Board, *Water Quality Status of Yamuna River*, 44.

71. Ibid., 9.

72. Ibid., 38.

73. Ibid., 18–19.

74. Ibid., 43.

75. Oswald Wood, *Final Report on the Settlement of Land Revenue in the Delhi District Carried on 1872–77 by Oswald Wood and Completed 1878–80 by R. Maconachie* (Lahore: Victoria Press, 1882), 5.

76. On a more hopeful note, I report that, under the Yamuna Action Plan, this drain has since been tapped and routed to a sewage treatment plant. So on a good day, when the system is functioning, sewage water no longer enters the Yamuna at this point. See chapter 5.

77. Conversation with anonymous merchant, Mathura, November 7, 2001.

78. Personal interview with Krishna Gopal Shukla, Vrindaban, December 1, 1999.

79. Halarnkar, "The Rivers of Death," 105–7.

80. Central Pollution Control Board, *Water Quality Status of Yamuna River*, 46.

81. Banerji and Martin, "Yamuna: The River of Death," 77.

82. Central Pollution Control Board, *Water Quality Status of Yamuna River*, 53.

83. Banerji and Martin, "Yamuna: The River of Death," 77.

84. *Hindustan Times* (Delhi), November 2, 2001.

85. Central Pollution Control Board, *Water Quality Status of Yamuna River*, 38 and 44.

86. Government of India, Central Water Commission, *Water Quality Studies*, 22.

87. *Hindustan Times* (Delhi), December 10, 2002.

88. Development Research and Action Group, *Rivers of Hope, Rivers of Despair* (New Delhi: Development Research and Action Group, 1994), 18. This pamphlet was produced by Paani Morcha.

4. GODDESS OF LOVE

Epigraph: "Arati Shri Jamuna Maiya ki," in Vrindaban Bihari Mishra, *Shri Yamuna Yasha Pachasa* (Vrindaban: Shivahari Press, 1999), 21.

1. For a more extensive introduction to the religious culture of the region of Braj, see my *Journey through the Twelve Forests* (New York: Oxford University Press, 1994).

2. Personal conversation with Chandramani Vedprakash, Yamunotri, September 16, 1999.

3. *Varaha Purana*, trans. S. Venkitasubramonia Iyer (Delhi: Motilal Banarsidass, 1985), pt. 2, pp. 445–46.

4. Nandalal Chaturvedi writes, "Shri Yamuna, the goddess of love and beloved of Krishna, is the chief goddess [*adhishthatri svamini-ji*] of the Pushti Marga." *Shri Yamuna Mahima* (Mathura: Shri Govardhan Granthmala Karyalay, 2004), 7.

5. Stated on a sign posted at Keshi Ghat and also published in pamphlets available at the Keshi Ghat Yamuna temple. Shri Yamuna Seva Samiti, *Shri Yamunashtakam evam Arati Sangraha* (Vrindaban: Shri Venkatesh Press, n.d.). For more on the story of the dismemberment of Sati, see David Kinsley, *Hindu Goddesses: Visions of the Divine Feminine in the Hindu Religious Tradition* (Berkeley: University of California Press, 1986), 38 ff.

6. Personal conversation with Brajesh Kumar Shukla, Vrindaban, December 1, 1999.

7. Gokulnath, *Chaurasi Baithak Charitra*, ed. Niranjandev Sharma (Mathura: Shri Govardhan Granthmala Karyalay, 1967), 1–2.

8. See Nandalal Nyati, *Shri Yamunashtakam* (Kota, Rajastan: Jyoti Printers, 1997), 3–4.

9. An *ashtakam* is a hymn composed of eight verses, with a ninth usually added to identify the benefits of singing the hymn. See the translation of this important hymn below.

10. Besides the Pushti Margiya Vaishnava followers of Vallabhacharya, the Nimbarki Vaishnava priests who attend the Yamuna temple at Keshi Ghat in Vrindaban, for example, sing Vallabhacharya's "Yamunashtakam"; the priests of the Yamuna temple in Yamunotri also sing this version of the hymn.

11. The Sanskrit terms I translate as "humble" and "assertive" lovers are *sura* and *asura*, respectively, which translate more literally as "gods" and "demons." I have chosen, however, to follow the commentary on this verse by Hariray and others who follow him. Hariray identifies these as female lovers (*svaminis*) who exhibit humility (*dainya-bhava*) and angry or forceful love (*mana-bhava*), respectively.

12. That is, while Lakshmi can grant the satisfaction of liberation, only Yamuna has the ability to grant the highest gift of blissful access to supreme love.

13. Personal conversation, Vrindaban, December 14, 1999.

14. Nandalal Chaturvedi, for example, writes, "There are two mothers in the Pushti Marga: One is Shri Yashoda Maiya and the other is Shri Yamuna Maiya. Shri Yashoda is the mother of the Lord and Shri Yamuna is the mother of the devotees" (*Shri Yamuna Mahima*, 7).

15. Shyam Manohar Goswamy's Hindi commentary in *Shri Yamunash-takam*, ed. Kedarnath Mishra (Banaras: Ananda Prakashan Sansthan, 1980), 109. He quotes *Bhagavata Purana* 10.45.22, which defines a mother as one who nourishes any children as her own.

16. This collection contains poems by ten different famous poets of the Pushti Margiya tradition. All forty-one poems are translated in appendix 1.

17. Ganga Bai, Poem number 30 in the "Forty-One Yamuna Poems" translated in appendix 1. See also Hariprasad Sharma, ed. and trans., *Shri Yamunashtakam evam Shri Yamuna-ji ke 40 Pada* (Mathura: Shri Pushti Margiya Sahitya Prakash Trust, 1999), 78–79.

18. Personal interview with Lakshman Das, Vrindaban, March 17, 2000.

19. Personal interview with Mohanlal, Gokul, April 17, 2000.

20. Personal interview with Giriraj, Gokul, April 17, 2000.

21. Personal interview with Mohanlal, Gokul, April 17, 2000.

22. Personal interview with Uddhava Bhai, Gokul, April 17, 2000.

23. Mishra, *Shri Yamuna Yasha Pachasa,* 15 and 2, respectively. This poem is also translated in its entirety in appendix 1.

24. Hariray, Poem number 2 in "Forty-One Yamuna Poems."

25. Personal interview with Deepu Pandit, Gokul, January 3, 2000.

26. See Tracy Pintchman, *The Rise of the Goddess in the Hindu Tradition* (Albany: State University of New York Press, 1994), particularly chapter 2. The classic text of the goddess tradition is the *Devi Mahatmya;* the goddess is identified as the mother of the world in this text. For a readable translation of this text, see Thomas Coburn, *Encountering the Goddess: A Translation of the Devi Mahatmya and a Study of Its Interpretation* (Albany: State University of New York Press, 1991).

27. For example, in the *Crest-Jewel of Discrimination* (*Viveka Chudamani*) attributed to Shankara, the world is compared to a scorching forest fire, and *maya,* which creates the world, is compared to a dangerous and illusory snake (Swami Prabhavananda and Christopher Isherwood, trans., *Shankara's Crest-Jewel of Discrimination* [Hollywood: Vedanta Press, 1947], 38 and 49).

28. Kinsley, *Hindu Goddesses,* 136.

29. "Yamuna Arati." See the end of appendix 1 for a complete translation of this *arati.*

30. Vrindaban Bihari Gosvami, *Yamuna evam Yamunashtaka* (Vrindaban: Vrindaban Research Institute, 1990), pt. 2, p. 89.

31. Personal interview with Brajendra Sharma, Vrindaban, April 24, 2000.

32. See, for example, *Bhagavata Purana* 1.3.28: "Krishna is Bhagavan himself" (Krishna tu Bhagavan svam). The long "a" in *Krishnaa* indicates the feminine, whereas the short "a" in *Krishna* indicates the masculine. *Krishnaa* is a common name for Yamuna. It appears as the third name, for example, in *Shri Yamuna Sahasra Nama,* a text composed of the thousand names of Yamuna. It also appears in the second verse of the "Shri Yamuna Yasha Pachasa." See appendix 1.

33. Govindaswami, Poem number 5 in "Forty-One Yamuna Poems."

34. Sharma, ed. and trans., *Shri Yamunashtakam evam Shri Yamuna-ji ke 40 Pada,* 35.

35. Mishra, *Shri Yamuna Yasha Pachasa,* 4. See verse 8 of this poem translated in appendix 1. The *Shri Yamuna Sahasra Nama* has been printed in many collections of Yamuna hymns. I translate from Vasudev Krishna Chaturvedi, ed., *Shri Yamuna Pujan Paddhati* (Mathura: Shri Sitaram Pushtakalaya, 2001), 44.

36. Krishnadas, Poem number 41 of the "Forty-One Yamuna Poems."

37. *Padma Purana,* trans. N. A. Deshpande (Delhi: Motilal Banarsidass, 1990), 1946.

38. See, for example, the *Taittiriya Upanishad* 2.71, which states that the ultimate is *rasa (raso vai sa)*. See Shyam Manohar Goswamy's Hindi commentary in *Shri Yamunashtakam,* ed. Kedarnath Mishra, 129, for an example of the classification of Yamuna as liquid *rasa.*

39. See *Bhagavata Purana* 10.21.11ff.

40. Specifically, the noun endings can be read either as feminine vocative endings or as masculine locative endings. Thus, the phrases are addressed to Yamuna so defined, as well as indicate such qualities in Krishna.

41. Shyam Manohar Goswamy's Hindi commentary in *Shri Yamunashtakam,* ed. Kedarnath Mishra, pt. 2, p. 91.

42. Devendra Sharma, "Yamuna and the Environment" (manuscript).

43. Shyam Manohar Goswamy's Hindi commentary in *Shri Yamunashtakam,* ed. Kedarnath Mishra, pt. 2, pp. 89–90.

44. See, for example, *Brihadaranyaka Upanishad* 1.4.

45. Summary translation by C. Mackenzie Brown, "The Theology of Radha in the Purana," in *The Divine Consort: Radha and the Goddesses of India,* ed. John S. Hawley and Donna M. Wulff (Berkeley: Graduate Theological Union, 1982), 57.

46. Shyam Manohar Goswamy in *Shri Yamunashtakam,* ed. Kedarnath Mishra, pt. 2, p. 91.

47. Told to me by Mohit Goswami of the main Radhavallabha temple in Vrindaban, March 12, 2000.

48. "Nita lila tum dekhana vari radha sama pyari." See appendix 1.

49. Personal interview with Anantadasi, Vrindaban, April 14, 2000.

50. See Poems number 5 and number 29 by Govindaswami and Ganga Bai, respectively, in the "Forty-One Yamuna Poems," appendix 1. See also verse 8 in Vallabhacharya's "Yamunashtakam" that appears earlier in this chapter.

51. Personal interview with Harekrishna, a priest at the Yamuna temple at Thakurani Ghat, Gokul, April 17, 2000.

52. I have translated this poem and placed it in appendix 1. See the section "Surdas's Famous Poem to Yamuna."

53. This story is told in *Bhagavata Purana* 10.58.16–29. Krishna meets Yamuna in the form of the beautiful young woman Kalindi while visiting the bank of the Yamuna River north of Indraprastha. Kalindi approaches Krishna for marriage, and Krishna takes her back to Dvaraka for the wedding celebration.

54. Many residents of Braj insist that Krishna never leaves Braj; thus, Yamuna and Krishna eternally remain lovers, not spouses.

55. Mount Govardhan is typically considered a solid or condensed form of *rasa* by many of the followers of Braj Vaishnavism. As they are both considered to be forms of *rasa,* the highest divinity, once again we observe the identification of Yamuna and Krishna. See Sharma, ed. and trans., *Shri Yamunashtakam evam Shri Yamuna-ji ke 40 Pada,* 3.

56. When Yamuna water is poured over a stone from Mount Govardhan, this love affair between these natural forms is being celebrated in ritual action. Here is worshipful participation in the love affair of the river and the mountain.

57. Govindaswami, Poem number 5 in "Forty-One Yamuna Poems," appendix 1.

58. Govindaswami, Poem number 8 in "Forty-One Yamuna Poems," appendix 1.

59. Chaturbhujadas, Poem number 14 in "Forty-One Yamuna Poems," appendix 1.

60. Chitaswami, Poem number 9 in "Forty-One Yamuna Poems," appendix 1.

61. Hariray, Poem number 4 in "Forty-One Yamuna Poems," appendix 1.

62. "Tumhari bunda bunda se krsna ko bas karti." This *arati* is translated in appendix 1.

63. Pannalal Purushottam Shastri, *Shri Yamuna Chalisa* (Gokul: Nivedana Prasar Mandal, 1948), p. 5, verse 8. For a translation of this text, see appendix 1.

64. Ganga Bai, Poem number 32 in "Forty-One Yamuna Poems."

65. Paramanandadas, Poem number 39 in "Forty-One Yamuna Poems."

66. Shyam Manohar Goswamy writes, "Lakshmi's story is that she is bound to a single limb of Shri Hari in Vaikuntha, as she is attached to his chest. But Shri Yamuna's story is greater, as she is bound to each and every limb of Krishna, each and every fiber of his being (Hindi commentary in *Shri Yamunashtakam,* ed. Kedarnath Mishra, 133).

67. Yamuna is often considered to be an ocean of the *rasa* of love (*raasa rasa ka sagar*) and is herself the essential divine form of the *rasa* of love (*rasa svarupa*). See Sharma, ed. and trans., *Shri Yamunashtaka evam Shri Yamuna-ji ke 40 Pad,* 76.

68. Verse 6 of Rupa Gosvamin's "Yamunashtakam," in Gosvami, *Yamuna evam Yamunashtaka,* 59. See appendix 1 for a translation of this text.

69. In *Shri Yamunashtakam,* ed. Kedarnath Mishra, pt. 2, pp. 132–33.

70. Personal communication, Chaibihari Sharma, Gokul, April 18, 2000.

71. Chitaswami, Poem number 11 in "Forty-One Yamuna Poems"; Sharma, ed. and trans., *Shri Yamunashtaka evam Shri Yamuna-ji ke 40 Pada,* 45–46.

72. Sharma, ed. and trans., *Shri Yamunashtaka evam Shri Yamuna-ji ke 40 Pada,* 46.

73. Govindaswami, Poem number 6 in "Forty-One Yamuna Poems," appendix 1.

74. Shastri, *Shri Yamuna Chalisa,* p. 9, verse 22. See appendix 1 for a translation of this text.

75. See Shyam Manohar Goswamy in *Shri Yamunashtakam,* ed. Kedarnath Mishra, pt. 2, p. 146.

76. Kumbhandas, Poem number 26 in "Forty-One Yamuna Poems," appendix 1.

77. Ibid., Poem number 25.

78. Ibid., Poem number 28.

79. Sharma, ed. and trans., *Shri Yamunashtaka evam Shri Yamuna-ji ke 40 Pada,* 75.

80. Personal interview, Gokul, April 17, 2000.

81. Personal interview, Mathura, April 21, 2000.

82. Hariray, Poem number 1 in "Forty-One Yamuna Poems," appendix 1.

83. Ibid., Poem number 3.

84. Nandadas, Poem number 18 in "Forty-One Yamuna Poems," appendix 1.

85. Krishnadas, Poem number 34 in "Forty-One Yamuna Poems," appendix 1.

86. Ganga Bai, Poem number 30 in "Forty-One Yamuna Poems," appendix 1.

87. Anonymous interview, Vrindaban, April 24, 2000.

88. A priest of the Yamuna temple at Keshi Ghat in Vrindaban told me about a young woman who was having difficulty getting married. Because of this, her mother told her to worship Yamuna on Sundays. After doing so for six Sundays in a row, she was approached for a successful marriage (Brajesh Kumar Shukla, personal interview, Vrindaban, December 1, 1999). Many women in the region of Braj perform the worship of Yamuna as part of their wedding celebrations.

89. Krishnadas, Poem number 41 in "Forty-One Yamuna Poems," appendix 1.

90. Personal interview with Vishuddhananda, Vrindaban, March 17, 2000.

91. See appendix 1 for a translation of this *arati* hymn.

92. See appendix 1 for a translation of this "Yamunashtakam" hymn.

93. The *Bhagavata Purana* narrates how the cowherd lovers of Krishna obtained him as a lover by bathing in the Yamuna. See 10.22.2ff.

94. The best of all spiritual powers is love of God. Poem number 41 in "Forty-One Yamuna Poems," appendix 1.

95. Personal interview with Vishnuswami, Mathura, April 21, 2000.

96. Shastri, *Shri Yamuna Chalisa*, 4, verse 1. See appendix 1.

97. The Radhavallabhis of Vrindaban consider Yamuna a girlfriend (*sakhi*) of Radha; therefore, for them she is said to increase love for Radha. The second verse of Hita Harivamsa's "Yamunashtakam" reads: "She perfects the devotion to the lotus feet of Radhika." But note that even here Yamuna is considered to be both a lover of Krishna herself (*Hari-priya*, verse 7) and a perfecter of love for Krishna (verse 9). Harivamsa's "Yamunashtakam" is included in Gosvami, *Yamuna evam Yamunashtaka*, pt. 2, pp. 65–68.

98. Personal interview with Lakshman Das, Vrindaban, March 17, 2000.

99. *Padma Purana* 3.29.47, trans. N. A. Deshpande, 1446.

100. For a translation of this story about Nandadas, told in the *Chaurasi Vaishnava ki Varta*, see Shyam Das, *Ashta Chhap: Lord Krishna's Eight Poet Friends* (Baroda: Shri Vallabha Publications, 1985), 259–67.

101. For more on this story, see my *Journey through the Twelve Forests*, 20–29. The Braj pilgrimage begins with a transformative bath in the Yamuna.

102. Nandadas, Poem number 17 in "Forty-One Yamuna Poems," appendix 1.

103. This body is often called the "perfected body" (*siddha-deha*) in Braj Vaishnavism. For more on this, see my *Acting as a Way of Salvation* (New York: Oxford University Press, 1988), especially chapters 5 and 7. Two views of this body can be found within the Pushti Margiya commentaries on Vallabhacharya's "Yamunashtakam." The commentator Purushottam emphasizes that this is the body the successful devotee is given upon death in order to enter and participate in Krishna's eternal love play, whereas the commentator Hariray claims that one acquires a "newness of body" in this very life. The latter says that an unfired clay pot cannot hold water, but after it is fired it is transformed from its previous state into a form that can hold water. Likewise, after contact with the Yamuna, one's body is transformed from an unfit state into one fit for a loving encounter with Krishna.

104. *Padma Purana* 3.29.35, trans. N. A. Deshpande, 1445.

105. Personal interview, Vrindaban, April 24, 2000.

106. Personal interview, Mathura, April 21, 2000.

107. Mishra, *Shri Yamuna Yasha Pachasa,* verse 13: "Jamuna jhaya pap sab katate." Also translated in appendix 1.

108. See verse 3 in Rupa's "Yamunashtakam," translated in appendix 1.

109. See verse 4 in Shankaracharya's "Yamunashtakam," translated in appendix 1.

110. See verse 2 in Rupa's "Yamunashtakam," translated in appendix 1; verse 13 in "Shri Yamuna Yasha Pachasa," translated in appendix 1.

111. For an example of this, see the commentary of Shyam Manohar Goswamy in *Shri Yamunashtakam,* ed. Kedarnath Mishra, pt. 2, pp. 70–71.

112. Here are a few examples of the ways "Daughter of the Sun" is expressed in Sanskrit: Surya-Putri, Padmabandho-Suta, Suraj-Beti, Dinkar Raj Dulari, Bhanu Tanaya.

113. Mishra, *Shri Yamuna Yasha Pachasa,* verse 1: "Jaya yamuna jaya bhanu dulari." See appendix 1.

114. Ibid., verse 4: "Ravi karate prakati jaga jani, taba hi dinkar kanya mani."

115. Verses 11 and 28. See appendix 1.

116. Rig Veda 10.10 is perhaps the most well-known text that presents Yama and Yamuna (or Yami) as twins.

117. Shastri, *Shri Yamuna Chalisa,* verse 3: "Mahima agama jaya nahi varani, yamahu dair jo avai sarani"; and verse 6: "Jo jamna jala majjana kari hai, ve yama phansa kabahu nahi pari hai." Yama uses his noose to draw souls off to the tortures of hell. See appendix 1.

118. Mishra, *Shri Yamuna Yasha Pachasa,* verse 15: "Jama ke duta nikata nahi ave, jo jamuna ji ko jasa gave."

119. "Jaha Yamuna, waha Yama na."

120. Mishra, *Shri Yamuna Yasha Pachasa,* verses 25–29.

121. *Padma Purana* 6.122.89–103. For an English translation, see *Padma Purana,* trans. N. A. Deshpande, 2742.

122. Jagadish Gupta, *Yama Dvitiya Vrat Katha* (Mathura: Prakash Press, n.d.). This account seems to be based on the narrative found in the *Skanda Purana* 2.4.11, a chapter titled "The Efficacy of Yama Dvitiya." See *The Skanda Purana,* trans. G. V. Tagare (Delhi: Motilal Banarsidass, 1994), pt. 6, pp. 107–12. The celebration of Bhai Duj fell on November 10 in the year 1999.

123. Michael Allaby, *Oxford Dictionary of Ecology* (New York: Oxford University Press, 1998), 321. This same dictionary defines a pollutant as "a by-product of human activities which enters or becomes concentrated in the environment, where it may cause injury to humans or desirable species."

124. While sitting on the bank of the river in Mathura one morning after viewing several moving rituals for worshipping Yamuna, I found myself pondering the cultural assertion that I had heard many times: that although the river is polluted it is still quite "pure" (*pavitra*). Although in this culture I think this means that human pollutants cannot ultimately affect divinity, it also dawned on me that even when pollutants are in the river the H_2O is still there too. Thus, even when carrying pollutants, Yamuna water remains fully present in the river.

125. Louis Dumont, *Homo Hierarchicus: The Caste System and Its Implications*, trans. Mark Sainsbury (London: University of Chicago Press, 1970), 46–61.

126. I once discovered this the hard way while living in Vrindaban many years ago. To fill my own bucket with water at a tap, I had to remove a bucket that had just been filled by a servant of a brahman. When the servant discovered that I had touched his bucket, he threw the water out angrily, washed the bucket, and refilled it.

127. Mysore N. Srinivas, *Religion and Society among the Coorgs of South India* (Oxford: Oxford University Press, 1952), 105. Emphasis added.

128. I continue to use the word *pollution* to refer to the domestic waste and industrial effluents physically affecting the ecological health of the river.

129. Lance E. Nelson, ed., *Purifying the Earthly Body of God: Religion and Ecology in Hindu India* (Albany: State University of New York Press, 1998), especially 331–44.

130. Personal interview with Bhagavan Devi, Vrindaban, April 5, 2000.

131. This ride took place in September 1999.

132. Kelly D. Alley, *On the Bank of the Ganga: When Wastewater Meets a Sacred River* (Ann Arbor: University of Michigan Press, 2002), 71.

133. Ibid., 98.

134. Ibid., 208. Rita Dasgupta Sherma concurs: "Thus, though motherhood is highly honored in Hindu kinship systems, it seems that this honor is based on her self-negation, the ability to endure privations for the family, and the willingness to nurture and give sustenance, no matter what the sacrifice, with no thought of her own needs. When the natural world is feminized, the above conception of maternal nature is projected onto the earth or any natural phenomenon that is considered sacred. Consequently, whether it is Bhumi Devi or Bharat Mata or a sacred grove, the expectation is that the sacred site will bless, nurture, purify or perform any other supportive maternal act without any requirement for sustenance in return" ("Sacred Immanence: Reflections of Ecofeminism in Hindu Tantra," in *Purifying the Earthly Body of God: Religion and Ecology in Hindu India*, ed. Lance E. Nelson [Albany: State University of New York Press, 1998], 97).

135. Personal interview with Kameshvar Chaturvedi, Mathura, October 7, 2001.

136. Personal interview with Mohanlal, Gokul, April 17, 2000.

137. *Hindustan Times* (Delhi), July 8, 2000.

138. Alley, *On the Bank of the Ganga*, 212.

139. Ibid., 219.

140. Ibid., 237.

141. David Kinsley, "Learning the Story of the Land," in *Purifying the Earthly Body of God*, ed. Lance E. Nelson (Albany: State University of New York Press, 1998), 234.

142. Personal interview with Vishuddhananda, Vrindaban, March 17, 2000.

143. Personal interview with Brajesh Kumar Shukla, Vrindaban, October 21, 1996.

144. Personal interview with Ananda Shukla, Vrindaban, October 11, 1999.

145. Personal interview with Vasishthagiri, Barkot, September 12, 1999.

146. Personal interview with Triloki Sharma, Gokul, April 18, 2000.

147. Personal interview with Deepu Pandit, Gokul, January 3, 2000. Deepu also told me that the physical river is like a church for those used to worshipping in it. If a church's doors are locked—or worse, if it burns down—worship will be very difficult for those people.

148. This might be compared to changing notions of the Hawaiian volcanic goddess Pele from a powerful goddess to one who might be injured. "You can't go shoving drills into her body like that. The old people say it will injure Pele and stop her creative force (Jerry Mander, *In the Absence of the Sacred* [San Francisco: Sierra Club Books, 1991], 333).

149. Personal interview with Lakshman Das, Vrindaban, March 17, 2000.

150. Personal interview with anonymous priest, Vrindaban, March 17, 2000.

151. Anonymous interview, Gokul, January 3, 2000.

152. Personal interview with Krishna Gopal Shukla, Vrindaban, December 1, 1999.

153. The copper pot of Yamuna water is carried on the head of a temple worker and is sheltered with a large red-and-white cloth umbrella while accompanied by musicians.

154. This is particularly true of the famous Shri Natha-ji temple of Nathdwara, but I have also seen truckloads of Yamuna water being delivered at the Krishna temple in Kankaroli.

155. Personal interview with Triloki Sharma, Gokul, April 18, 2000.

156. Personal interview with Prakash Sharma, Mathura, April 4, 2000.

157. Anonymous interview, Vrindaban, March 8, 2000.

158. Personal interview with Ramu Parek, Vrindaban, November 17, 1999.

159. This occurred in Vrindaban, November 5, 2001.

160. Personal interview with anonymous *baba*, Vrindaban, October 7, 2001.

161. "Pandas do not say that gandagi is dangerous for Ganga" (Alley, *On the Banks of the Ganga*, 89).

162. "World's Most Effective Environmental Attorney," interview in *Hinduism Today* (October 1997): 26.

163. Personal interview with Krishna Gopal Shukla, Vrindaban, October 17, 2001.

164. Personal interview with Gopeshwar Nath Chaturvedi, Mathura, December 4, 1999.

5. SIGNS OF HOPE

Epigraph: personal interview, M. C. Mehta, New Delhi, December 28, 1999.

1. In Hindi, these signs read:

Ghar ghar yah abhiyan chalao
  yamuna maiya shuddha banao.

Kahate hain sab veda purana
  bina sudhha yamuna jal ke nahi kalyana.

Yamuna bharat ki hai shan
  aur svacchata is ki jan.

Bahut diya hai yamuna maiya ne
  ab yamuna mange seva.

2. Personal interview with Gopeshwar Nath Chaturvedi, Mathura, December 4, 1999.

3. *Hinduism Today* (October 1997): 26.

4. Personal interview with M. C. Mehta, New Delhi, December 28, 1999.

5. Ganges Action Plan and Yamuna Action Plan.

6. Anonymous boatman, Vrindaban, January 6, 2000.

7. When I returned to Mathura and Vrindaban during the fall of 2001, I learned that all the sewage treatment plants were operational.

8. Narrated in *Bhagavata Purana* 10.16.

9. This refers to the identification of Krishna with the *ashvattha* or *pipal* tree in Bhagavad-gita 10.26.

10. Interview recorded in Ranchor Prime, *Hinduism and Ecology* (Delhi: Motilal Banarsidass, 1994), 16.

11. Ibid., 19.

12. Friends of Vrindaban organized a 525-mile bicycle ride from Yamunotri to Vrindaban that took place October 5–26, 1996. I participated in this ride, which allowed me to formulate a preliminary sketch of the more detailed research that was to follow.

13. For examples of her work, see Nicholas Barnard, *Arts and Crafts of India,* with photographs by Robyn Beeche (London: Conran Octopus, 1993); and Shrivatsa Goswami, *Celebrating Krishna,* with photographs by Robyn Beeche (Vrindaban: Shri Caitanya Prema Samsthana, 2001).

14. The two made a documentary film titled *Holi: Festival of Colours.* Unfortunately, the film, although available for viewing, was never finished for commercial distribution.

15. For example, see "Personality of the Week: Michael Duffy," *The Pioneer* (New Delhi), September 8, 1996.

16. Personal interview with Michael Duffy, Vrindaban, December 2, 1999.

17. Personal interview, Vrindaban, November 5, 2001.

18. Shrivatsa Goswami, "Vrindavana as a Model Environment" (paper delivered at the Conference on Hinduism and Ecology, Harvard University, Center for the Study of World Religions, October 1997), 5.

19. The quotations that follow are from a personal interview with Shrivatsa Goswami in Vrindaban, January 14, 2000.

20. Goswami, "Vrindavana as a Model Environment," 1.

21. Shrivatsa Goswami, "Lord Krishna: Preserver and Protector of the Environment," *India Magazine of Her People and Culture* 12 (August 1992): 83.

22. Goswami, "Vrindavana as a Model Environment," 2.

23. Ibid., 3.

24. Personal interview, Vrindaban, January 14, 2000.

25. Shrivatsa Goswami, "Religion and Environment," in *Jnana-Pravaha Bulletin* (Centre for Cultural Studies, Banaras) (1998–99): 60. This published lecture was delivered at Jnana-Pravaha Centre for Cultural Studies, Banaras, October 10, 1998.

26. Ibid., 60.

27. Goswami, "Lord Krishna: Preserver and Protector of the Environment," 83.

28. Goswami, "Vrindavana as a Model Environment," 2.

29. Goswami, "Lord Krishna: Preserver and Protector of the Environment," 81.

30. Personal interview, Vrindaban, January 14, 2000.

31. Goswami, "Religion and Environment," 65.

32. Goswami, "Lord Krishna: Preserver and Protector of the Environment," 83.

33. Goswami, "Vrindavana as a Model Environment," 4.

34. Goswami, "Religion and Environment," 71.

35. Ibid., 76.

36. Goswami, "Vrindavana as a Model Environment," 5.

37. Goswami, "Religion and Environment," 66.

38. Ibid., 66. Goswami is here referring to the fact that Yamuna is regarded as Krishna's lover (*patarani*) in Braj religious culture.

39. Government statistics indicate that more people visit Vrindaban daily than India's most visited tourist site, the Taj Mahal, located just forty miles downstream from Vrindaban.

40. Goswami, "Vrindavana as a Model Environment," 5.

41. On Yamuna Chath (Yamuna's birthday celebration; also known as Yamuna Jayanti) of 2005 (April 14 that year), Friends of Vrindaban launched a daily program of worship they named "Yamuna Maha Arati," on the bank of the Yamuna at Bhramar Ghat, a ghat located within Shrivatsa Goswami's *ashram*. This accompanied the start of the "Yamuna Kar Seva," a program to clear up garbage from the riverbank. An e-mail message that was sent out to announce this program stated that Friends of Vrindaban were intentionally "linking religious faith of Yamuna with environmental activism" (Friends of Vrindaban, e-mail, April 11, 2005).

42. Shrivatsa Goswami, for example, writes, "Once again, Vrindavana does not get the river it deserves—none of Yamuna's water gets past Delhi, and what passes Vrindavana is the effluent from Okhla" ("Vrindavana as a Model Environment," 4).

43. "Jana-jana ki priya pavana Yamuna. Nirmal shital jal ki Yamuna."

44. Government of India, Ministry of Environment and Forests, *Yamuna Action Plan* (New Delhi: Government of India, Ministry of Environment and Forests, 1993).

45. Anil Agarwal, Sunita Narain, and Srabani Sen, eds., *The Citizens' Fifth Report* (New Delhi: Centre for Science and Environment, 1999), 92.

46. Ibid.

47. Ibid.

48. Personal interview with O. P. Singhal, Mathura, April 26, 2000.

49. "Yamuna ko shuddha rakhana apka kartavya hai. Yamuna me pradushan phailana dandaniya aparadha hai."

50. "Yamuna ko nirmal rahane do. Yamuna ko aviral bahane do."

51. "Hindu-muslim sab mil jao; Yamuna pradushan dur bhagao."

52. "Jana-jana ki priya pavana Yamuna. Nirmal shital jal ki Yamuna."

53. "Jala prakrti ki amulya dharohara hai. Ise apna prema va sanrakshana de."

54. "Bahut diya hai Yamuna Maiya ne. Ab Yamuna mange seva."

55. Personal interview with O. P. Singhal, Vrindaban, November 5, 2001.

56. Another noteworthy environmental organization based in Delhi is We for Yamuna, composed of Delhi University students dedicated to cleaning the Yamuna.

57. Personal interview with Sureshwar Sinha, Vrindaban, November 24, 1999.

58. See Agarwal, Narain, and Sen, eds., *The Citizens' Fifth Report,* 360.

59. Ibid., 362.

60. Ibid., 363.

61. Rajeev Dhavan, senior advocate, Supreme Court, quoted in Agarwal, Narain, and Sen, eds., *The Citizens' Fifth Report,* 378.

62. Ibid., 384.

63. *Hindustan Times* (Delhi), "Saturday Interview," April 20, 1996.

64. Agarwal, Narain, and Sen, eds., *The Citizens' Fifth Report,* 384.

65. Personal interview with Veer Bhadra Mishra, Banaras, January 6, 2003.

66. *Hindustan Times* (Delhi), April 9, 1998.

67. *Times of India* (New Delhi), September 20, 1999.

68. See "800 Polluting Units Served Notices," *Hindustan Times* (Delhi), January 28, 2000.

69. *Hindustan Times* (Delhi), December 24, 1999.

70. *Hindustan Times* (Delhi), January 24, 2000.

71. *Hindustan Times* (Delhi), May 12, 2000.

72. *Times of India* (New Delhi), May 13, 2000.

73. *The Hindu* (Delhi), July 10, 2000.

74. *Times of India* (Bombay), August 5, 2000.

75. Reported in *Hindustan Times* (Delhi), April 11, 2001. The bench was composed of Justice B.N. Kirpal, Justice Ruma Pal, and Justice Brijesh Kumar.

76. *Indian Express* (New Delhi), April 11, 2001 (the ruling was given, and the article was written, on April 10, 2001).

77. "Sewer River," *Down to Earth* (Centre for Science and Environment, New Delhi) (May 15, 2001): 7.

78. *Asian Age* (Delhi), July 8, 2000.

79. *Hindustan Times* (Delhi), June 25, 2000.

80. *Hindustan Times* (Delhi), June 4, 2000.

81. *Business Line* (New Delhi), July 13, 2002.

82. "The Great Sham," *Down to Earth* (Centre for Science and Environment, New Delhi) (June 30, 2001): 6.

83. This is a common wordplay on the abbreviation for the Yamuna Action Plan. See also the political cartoon in Agarwal, Narain, and Sen, eds., *The Citizens' Fifth Report,* 57.

84. *Hindustan Times* (Delhi), December 10, 2002.

85. *Hindustan Times* (Delhi), December 15, 2002.

86. Especially e-mail communications from Sureshwar Sinha following this date.

87. E-mail from Subijoy Dutta, March 25, 2004.

88. A story in the *Chaitanya Charitamrta* tells how the saint Chaitanya was informed in Banaras that the Ganges was the Yamuna; he bathed in the river with ecstatic joy. He then discovered that the river there was called the Ganges and felt deceived. A companion of his, however, explained, "There was no

falsity in the words of Sripada; just now you have bathed in the Yamuna. The Ganga and the Yamuna flow together in a single stream; on the west the Yamuna flows, and on the east the Ganga" (*Caitanya Caritamrta of Krsnadasa Kaviraja*, ed. Tony K. Stewart, trans. Edward C. Dimock [Cambridge: Harvard University Press, 1999], 370).

89. Personal interview with Veer Bhadra Mishra, Banaras, December 17, 1999.

90. This is clear from many Uttar Pradesh Jal Nigam reports. Kanpur was listed as one of the top ten most polluted cities in the world by the World Health Organization in a 1996 survey.

91. Personal interview with Rakesh Jaiswal, Kanpur, March 3, 2000.

92. Parmarth Niketan Ashram. *Kumbha Mela: Festival of the Nectar of Immortality* (Rishikesh: Parmarth Niketan Ashram, Swami Shukdevanand Trust, 2001), 11.

93. Ibid., 9.

94. Personal interview, Rishikesh, October 31, 2001.

95. It would be easy to add more voices to this growing group of religious leaders. Tavleen Singh, in an article in *India Today* titled "It's Time to Clean Up the Act," reported that the influential Shankaracharya of Kancheepuram had been making the connection between religion and environmental considerations in his speeches. "The Shankaracharya did not mince his words. He said it was a sin that a river as sacred as the Ganga should be polluted by industrial wastes and sewage. 'Any Hindu responsible for doing this is a sinner,' he said" (June 28, 1999, 10).

6. A MATTER OF BALANCE

Epigraphs: Member of the American Rivers Conservation Council, quoted in Tim Palmer, *Endangered Rivers and the Conservation Movement* (Berkeley: University of California Press, 1986), 151; personal interview with Deepu Pandit, Vrindaban, January 3, 2000.

1. Personal interview with Krishna Gopal Shukla, Vrindaban, October 17, 2001.

2. Personal interview with shrine priest near Keshi Ghat in Vrindaban, March 17, 2000.

3. Personal interview, Kanpur, March 4, 2000.

4. *Indian Express* (New Delhi), December 10, 2001.

5. Personal interview with Kameshvar Chaturvedi, Mathura, October 7, 2001.

6. Lina Gupta, "Ganga: Purity, Pollution, and Hinduism," in *Ecofeminism and the Sacred*, ed. Carol Adams (New York: Continuum, 1993), 109.

7. Kelly D. Alley, *On the Bank of the Ganga: When Wastewater Meets a Sacred River* (Ann Arbor: University of Michigan Press, 2002), 219.

8. See "Search for the Sarasvati," *India Today* (September 28, 1998): 64 ff. See also K. S. Valdiya, *Saraswati: The River That Disappeared* (Hyderabad: Universities Press, 2002).

9. Personal interview with Chamanlal Bhatta, Mathura, January 9, 2000.

10. Vasudha Narayanan, "Water, Wood, and Wisdom: Ecological Perspectives from the Hindu Traditions," *Daedalus* 130, no. 4 (Fall 2001): 188.

11. Bruce Sullivan, "Theology and Ecology at the Birthplace of Krsna," in *Purifying the Earthly Body of God,* ed. Lance Nelson (Albany: State University of New York Press, 1998), 261.

12. Personal interview with Muni-ji (Swami Chidanand Saraswati), Rishikesh, October 31, 2001.

13. Christopher Chapple, "Toward an Indigenous Indian Environmentalism," in *Purifying the Earthly Body of God,* ed. Lance Nelson (Albany: State University of New York Press, 1998), 20.

14. Personal interview with Veer Bhadra Mishra, Banaras, December 17, 1999.

15. Quoted in Kazimuddin Ahmed, Suverchala Kashyap, and Samir Kumar Sinha, "Pollution of Hinduism," *Down to Earth* (Centre for Science and Environment, New Delhi) (February 15, 2000): 35.

16. Personal interview with Muni-ji, Rishikesh, October 31, 2001.

17. Al Gore, *Earth in the Balance: Ecology and the Human Spirit* (New York: Houghton Mifflin, 1992).

18. *The World Scientists' Warning to Humanity,* 1992, available on many Web sites, including that of the Union of Concerned Scientists: www.ucsusa.org.

19. He has written an article by this name: Edward O. Wilson, "Is Humanity Suicidal?" *New York Times Magazine,* May 30, 1993.

20. *The World Scientists' Warning to Humanity.*

21. Particularly within circles influenced by deep ecology.

22. Alan Drengson and Yuichi Inoue, eds., *The Deep Ecology Movement: An Introductory Anthology* (Berkeley: North Atlantic Books, 1995), 49. Emphasis added.

23. John Cronin and Robert F. Kennedy Jr., *The Riverkeepers* (New York: Scribner, 1997), 18.

24. See David James Duncan, *My Story as Told by Water* (San Francisco: Sierra Club Books, 2001), and his novel *The River Why* (San Francisco: Sierra Club Books, 1983).

25. John A. Murray, ed., *The River Reader: A Nature Conservancy Book* (New York: Lyons Press, 1998).

26. Personal interview with Veer Bhadra Mishra, Banaras, December 12, 1999.

27. Alexander Stille, "The Ganges' Next Life," *New Yorker* (January 19, 1998): 65–67.

28. Personal interview, Barkot, September 1999.

29. Conversation with anonymous boatman, Vrindaban, September 9, 1999.

30. Personal interview with Gopeshwar Nath Chaturvedi, Mathura, November 5, 2001. Deepu Pandit said something very similar: "The goddess is in all forms on Earth, but the pollution hides her. It is like the embodied form [*murti*] being broken in a temple. God is not affected by this, but our love [*bhava*] is affected. Here the water is like the embodied form [*murti*]" (Gokul, January 3, 2000).

31. See "Yamunashtakam" by Rupa Gosvamin, verse 8, in appendix 1.

32. Specifically, Hariray connects this with *Brihadaranyaka Upanishad* 4.4.5. See Kedarnath Mishra, ed., *Shri Yamunashtakam* (Banaras: Ananda Prakashan Sansthan, 1980), 147.

33. Personal interview with Dinesh Chaturvedi, Mathura, April 21, 2000.

34. Personal interview with Chaibihari Sardar, Gokul, April 18, 2000.

35. Personal interview with Muni-ji, Rishikesh, October 31, 2001.

36. Personal interview with Vasishthagiri, Barkot, September 1999.

37. There is also a reciprocal circularity about the relationship between rivers and cultures that worship them. Veer Bhadra Mishra explained to me, "Our culture is dying as these rivers—Yamuna and Ganga—are dying. If we cannot save these rivers, then we cannot save our culture" (Banaras, March 13, 2000). Or stated in a reverse fashion: cultures that love rivers will save the rivers, and the continued existence of the rivers will save the cultures that love them.

38. Narayanan, "Water, Wood, and Wisdom," 202.

39. Personal interview with Giriraj, Gokul, April 17, 2000.

40. Personal interview with Harekrishna, Gokul, April 17, 2000.

41. Personal interview with Brajesh Shukla, Vrindaban, March 17, 2000.

42. Personal interview with Deepu Pandit, Vrindaban, January 3, 2000.

43. Personal interview with Anantadasi, Vrindaban, April 24, 2000.

44. Personal interview with Giriraj, Gokul, April 17, 2000.

45. Personal interview with Chaibihari Sardar, Gokul, April 18, 2000.

46. See my "A Theology of Place: Pilgrimage in the Caurasi Baithak Caritra," in *Studies in Early Modern Indo-Aryan Languages, Literature, and Culture,* ed. Alan Entwistle et al. (New Delhi: Manohar Publishers, 1999), 157–66. This is also very much in line with the teaching expressed in the second canto of the *Bhagavata Purana,* which says that the world is the physical body of God.

47. "Nadi aur devi to ek hi hai!" Personal interview with Anantadasi, Vrindaban, April 24, 2000.

48. Personal interview with Ghanashyam Sharma, Gokul, April 18, 2000.

49. Personal interview with Paramananda Sharma, Gokul, April 18, 2000.

50. Bill Aitken, *Seven Sacred Rivers* (New Delhi: Penguin Books, 1992), 8.

51. Some of this also has to do with strategies for motivating people to take effective action. Shrivatsa Goswami of Vrindaban told me, "I have a very special responsibility. It takes thousands of years to build up a culture that worships rivers as goddesses, but you might kill the goddess in a second by telling people how polluted the river is. My challenge is to give them enough information to move them to action, but not so much that it kills their faith" (Vrindaban, November 7, 1999).

52. See Burton Watson, trans., *The Complete Works of Chuang Tzu* (New York: Columbia University Press, 1968), 186–87.

53. The way this is expressed in Bhagavad-gita 2.47 is that the karma yogi avoids both ordinary action, wherein one is attached to the fruits of actions, and ascetic withdrawal or inaction.

54. See, for example, Bhagavad-gita 7.4, 8.4, and 15.16.

55. This philosophical position is often identified as *bhedabheda,* "difference-in-nondifference."

56. This brings to mind Arundhati Roy's notion of the small. "We have to support our small heroes. (Of these we have many. Many.) We have to fight specific wars in specific ways. Who knows, perhaps that's what the twenty-first century has in store for us. The dismantling of the Big. Big bombs, big dams, big ideologies, big contradictions, big countries, big wars, big heroes, big mistakes. Perhaps it will be the Century of the Small. Perhaps right now, this very minute, there's a small god up in heaven readying herself for us" (*The Greater Common Good* [Bombay: India Book Distributors, 1999], 4–5.).

57. Personal communication, Bloomington, Indiana, June 6, 1998.

58. Freya Matthews, "Conservation and Self-Realization: A Deep Ecological Perspective," in *The Deep Ecology Movement: An Introductory Anthology,* ed. Alan Drengson and Yuichi Inoue (Berkeley: North Atlantic Books, 1995), 125.

59. Sallie McFague, *The Body of God: An Ecological Theology* (Minneapolis: Fortress Press, 1993), 132.

60. The literature on Yamuna suggests that this river eventually mingles with all bodies of water on Earth. See Rupa Gosvamin's "Yamunashtakam," verse 4; Shankaracharya's "Yamunashtakam," verse 3; and the "Shri Yamuna Chalisa," verse 20, in appendix 1. Moreover, as noted in chapter 4, Yamuna is identified with the whole world.

61. Personal interview with Shrivatsa Goswami, Vrindaban, January 14, 2000.

APPENDIX I

1. This Sanskrit hymn is reproduced in Vrindaban Bihari Gosvami, *Yamuna evam Yamunashtaka* (Vrindaban: Vrindaban Research Institute, 1990), pt. 2, pp. 57–60.

2. This Sanskrit hymn is reproduced in ibid., pt. 2, pp. 49–52.

3. I translated the forty-one poems from the collection included in Kedarnath Mishra, ed., *Shri Yamunashtakam* (Varanasi: Ananda Prakash Sansthan, 1980), 81–108. I also used *Shri Yamunashtakam evam Shri Yamuna-ji ke 40 Pada,* ed. and trans. Hariprasad Sharma (Mathura: Shri Pushti Margiya Sahitya Prakash Trust, 1999), as an interpretive guide when in doubt about the translation of a line. I took the order of the forty-one poems—which varies from collection to collection—from Mishra's text. For some reason Sharma did not include the last poem in his collection. I thank my friend Shyam Das for checking these poems and making valuable suggestions based on his keen knowledge of them.

4. This is a very difficult line to translate. I have followed Sharma's commentary in producing this translation. An alternative translation is: "She gives her bliss to everyone. She signals for a meeting with her beloved, and my heart is overjoyed when I hear her speak." Another alternative is: "She gives her bliss to everyone. She rests with her beloved, and my heart is overjoyed when she speaks."

5. Rasika Pritama is the pen name of Hariray, author of the first four poems.

6. "The Beloved of Rasika Pritama" refers to Krishna, who is under the control of Yamuna's powerful love.

7. A quiver in the left arm of a woman indicates auspiciousness or delight, that something very good has just happened. Yamuna experiences this when a

soul takes the Brahma-Sambandha mantra that initiates it into the loving service (*seva*) of Krishna.

8. The poet Govindaswami is the author of this and the next four poems. While Govinda is a common name for Krishna, this line also indicates that the author, too, is happy while looking at Yamuna.

9. This is the signature line of Chitaswami, the author of this and the next four poems. Vitthal is a common name for Krishna as well as his guru.

10. Although the verb in this line is *harata* in Mishra's edition, it is *viharata* in all other collections.

11. This refers to a body suitable for loving service (*seva*) to Krishna. It is frequently called the *siddha-deha* or *siddha-rupa*. For more on it, see my *Acting as a Way of Salvation*.

12. Shesha is Vishnu's thousand-headed cobra. He worships the Lord as a majestic king, not as Yamuna's Beloved.

13. The point here is that, while *svati* rainwater is inconsistent and unreliable, Yamuna is a vast and constant source of grace.

14. The meaning of this poem seems to be that to bathe in Yamuna without love and understanding is worthless.

15. See note 11.

16. Her vow is a promise to save all beings who seek her shelter.

17. I translate *dharata* as "mother," based on conversations in Braj. The word can also mean "support" or "earth."

18. Shri Vitthal is the signature name of the female poet Ganga Bai.

19. Although this is typically said of Ganges, here it is said of Yamuna as an indication of Shiva's respect.

20. This poem is reproduced in Hariprasad Sharma, *Manasi Seva ko Prakar* (Udaipur: Ramanlal Parikh, 2000), 15. It is the only Yamuna poem to be included in the collection of Pushti Margiya sacred texts, Vaishnava Mitra Mandala Sarvajanik Nyas, eds., *Nitya Stotra evam Pada Sangraha* (Indore: Vaishnava Mitra Mandala, 2003), 112.

21. Pannalal Purushottam Shastri, *Shri Yamuna Chalisa* (Gokul: Nivedana Prasar Mandal, 1948).

22. Vrindaban Bihari Mishra, *Shri Yamuna Yasha Pachasa* (Vrindaban: Shivahari Press, 1999).

23. Since the long "a" in *Krishnaa* indicates a feminine noun, the name refers here to Yamuna.

24. I assume that *Brahmakunda* is another name for Saptarishi Kund, mentioned in chapter 2.

25. This refers to a story that appears in *Bhagavata Purana* 10.58.16–29.

26. The Yamuna actually curves at Vrindaban, enclosing it on three sides.

27. Gangasagar is where the combined rivers empty into the ocean.

28. I translated it from a reproduction in B. K. Chaturvedi, *Yamuna*, Gods and Goddesses of India, no. 12 (Delhi: Books for All, 1998), 98.

Glossary

ADHIBHUTA The manifest and transitory dimension of ultimate reality. An important technical term that appears in the Bhagavad-gita, in Yamuna theology the *adhibhuta* form (*adhibhautika-rupa*) is considered to be the physical river itself.

ADHIDAIVA The all-inclusive divine dimension of ultimate reality. An important technical term that appears in the Bhagavad-gita, in Yamuna theology the *adhidaiva* form (*adhidaivika-svarupa*) is considered to be Yamuna as a loving goddess.

ADHYATMA The unmanifest and unchanging dimension of ultimate reality. An important technical term that appears in the Bhagavad-gita, in Yamuna theology the *adhyatma* form (*adhyatmika-rupa*) is considered to be the spiritual power of the river that cleanses pilgrims of their sins.

ALLAHABAD City where the Yamuna joins the Ganges (and the mythical river Sarasvati). Called Prayag in older Sanskritic literature, it is a major pilgrimage destination and site of the famous Kumbha Mela, a religious gathering every twelve years that attracts millions for a holy dip in the confluence of these two important sacred rivers.

ARATI A reverential waving of a sacred lamp before a deity, or a short hymn of praise for a particular deity.

BABA A wandering holy man who has typically renounced ordinary life.

BARRAGE A dam designed to regulate with huge gates the flow of water into channels used either for agricultural irrigation or the generation of electricity.

BOD Biochemical oxygen demand. This indicator of water pollution is a measure of the amount of organic matter in a body of water that requires oxygen to break it down. The greater the volume of organic matter, the greater will be the demand for dissolved oxygen (DO) in the water.

BRAJ A sacred region centered on the Yamuna River about one hundred miles south of Delhi. This area is identified as the playground of Krishna and is also a major center for Yamuna worship. There are more Yamuna temples in Braj than anywhere else, and here Yamuna's theological traditions were most fully developed. Many poems celebrating Yamuna were composed in Braj Bhasha, the distinctive language of this area usually considered to be a dialect of Hindi.

CHAMBAL RIVER A major tributary that joins the Yamuna about three hundred miles downstream from Delhi.

CHATTI A resting place built to accommodate the needs of mountain pilgrims.

CPCB Central Pollution Control Board. Set up as a response to India's environmental legislation of the 1970s to check pollution, it is roughly equivalent to the United States Environmental Protection Agency.

DARSHAN "Seeing." In this form of visual communion, the worshipper views a divinity.

DELHI The national capital of the state of India, located on the Yamuna River. Delhi now has a population of more than fifteen million people.

DEVI "Goddess." This is the feminine form of divinity within Hindu traditions. As a goddess, Yamuna is referred to as Yamuna Devi.

DO Dissolved oxygen. This indicator of water pollution determines the amount of dissolved oxygen required to support the aerobic bacteria necessary to break down organic pollutants in a body of water.

GANGA Ganges River and goddess. The latter is called Ganga Ma or Ganga Devi.

GANGOTRI The source, or "mouth," of the Ganges; a major pilgrimage destination.

GAUDIYA VAISHNAVA A follower of one of the principal Braj denominations of Vaishnavism founded in the sixteenth century by the Bengali saint Chaitanya.

GHAT A series of steps that give bathers and worshippers access to a body of water.

GIRIRAJ "King of the Mountains." This term refers to a hill in the Braj region used by Krishna to shelter the people of Braj from a fierce rainstorm. Known also as Govardhan, Giriraj is the sacred center of Braj and is identified as a natural form of Krishna, the Beloved of Yamuna. Stones from this sacred mountain are worshipped in temples and shrines as natural embodiments of divinity.

GOKUL A temple town located on the Yamuna in Braj. This major center for Pushti Margiya Vaishnavas is on the opposite bank of the river and downstream from Mathura.

HARIRAY The great-grandson of Vallabhacharya who wrote an important commentary on his great-grandfather's "Yamunashtakam" and some of the Yamuna poems in the "Forty-One Yamuna Poems."

JAGAT Manifest reality; the "world."

KESHI GHAT The main bathing ghat providing access to the Yamuna in the town of Vrindaban.

KRISHNA The Dark Lord, who is considered by many Hindus (especially Vaishnavas) to be the highest divinity and the ultimate, all-inclusive reality. He is a playful god of love associated with the region of Braj and is the Beloved of Yamuna.

LINGAM The aniconic form of the Hindu god Shiva. It is typically found in the center of any temple dedicated to Shiva.

MATHURA The major pilgrimage center and largest city in the region of Braj. Mathura is celebrated as the birthplace of Krishna.

MOKSHA "Liberation." This much-debated term in Hindu religious traditions is often taken to mean realizing a state of identity with ultimate reality.

MURTI "Embodied form" of divinity: the physical body of a god or goddess accessible to devotees.

PATARANI Can mean "main wife," but, in the context of Yamuna theology, usually refers to Yamuna's position as the "Chief Lover" of Krishna.

PUJA The distinctive form of Hindu worship in which worshippers show their appreciation for a divinity through offerings of such things as food, flowers, clothing, incense, and hymns.

PURANA Literally means "ancient." It refers to an important genre of Hindu scripture that dates back to early in the first millennium. These fluid texts were compiled by multiple authors over long periods of time and give expression to much of the religious thought and practices that make up the living traditions of Hinduism today.

PUSHTI MARGA An important Braj denomination of Vaishnavism founded by the sixteenth-century saint Vallabhacharya and followed by Pushti Margiya Vaishnavas. Yamuna goddess theology is more central to this denomination than any other.

RADHA The feminine aspect of ultimate divinity, and Krishna's favorite cowherd lover. Some worshippers of Yamuna identify her with Radha.

RUPA GOSVAMIN One of the chief theologians of Gaudiya Vaishnavism centered in Vrindaban; author of a "Yamunashtakam."

SAMSARA Circuit of alienated mundane existence; troubled life; heavily conditioned and ongoing existence.

SARASVATI A mythical river said to join the Yamuna and Ganges at Allahabad. Sarasvati is also a goddess of the arts and higher learning.

SEVA "Loving service." Seva often refers to an act of worship, but in the context of the sacred rivers of northern India it is increasingly coming to mean environmental activism.

SHANKARA; ALSO SHANKARACHARYA The legendary ninth-century systematizer of Advaita Vedanta, a philosophical school that informs important traditions of asceticism in India and that captured the attention of early Western scholars of Hinduism.

SVARUPA "Essential form." The term refers to a divinity or ultimate reality.

THAKURANI GHAT The main bathing ghat providing access to the Yamuna in the town of Gokul.

VAISHNAVA "Related to Vishnu." This term refers to those who worship Vishnu—often identified as Krishna—as the highest divinity or ultimate, all-inclusive reality. These are also called Bhagavatas in early texts.

VALLABHACHARYA The sixteenth-century founder-saint of Pushti Margiya Vaish-navism. He authored the most influential and well-known "Yamunashtakam."

VEDANTA A philosophical school of Hindu thought based on the nondual teachings of the Upanishads, *Brahma Sutras,* and Bhagavad-gita.

VISHRAM GHAT The main bathing ghat providing access to the Yamuna in the city of Mathura.

VITTHALNATH The son of Vallabhacharya and major leader of the Pushti Margiya Vaishnavism.

VRINDABAN A temple town located on the Yamuna in Braj. This town was de-veloped primarily by the Gaudiya Vaishnavas and is usually identified as a forest of love.

YAMA Lord of Death. He is also know as Dharma-raja, "Lord of Righteousness," and is the elder, twin brother of Yamuna.

"YAMUNASHTAKAM" An eight-versed Sanskrit hymn that praises Yamuna.

YAMUNOTRI The source, or "mouth," of the Yamuna; a major pilgrimage destination.

YAP Yamuna Action Plan; a governmental initiative begun in 1993 to stop pollution of the Yamuna, primarily by building municipal waste treatment plants for cities located along the river. Technically YAP is part of Phase II of GAP, the Ganga Action Plan, launched in 1985 to rid the Ganges of pollution.

Bibliography

Agarwal, Anil, Sunita Narain, and Srabani Sen, eds. *The Citizens' Fifth Report: State of India's Environment.* New Delhi: Centre for Science and Environment, 1999.

Agni Purana. Trans. N. Gangadharan. Delhi: Motilal Banarsidass, 1984.

Ahmed, Kazimuddin, Suverchala Kashyap, and Samir Kumar Sinha. "Pollution of Hinduism." *Down to Earth* (Centre for Science and Environment, New Delhi) (February 15, 2000): 27–37.

Aitken, Bill. *Seven Sacred Rivers.* New Delhi: Penguin Books, 1992.

Allaby, Michael. *Oxford Dictionary of Ecology.* New York: Oxford University Press, 1998.

Alley, Kelly D. *On the Bank of the Ganga: When Wastewater Meets a Sacred River.* Ann Arbor: University of Michigan Press, 2002.

Anand, Mulk Raj. *Untouchable.* London: Penguin Books, 1940.

Ayres, Ed. *God's Last Offer.* New York: Four Walls Eight Windows, 1999.

Bahuguna, Sunderlal. *Chipko: The People's Movement with a Hope for the Survival of Humankind.* Tehri-Garhwal: Chipko Information Centre, n.d.

————. *The Message of Aranya Culture and Tradition: A Continual Renewal.* Tehri-Garhwal: Chipko Information Centre, n.d.

Banerji, Rajat, and Max Martin. "Yamuna: The River of Death." In *Homicide by Pesticides,* ed. Anil Agarwal, 47–98. New Delhi: Centre for Science and Environment, 1997.

Barnard, Nicholas. *Arts and Crafts of India.* With photographs by Robyn Beeche. London: Conran Octopus, 1993.

Berry, Thomas. *The Dream of the Earth.* San Francisco: Sierra Club Books, 1990.

Bhandarkar, Ramkrishna Gopal. *Vaisnavism, Saivism, and Minor Religious Systems*. New Delhi: Asian Educational Services, 1987.

Bhardwaj, Surinder. *Hindu Places of Pilgrimage in India*. Berkeley: University of California Press, 1983.

Bord, Janet, and Colin Bord. *Sacred Waters*. London: Granada Publishing, 1985.

Bowen, Robert. *Geothermal Sources*. London: Elsevier Applied Science, 1989.

Brown, C. Mackenzie. "The Theology of Radha in the Puranas." In *The Divine Consort: Radha and the Goddesses of India*, ed. John S. Hawley and Donna M. Wulff, 57–71. Berkeley: Graduate Theological Union, 1982.

Brown, Lester, and Ed Ayres, eds. *The World Watch Reader on Global Environmental Issues*. New York: W. W. Norton, 1998.

Bruun, Ole, and Arne Kalland. "Images in Nature: An Introduction to the Study of Man-Environment Relations in Asia." In *Asian Perceptions of Nature*, ed. Ole Bruun and Arne Kalland, 1–24. Richmond, U.K.: Curzon Press, 1995.

Caitanya Caritamrta of Krsnadasa Kaviraja. Ed. Tony K. Stewart, trans. Edward C. Dimock. Cambridge: Harvard University Press, 1999.

Central Pollution Control Board. *Water Quality Status of Yamuna River*. Delhi: Central Pollution Control Board, 2000.

Chapple, Christopher. "Hinduism and Deep Ecology." In *Deep Ecology and World Religions*, ed. David Barnhill and Roger Gottlieb, 59–76. Albany: State University of New York, 2001.

———. "Toward an Indigenous Indian Environmentalism." In *Purifying the Earthly Body of God*, ed. Lance Nelson, 13–37. Albany: State University of New York Press, 1998.

Chaturvedi, B. K. *Yamuna*. Gods and Goddesses of India, no. 12. Delhi: Books for All, 1998.

Chaturvedi, Nandalal. *Shri Yamuna Mahima*. Mathura: Shri Govardhan Granthmala Karyalay, 2004.

Chaturvedi, Vasudev Krishna, ed. *Shri Yamuna Pujan Paddhati*. Mathura: Shri Sitaram Pustakalaya, 2001.

Coburn, Thomas. *Encountering the Goddess: A Translation of the Devi Mahatmya and a Study of Its Interpretation*. Albany: State University of New York, 1991.

Colebrooke, H. T. "On the Vedas, or Sacred Writings of the Hindus." *Asiatic Researches* 8 (1808): 377–497.

Cronin, John, and Robert F. Kennedy Jr. *The Riverkeepers*. New York: Scribner, 1997.

Cummings, Charles. *Eco-Spirituality*. New York: Paulist Press, 1991.

Das, Shyam. *Ashta Chhap: Lord Krishna's Eight Poet Friends*. Baroda: Shri Vallabha Publications, 1985.

———, trans. *Ocean of Jewels: Prameyaratnarnava of Lallu Bhatta*. Baroda: Shri Vallabha Publications, 1986.

Dasgupta, Surendranath. *A History of Indian Philosophy*. 5 vols. Delhi: Motilal Banarsidass, 1975.

Davis, Richard H. *Ritual in an Oscillating Universe: Worshiping Siva in Medieval India*. Princeton: Princeton University Press, 1991.

Deussen, Paul. *Outline of the Vedanta*. London: Luzac and Company, 1907.

Devall, Bill. "The Ecological Self." In *The Deep Ecology Movement: An Introductory Anthology*, ed. Alan Drengson and Yuichi Inoue, 101–23. Berkeley: North Atlantic Books, 1995.

Development Research and Action Group. *Rivers of Hope, Rivers of Despair.* New Delhi: Development Research and Action Group, 1994.

Doniger, Wendy. "Saranyu/Samjna: The Sun and Shadow." In *Devi: Goddesses of India*, ed. John S. Hawley and Donna M. Wulff, 154–72. Berkeley: University of California Press, 1996.

Drengson, Alan, and Yuichi Inoue, eds. *The Deep Ecology Movement: An Introductory Anthology.* Berkeley: North Atlantic Books, 1995.

Dugan, Patrick R. *Biochemical Ecology of Water Pollution.* New York: Plenum Press, 1972.

Dumont, Louis. *Homo Hierarchicus: The Caste System and Its Implications.* Trans. Mark Sainsbury. London: University of Chicago Press, 1970.

Duncan, David James. *My Story as Told by Water.* San Francisco: Sierra Club Books, 2001.

———. *The River Why.* San Francisco: Sierra Club Books, 1983.

Eck, Diana L. *Banaras: City of Light.* Princeton: Princeton University Press, 1983.

———. "Ganga: The Goddess in Hindu Sacred Geography." In *Devi: Goddesses of India*, ed. John S. Hawley and Donna M. Wulff, 137–53. Berkeley: University of California Press, 1996.

Eliade, Mircea. *Patterns in Comparative Religion.* New York: Meridian Books, 1963.

Farago, M. E., A. Mehra, and D. K. Banerjee. "A Preliminary Investigation of Pollution in the River Yamuna, Delhi, India: Metal Concentrations in River Bank Soils and Plants." *Environmental Geochemistry and Health* 11, no. 3–4 (1989): 149–56.

Feldhaus, Anne. *Water and Womanhood: Religious Meanings of Rivers in Maharashtra.* New York: Oxford University Press, 1995.

Fox, Matthew. *Original Blessing.* Santa Fe: Bear and Company, 1983.

Fox, Warwick. *Toward a Transpersonal Ecology: Developing New Foundations for Environmentalism.* Albany: State University of New York Press, 1995.

Gadgil, Madhav, and Ramachandra Guha. *Ecology and Equity.* New Delhi: Penguin Books, 1995.

Gandhi, Mohandas K. *All Men Are Brothers.* Lausanne: United Nations Educational, Scientific, and Cultural Organization, 1958.

———. *An Autobiography: The Story of My Experiments with Truth.* Boston: Beacon Press, 1957.

———. *The Bhagavad Gita, According to Gandhi.* Ed. John Strohmeier. Berkeley: Berkeley Hills Books, 2000.

Gardner, Gary. *Invoking the Spirit: Religion and Spirituality in the Quest for a Sustainable World.* Worldwatch Paper 164. Washington, DC: Worldwatch Institute, 2002.

Giani, Bhajan Singh. *Gurdwara Sri Paonta Sahib: A Short History.* Paonta Sahib, Himachal Pradesh: Parbandhak Committee, 1997.

Gokulnath. *Chaurasi Baithak Charitra.* Ed. Niranjandev Sharma. Mathura: Shri Govardhan Granthmala Karyalay, 1967.

Gonda, Jan. *Visnuism and Sivaism.* London: University of London, 1970.

Gonzalez-Wippler, Migene. *Santeria: The Religion.* St. Paul, MN: Llewellyn Publications, 1994.

Gopal, Brij, and Malavika Sah. "Conservation and Management of Rivers in India: Case-Study of the River Yamuna." In *Environmental Conservation* 20, no. 3 (Autumn 1993): 243–54.

Gore, Al. *Earth in the Balance: Ecology and the Human Spirit.* New York: Houghton Mifflin, 1992.

Gosvami, Vrindaban Bihari. *Yamuna evam Yamunashtaka.* Vrindaban: Vrindaban Research Institute, 1990.

Goswami, Shrivatsa. *Celebrating Krishna.* With photographs by Robyn Beeche. Vrindaban: Shri Caitanya Prema Samsthana, 2001.

————. "Lord Krishna: Preserver and Protector of the Environment." *India Magazine of Her People and Culture* 12 (August 1992): 78–83.

————. "Religion and Environment." *Jnana-Pravaha Bulletin* (Centre for Cultural Studies, Banaras) (1998–99): 54–82.

————. "Vrindavana as a Model Environment." Paper delivered at the Conference on Hinduism and Ecology, Harvard University, Center for the Study of World Religions, October 1997.

Government of India, Central Water Commission. *Water Quality Studies: Yamuna System, Status Report, 1978–1990.* New Delhi: Government of India, Central Water Commission, 1991.

Government of India, Ministry of Environment and Forests. *Yamuna Action Plan.* New Delhi: Government of India, Ministry of Environment and Forests, 1993.

Griffith, Ralph T. H. *The Hymns of the Rig Veda.* London, 1889. Reprint, Delhi: Motilal Banarsidass, 1973.

Guha, Ramachandra. "Mahatma Gandhi and the Environmental Movement in India." In *Environmental Movements in Asia,* ed. Arne Kalland and Gerard Persoon, 65–82. Richmond, U.K.: Curzon Press, 1998.

————. *The Unquiet Woods: Ecological Change and Peasant Resistance in the Himalaya.* New Delhi: Oxford University Press, 1999.

Gupta, Jagadish. *Yama Dvitiya Vrat Katha.* Mathura: Prakash Press, n.d.

Gupta, Lina. "Ganga: Purity, Pollution, and Hinduism." In *Ecofeminism and the Sacred,* ed. Carol Adams, 99–116. New York: Continuum, 1993.

Haberman, David L. *Acting as a Way of Salvation.* New York: Oxford University Press, 1988.

————. *Journey through the Twelve Forests: An Encounter with Krishna.* New York: Oxford University Press, 1994.

————. "On Trial: The Love of the Sixteen Thousand Gopees." *History of Religions* 33, no. 1 (August 1993): 44–70.

————. "A Theology of Place: Pilgrimage in the Caurasi Baithak Caritra." In *Studies in Early Modern Indo-Aryan Languages, Literature, and Culture,* ed. Alan Entwistle et al., 157–66. New Delhi: Manohar Publishers, 1999.

Halarnkar, Samar. "The Rivers of Death." *India Today* (Delhi) (January 15, 1997): 102–7.

Hayden, Tom. *The Lost Gospel of the Earth*. San Francisco: Sierra Club Books, 1996.

Heimann, Betty. *Facets of Indian Thought*. London: George Allen and Unwin, 1964.

Inden, Ronald. *Imagining India*. Oxford: Blackwell Publishers, 1990.

Jacobsen, Knut A. "*Bhagavadgita*, Ecosophy T, and Deep Ecology." *Inquiry* 39 (June 1996): 219–38.

Jha, P. K., V. Subramanian, R. Sitasawad, and R. Van Grieken. "Heavy Metals in Sediments of the Yamuna River." *Science of the Total Environment* 95 (1990): 7–27.

Kaul, H. K., comp. and ed. *Historic Delhi*. Delhi: Oxford University Press, 1996.

Kinsley, David. *Ecology and Religion: Ecological Spirituality in Cross-Cultural Perspective*. Englewood Cliffs, NJ: Prentice Hall, 1995.

————. *Hindu Goddesses: Visions of the Divine Feminine in the Hindu Religious Tradition*. Berkeley: University of California Press, 1986.

————. "Learning the Story of the Land." In *Purifying the Earthly Body of God*, ed. Lance E. Nelson, 225–46. Albany: State University of New York Press, 1998.

Kopf, David. *British Orientalism and the Bengal Renaissance*. Berkeley: University of California Press, 1969.

Mander, Jerry. *In the Absence of the Sacred*. San Francisco: Sierra Club Books, 1991.

Manes, Christopher. *Green Rage: Radical Environmentalism and the Unmaking of Civilization*. Boston: Little, Brown, and Company, 1990.

Margulis, Lynn. *Symbiotic Planet: A New Look at Evolution*. New York: Basic Books, 1998.

Marshall, Peter. *Nature's Web: Rethinking Our Place on Earth*. London: Simon and Shuster, 1992.

Matsubara, Mitsunori. *Pancaratra Samhitas and Early Vaisnava Theology*. Delhi: Motilal Banarsidass, 1994.

Matthews, Freya. "Conservation and Self-Realization: A Deep Ecological Perspective." In *The Deep Ecology Movement: An Introductory Anthology*, ed. Alan Drengson and Yuichi Inoue, 124–35. Berkeley: North Atlantic Books, 1995.

McCully, Patrick. *Silenced Rivers: The Ecology and Politics of Large Dams*. London: Zed Books, 2001.

McFague, Sallie. *The Body of God: An Ecological Theology*. Minneapolis: Fortress Press, 1993.

Merh, Kusum P. *Yama: The Glorious Lord of the Other World*. New Delhi: D. K. Printworld, 1996.

Mishra, Kedarnath, ed. *Shri Yamunashtakam*. Banaras: Ananda Prakashan Sansthan, 1980.

Mishra, Pandit. *Shri Bateshwar Nath va Shauripur*. Shikohabad: Jaya Ma Enterprises, 1983.

Mishra, Vrindaban Bihari. *Shri Yamuna Yasha Pachasa*. Vrindaban: Shivahari Press, 1999.

Mumme, Patricia. "Models and Images for a Vaisnava Environmental Theology: The Potential Contribution of Srivaisnavism." In *Purifying the Earthly Body of God*, ed. Lance Nelson, 133–61. Albany: State University of New York Press, 1998.

Murray, John, A., ed. *The River Reader: A Nature Conservancy Book*. New York: Lyons Press, 1998.

Naess, Arne. "The Deep Ecological Movement: Some Philosophical Aspects." In *Deep Ecology for the 21st Century*, ed. George Sessions, 64–84. Boston: Shambala, 1995.

———. *Ecology, Community, and Lifestyle: Outline of an Ecosophy*. Trans. David Rothenberg. Cambridge: Cambridge University Press, 1989.

———. *Gandhi and Group Conflict: An Exploration of Satyagraha*. Oslo: University of Oslo, 1974.

———. *Gandhi and the Nuclear Age*. Totowa, NJ: Bedminister Press, 1965.

———. "Self-Realization: An Ecological Approach to Being in the World." In *The Deep Ecology Movement: An Introductory Anthology*, ed. Alan Drengson and Yuichi Inoue, 13–30. Berkeley: North Atlantic Books, 1995.

———. "The Shallow and the Deep, Long-Range Ecology Movement: A Summary." *Inquiry* 16 (1973): 95–100.

Narada Purana. Trans. G. V. Tagare. Delhi: Motilal Publishers, 1980.

Narayanan, Vasudha. "Water, Wood, and Wisdom: Ecological Perspectives from the Hindu Tradition." *Daedalus* 130, no. 4 (Fall 2001): 179–206.

Nash, Roderick. *The Rights of Nature*. Madison: University of Wisconsin Press, 1989.

Nattier, Jan. *A Few Good Men: The Bodhisattva Path according to* The Inquiry of Ugra. Honolulu: University of Hawai'i Press, 2003.

Nelson, Lance E., ed. *Purifying the Earthly Body of God: Religion and Ecology in Hindu India*. Albany: State University of New York Press, 1998.

———. "Reading the Bhagavadgita from an Ecological Perspective." In *Hinduism and Ecology*, ed. Christopher Key Chapple and Mary Evelyn Tucker, 127–64. Cambridge: Harvard University Press, 2000.

Nyati, Nandalal. *Shri Yamunashtakam*. Kota, Rajasthan: Jyoti Printers, 1997.

Padma Purana. Trans. N. A. Deshpande. Delhi: Motilal Banarsidass, 1990.

Palmer, Tim. *Endangered Rivers and the Conservation Movement*. Berkeley: University of California Press, 1986.

Parmarth Niketan Ashram. *Kumbha Mela: Festival of the Nectar of Immortality*. Rishikesh: Parmarth Niketan Ashram, Swami Shukdevanand Trust, 2001.

Pavitrananda, Swami. "Pilgrimage and Fairs." In *The Cultural Heritage of India*, vol. 4, pp. 495–502. Calcutta: Ramakrishna Mission, 1956.

Pedersen, Poul. "Nature, Religion, and Cultural Identity: The Religious Environmental Paradigm." In *Asian Perceptions of Nature*, ed. Ole Bruun and Arne Kalland, 258–76. Richmond, U.K.: Curzon Press, 1995.

Peritore, N. Patrick. "Environmental Attitudes of Indian Elites: Challenging Western Postmodern Values," *Asian Survey* 33, no. 8 (1993): 804–18.

Pintchman, Tracy. *The Rise of the Goddess in the Hindu Tradition*. Albany: State University of New York Press, 1994.

Prabhavananda, Swami, and Christopher Isherwood, trans. *Shankara's Crest-Jewel of Discrimination*. Hollywood: Vedanta Press, 1947.

Prayag Mahatmya. Allahabad: Shri Durga Pustak Bhandar, n.d.

Prime, Ranchor. *Hinduism and Ecology*. Delhi: Motilal Banarsidass, 1994.

Rambharosa. *Sadhana Paddhati*. Haridwar: Paliwal Press, 1998.

Rattue, James. *The Living Stream: Holy Wells in Historical Context*. Woodbridge, U.K.: Boydell Press, 1995.

The Rig Veda. Trans. Wendy Doniger (O'Flaherty). Middlesex, U.K.: Penguin Books, 1981.

Rocher, Ludo. *The Puranas*. The History of Indian Literature, no. 2, ed. Jan Gonda. Wiesbaden: Otto Harrassowitz, 1986.

Roy, Arundhati. *The Greater Common Good*. Bombay: India Book Distributors, 1999.

Ruether, Rosemary Radford. *Gaia and God: An Ecofeminist Theology of Earth Healing*. San Francisco: Harper, 1992.

Sessions, George, and Bill Devall. *Deep Ecology: Living as If Nature Mattered*. Salt Lake City: Gibbs Smith, 1985.

Sharma, C. V. J., ed. *Modern Temples of India: Selected Speeches of Jawaharlal Nehru at Irrigation and Power Projects*. New Delhi: Central Board of Irrigation and Power, 1989.

Sharma, Devendra. "Yamuna and the Environment." Manuscript.

Sharma, Hariprasad. *Manasi Seva ko Prakar*. Udaipur: Ramanlal Parikh, 2000.

————, ed. and trans. *Shri Yamunashtakam evam Shri Yamuna-ji ke 40 Pada*. Mathura: Shri Pushti Margiya Sahitya Prakash Trust, 1999.

Shastri, J. L., ed. *Upanishatsamgraha*. Delhi: Motilal Banarsidass, 1980.

Shastri, Pannalal Purushottam. *Shri Yamuna Chalisa*. Gokul: Nivedana Prasar Mandal, 1948.

Sherma, Rita Dasgupta. "Sacred Immanence: Reflections of Ecofeminism in Hindu Tantra." In *Purifying the Earthly Body of God: Religion and Ecology in Hindu India*, ed. Lance E. Nelson, 89–131. Albany: State University of New York Press, 1998.

Shiva, Vandana. *The Violence of the Green Revolution: Third World Agriculture, Ecology, and Politics*. London: Zed Books, 1991.

Siegel, Lee. *Sacred and Profane Dimensions of Love in Indian Traditions as Exemplified in the Gitagovinda of Jayadeva*. Delhi: Oxford University Press, 1978.

Singh, Abha. "Irrigating Haryana: The Pre-Modern History of the Western Yamuna Canal." In *Medieval India: Researches in the History of India, 1200–1750*, ed. Irfan Habib, 49–61. Delhi: Oxford University Press, 1999.

Sivaramamurti, C. *Ganga*. New Delhi: Orient Longman, 1976.

Skanda Purana. Trans. G. V. Tagare. 15 vols. Delhi: Motilal Banarsidass, 1992–2001.

Spear, Percival. *A History of India*. Vol. 2. London: Penguin Books, 1978.

Srinivas, Mysore N. *Religion and Society among the Coorgs of South India*. Oxford: Oxford University Press, 1952.

Stietencron, Heinrich von. *Ganga und Yamuna Zur symbolischen Bedeutung der Flussgottinnen an indischen Tempeln*. Wiesbaden: Otto Harrassowitz, 1972.

Stille, Alexander. "The Ganges' Next Life." *New Yorker* (January 19, 1998).
Sullivan, Bruce. "Theology and Ecology at the Birthplace of Krsna." In *Purifying the Earthly Body of God,* ed. Lance Nelson, 247–67. Albany: State University of New York Press, 1998.
Thapar, Romila. *A History of India.* Vol. 1. Middlesex, U.K.: Penguin Books, 1966.
Thoreau, Henry David. *The River: Selections from the Journal of H. D. Thoreau.* New York: Bramhall House, 1963.
Tirosh-Samuelson, Hava. "Nature in the Sources of Judaism." *Daedalus* 130, no. 4 (Fall 2001): 99–124.
Tuck, Andrew. *Comparative Philosophy and the Philosophy of Scholarship.* New York: Oxford University Press, 1990.
Uttar Pradesh Irrigation Department. *Yamuna Hydro Electric Project.* Dehra Dun: Uttar Pradesh Irrigation Department, n.d.
Vaishnava Mitra Mandala Sarvajanik Nyas, eds. *Nitya Stotra evam Pada Sangraha.* Indore: Vaishnava Mitra Mandala, 2003.
Valdiya, K. S. *Saraswati: The River That Disappeared.* Hyderabad: Universities Press, 2002.
Van Buitenen, J. A. B. *Ramanuja on the Bhagavadgita.* Delhi: Motilal Banarsidass, 1968.
Varaha Purana. Trans. S. Venkitasubramonia Iyer. Delhi: Motilal Banarsidass, 1985.
Varenne, Jean. *Yoga and the Hindu Tradition.* Chicago: University of Chicago Press, 1976.
Wallace, Mark. *Finding God in the Singing River: Christianity in an Ecological Age.* Minneapolis: Fortress Press, 2005.
Watson, Burton, trans. *The Complete Works of Chuang Tzu.* New York: Columbia University Press, 1968.
White, Lynn. "Continuing the Conversation." In *Western Man and Environmental Ethics,* ed. Ian G. Barbour, 55–64. Reading, MA: Addison-Wesley, 1973.
———. "The Historical Roots of Our Ecologic Crisis." *Science* 155, no. 3767 (March 1967): 1203–7.
Wilson, Edward O. *The Diversity of Life.* New York: W. W. Norton, 1999.
Wolpert, Stanley. *A New History of India.* New York: Oxford University Press, 1982.
Wood, Oswald. *Final Report on the Settlement of Land Revenue in the Delhi District Carried on 1872–77 by Oswald Wood and Completed 1878–80 by R. Maconachie.* Lahore: Victoria Press, 1882.

Index

Text: 10/13 Sabon
Display: Sabon
Compositor: International Typesetting and Composition
Cartographer: Bill Nelson